The Female-
Impersonators

The Female-Impersonators
Earl Lind

MINT EDITIONS

The Female-Impersonators was first published in 1922.

This edition published by Mint Editions 2021.

ISBN 9781513209104 | E-ISBN 9781513298474

Published by Mint Editions®

 MINT
EDITIONS

minteditionbooks.com

Publishing Director: Jennifer Newens
Design & Production: Rachel Lopez Metzger
Project Manager: Micaela Clark
Typesetting: Westchester Publishing Services

Inscribed to Nature's Step-Children—the sexually abnormal by birth—in the hope that their lives may be rendered more tolerable through the author's efforts to enlighten thinking men on these step-children's psychology and life experience.

"But this is a people robbed and spoiled; they are all of them snared in holes, and they are hid in prison houses; they are for a prey, and none delivereth; for a spoil, and none saith, Restore.

"Who among you will give ear to this? Who will hearken and hear for the time to come?"

—Isaiah XLII, v. 22, 23.

Contents

Introduction

When, in 1918, I agreed to publish the author's Autobiography of an Androgyne, I did so because persuaded that androgynism was not sufficiently understood and that therefore androgynes were unjustly made to suffer.

Owing to the subject matter, or rather on account of the way in which it was presented by the author, I was obliged to restrict the sale of the book to physicians, lawyers, legislators, psychologists, and sociologists.

The sale of the book, while not as large as it ought to have been, showed however that the interest of the professional man could be awakened, and he be made to realize that the androgyne is no more to be punished for his harmless sexual transgressions than a congenital physical cripple for the latter's unæsthetic physique.

Hardly had the Autobiography of an Androgyne been published, when the author (who, it must be understood, belongs to that despised class of sexual cripples) started, to use his own words, "to peddle the script" of The Female-Impersonators around to general book publishers, and continued to do so for two years, until ten publishers had returned it to him as unsuited for general circulation.

It must be understood that the author wrote The Female-Impersonators for the general reader as he felt that, although propaganda among scientists was necessary, and would undoubtedly do some good, really to help the suffering androgyne quickly, it was necessary to reach the general public.

In this idea the author was not wrong. During the last few years several suicides and murders of androgynes have come to my personal notice, and although a change of laws, which would do away with the punishment of androgynes for their harmless sexual lapses, would do a great deal to ameliorate the conditions surrounding their lives (particularly prevent much blackmail, from which they continually suffer) yet the suicides of androgynes are almost always due, not to fear of punishment by the law, but to fear of exposure, which would cause the loss of their positions and insure their being shunned by "decent" society.

As to the frequent murders of androgynes, these surely have not been committed by members of the medical, legal or other learned professions, but by men belonging to "the general public"—men more or less "civilized," but altogether brutal.

It can not be doubted that a repeal of those laws which prescribe punishment for sexual lapses of these "pseudo-men" would do good, as it would not only save them from prison terms, but also enable the braver of them to prosecute and stop blackmailers, who make a regular business of draining the resources of androgynes.

It is however impossible to achieve all that is desirable until the general public has been thoroughly impregnated with the fact that androgynism (as well as its correlative, gynandrism) is a *psychopathia sexualis,* a mental twist, as harmless to society as anything can be, because it is neither infectious nor contagious, and can not be induced in anybody through either association with androgynes or through quasi-philosophical (that is, sophistical) teachings or cults.

It must be understood that a normal man can not develop sexual feelings or desires for another man, although it must be admitted that homosexuality is occasionally practiced under conditions where access to the opposite sex is impossible (or next to impossible), as, for example, among soldiers on campaigns, among sailors during long voyages on sailing vessels, in boarding-schools for adolescents, etc. This species of homosexuality is indulged in only from "necessity"—so to say— and is not considered by those indulging as much different from self-manustupration. It is gladly abandoned as soon as access to the opposite sex has become possible.

An ultra-androgyne however, although he has the male primary physical attributes, never feels himself to be a real male, but a female incarnated in a male body (often with feminine earmarks), and would no more be able to develop sexual feelings for a female than a normal man for another male.

It is therefore a consummation devoutly to be wished that a book setting forth the facts of androgynism could be distributed among the general public. The author tried to write a compendium for such readers, and THE FEMALE-IMPERSONATORS is the result.

That he has failed in his attempt is to me not only very apparent, but also quite natural.

To the author nothing that he has written about the practices of androgynes seems what we call immoral or revolting. Because their own congenital sexual tendencies appear to androgynes as the full-fledged man's appear to the latter.

To the author of THE FEMALE-IMPERSONATORS it is as natural to fall in love with another male (bearing in mind however that the androgyne is only a "pseudo-male") and write, what he calls poems, dedicated to his "hero-boys" (who to me appear nothing but low ruffians, blackmailers, and grafters) as it would be for a normal man to fall in love with some good-looking female, and write "poetry" about her, perhaps in some of his later "poems" to bewail the fact that she has proven herself "faithless, truthless, and makes a sale of that which men call love, to him who bids the highest."

It is therefore but natural that, since the author sees human beings, as it were, distorted through his own mental astigmatism, namely females as belonging to his own sex and males to the opposite, his second book, THE FEMALE-IMPERSONATORS, contains a great deal which to the average reader would be "shocking", and thus, instead of accomplishing the result which he intended, would cause disgust, and make the treatment of the androgyne even worse than at present.

After the author had submitted the manuscript of his book to numerous publishers, trying in vain (as I had predicted to him) to induce one of them to bring out the book for general circulation, I agreed to publish it for restricted sale.

Not because I really felt that the book presents a great deal of new material of scientific interest, but because, by describing the life experience of various other androgynes, their viewpoints, their sufferings, it continues the missionary work begun by the author in his AUTOBIOGRAPHY OF AN ANDROGYNE and thus helps in keeping up the good work. For, to achieve results, it is not only necessary to awaken interest in a subject, but also to keep that interest alive.

Gutta cavat lapidem, non vi, sed saepe cadendo. "A drop of water wears a hole in a stone, not by force, but by frequently falling."

That the author is really doing missionary work can not be doubted by me, for I know that he does not derive any financial benefit from the publication of his AUTOBIOGRAPHY OF AN ANDROGYNE, nor do I expect he will from the publication of the present sequel.

Every cent which I have turned over to him as royalties from the sale of his AUTOBIOGRAPHY he has returned to me to be expended for advertisements in various medical journals and, owing to the slight interest in the subject which exists among physicians, I am sorry to say that those advertisements have not been financially remunerative.

As the author however feels that he has a mission to fulfill; that he has been created by Providence one of the despised androgynes for the purpose of taking up their cause and ameliorating their state of almost unparalleled sufferings, the missionary work will go on, as it has begun.

As in the case of the first of the present trilogy, THE FEMALE-IMPERSONATORS is published practically as its author wrote it.

For my impressions of the author's personality, I refer to my *Introduction* in his AUTOBIOGRAPHY OF AN ANDROGYNE.

ALFRED W. HERZOG
March, 1922

PART I

THE THIRD SEX

I

How This Book Came to Be Written

My motive was humanitarian. My aim was to save thousands of innocent stepchildren of Nature from an aggregate of tens of thousands of years in prison, and bring about a repeal of the laws under which they are incarcerated and which are still in the codes because civilized man has not yet entirely emerged from the prejudice and superstition of the Dark Ages. My second aim was to put a stop to the continuous string of murders of these stepchildren, the assassins laboring under the delusion that homosexuality is due to deepest moral depravity, and feeling that they are mandatories of society in ridding the world of these "monsters." My third aim was to save hundreds of these superlatively melancholy sexual intermediates from suicide as the result of bitter persecution by those who pride themselves on the fact that in their own case, sex has been thoroughly differentiated.

The problem of the bisexual girl-boy or androgyne has been presented for the *learned professions* in my Autobiography of an Androgyne and The Riddle of the Underworld. But to accomplish my three aims, it is necessary that the *general reader* have instilled into his mind that sexual intermediates are not to blame for their cross-sex idiosyncrasies. Such knowledge could not besmirch the soul of the general reader, but only benefit him morally.

In the present work I have a message for the general reader such as, in nearly every individual case, has never yet reached him. My God-given mission is to be one of the first to cry: "Child of English culture,[1] reflect a moment, and ask yourself whether you are at last, in this the most enlightened century of man's existence, willing to grant justice and humane treatment to the androgyne and gynander? Do you still insist that these sexual cripples continue to suffer physical and mental torture for another century because your own pleasure bulks too large for you to hear and bear the truth about the despairing cross-sexed?"

---

1. Continental European civilizations are, on this subject, a half-century ahead of Anglo-American.

Why should the Christian and the Jew have always regarded as the one unpardonable sin the union in one human body of the distinctive physical and psychic earmarks of the two recognized sexes? Why should they have pitied and assisted the club-footed and the deaf-mute, but always endeavored to grind sexual cripples to powder under their heels?

There is indeed no worse crippling than the sexual. This is because sex, with all that it implies, is the principal physiological factor in life. Any abnormality of sex is truly the greatest of tragedies.

Reader, what would have been your own attitude on this question if God had created you, or your son or daughter, a sexual intermediate, instead of some stranger about whose banishment, suicide, or murder you have read in the paper? Would you have driven the ill-starred son or daughter from home, and henceforth treated them as dead? Or would you, when their dead body was fished out of the river, be able to feel pity as did a father I read about in a New York paper, who exclaimed at sight of it: "Poor Jimmie! How you must have suffered!"[2]

2. See Part VI, chapter III.

My first three books on sexology form a trilogy. They together set forth all phases of the life experience of a bisexual university "man." To only a trifling extent do they overlap. Thus the scientist wishing a full account of my unique life experience must read the entire trilogy. For I was predestined to an unusual role in the great drama we call "life." I was brought into the world as one of the rare humans who possess a strong claim, on anatomic grounds as well as psychic, to membership in both the recognized sexes. I was foreordained to live part of my life as man and part as woman.

The first of the trilogy, the AUTOBIOGRAPHY OF AN ANDROGYNE, was published in January, 1919. In the following June, I began a supplement, THE FEMALE-IMPERSONATORS. Before September, I began to submit it to publishers. But they refused to do anything toward ameliorating the condition of the world's most oppressed class. It seemed to be their opinion that the world must have its scapegoat—to punish, vicariously, for the world's own sins. For centuries, sexual intermediates had served the world in that capacity.

After I had peddled the script around for two years to a total of ten regular book publishers, the MEDICO-LEGAL JOURNAL, publisher of my first book, consented to make the work available for those interested. The long delay in publication was utilized by myself in improving the form.

The third of the trilogy, THE RIDDLE OF THE UNDERWORLD, has been elaborated simultaneously with THE FEMALE-IMPERSONATORS. Into the latter, I put the "milk for babes" (in St. Paul's language); into the former, the "meat for strong men." I wrote the latter in a popular style because addressed primarily to the general reader; the former more in the style suitable for scientists.

In my AUTOBIOGRAPHY, I was almost exclusively occupied with a frank exposition of what life meant to me personally. In the two supplements, I have been chiefly occupied in depicting characters with whom I associated in the Underworld. The Bible says: "Man is altogether born in sin!" But in Christendom this is really true of only the one-tenth of the race who people the Underworld. The other nine-tenths are comparatively saints. But there exists no reason for the latter's prevalent Phariseeism. For the most part their moral superiority is hereditary and environmental.

Because of my innate appetencies and avocation of female-impersonator, I was fated to be a Nature-appointed amateur detective. I enjoyed entrée to the hearts of both male and female denizens of the Underworld, my stamping-ground when I surrendered my bisexual body to the feminine side of my dual psyche. They would whisper into my ears their innermost secrets. Those who happened to be Roman Catholics (because some whom I met in the Underworld were only chance and rare visitors, and ordinarily able to live up to high ideals) have doubtless revealed the mysteries of their inner life to their priest in the vaguest terms. But with me, because as a rule ignorant of the confessor's identity and not likely to meet him in Overworld life, the confessions of Roman Catholic, Protestant, Jew, and atheist were detailed and exhaustive. Surely my having been thus favored by Providence ought to qualify me to depict little known human types for those who have missed the opportunity of meeting all kinds of people.

Of course, after the lapse of more than a score of years, I can not recall verbatim the individual confessions and conversations. I remember only their general drift. As outlined by me, they are merely representative. But Nature has endowed me with a rare memory. The earliest ascertainable date is the age of two years and three months, when I recall having seen the coffin of a great-grandmother carried out of the house. I still preserve earlier memories, such as being held on my mother's lap and contemplating her mountainous bare breast. I remember hearing the moon whistle shrilly (the six P.M. factory whistles as I gazed at the crescent moon).

No reader should conclude from my trilogy that New York has been particularly immoral. Conditions are about the same in all great cities, except that those of the United States are puritan towns compared with Europe. I have explored the Underworld in many cities of both continents, being temperamentally qualified. But in America's smaller cities west of the meridian of Kansas City, the sexual Underworld is more bold and wields more political power than anywhere else in the United States or Europe.

An Underworld exists in all cities of any size because human nature is what it is, and because of the social usages decreed by the blind Overworld, which happens to include the vast majority of mankind. Man is descended from the beasts, and still retains many of their instincts—particularly true of the atypic or atavic who throng the red-light districts.

As the MEDICAL WORLD said of my AUTOBIOGRAPHY OF AN ANDROGYNE, the present work also "will be found a revelation of things undreamed of by most people. It is a contribution to the almost unexplored field of abnormal psychology."

II

The Place of the Androgyne in the Male Sex Scale

Throughout the ages that mankind have trod the earth, a broad and endless stream of masculinity has coursed along until swallowed in the ocean of eternity. In all streams—whether of water, lava, or manhood—the particles at the center flow most rapidly and the speed gradually decreases toward the banks. At occasional points along the latter, the particles are stationary, or there is even an eddy.

(1) The Tremendously Virile cause the surging rapids at the center of the masculine river. Their pre-eminent characteristic lies in excessive venery and excessive promiscuity. Sex holds by far the chief place in their thoughts. A large part of their waking hours is spent in the torture of unsatisfied longing. Their conversation with business intimates tends to sexual lines. They are the "black sheep" of families, never letting an opportunity go by without improving it. They are the seducers of girls under puberty. They are largely instrumental in securing a continuous flow of recruits to the rapidly decimating demimonde. Indeed the tremendously virile constitute the latter's chief *raison d'etre*.

Their ambition being to be "the husbands of all women," the tremendously virile, among Christian nations, often do not marry. If they do, a separation or divorce follows within a few years.

As a rule, only these free lances—as long as under thirty—appeal to androgynes as "heroes." To them alone do these pseudo-men yearn to devote themselves as slaves.

As a rule, the tremendously virile are not *gentle*-men. For they possess not even a vestige of mild or semi-feminine traits. They are overbearing, quarrelsome, and pugnacious. They will not take a back seat for any one. They constitute the raw material for the roughest, rudest, and most death-defying occupations, as volunteer soldiers and sailors, pugilists, highwaymen, and burglars. They abhor prosaic work.

As a rule, the tremendously virile are men of only three interests in life: fighting (including the slaughter of dumb beasts, in their inability to give the same treatment to their fellow man); sport in the usual sense of that word; and the sexual instinct. But a mere handful, whom Nature endowed with unusual brain power, have been leaders in war and politics. In the United States, I dare instance only Mohammed, Henry the Eighth, Louis the Fourteenth, and Bismarck. But leaders of the American nation have belonged to this tremendously virile class. I dare not name them because cultured society, with their present mediæval ideas on sex, severely censure men of this class as "bestial." But the latter are fundamentally irresponsible.

In absolute monarchies and aristocracies almost throughout history, the tremendously virile have been at the helm of the ship of state. Because they have been, by birth, the greatest fighters. They thus forged to the front and pre-empted for themselves and their posterity the best things of life. Their constituting themselves the ruling class has rendered history, for the most part, a record of wars. Tremendous virility, combined with unusual brain power, makes the born leader of men, before whose will the masses bow unquestioningly and they blindly turn themselves into "cannon fodder" at his beck and call. Only since the dawn of the nineteenth century have the mildly virile been coming into their own, and brain and science beginning to get the upper hand over brute force. The recent World War was the final resurgence of the tremendously virile as moulders of the destinies of nations, as well as the death blow to their ambitions in this direction.

As the status of peoples descends from the enlightened to the savage, the proportion that this class forms of the entire male sex gradually increases. Among enlightened nations, I estimate it at five per cent on the basis of my intimate mingling, in the role of a soubrette, with several thousand young bachelors belonging exclusively to either the tremendously or ultra-virile class, while nearly all my every-day associates have belonged to the mildly virile.

On the basis of my reading in anthropology, I estimate the proportion among savages at seventy-five per cent. Among the adult males, I have read that women constitute almost the sole topic of conversation. Fighting and sport fill up the rest of life. When an explorer has visited a savage or barbarous tribe, the outstanding hospitality is the provision of a bed-fellow belonging to the gentle sex.

(2) The Ultra-Virile, on either side of the sexually fastest flowing particles just described, take their less rapid course in the stream of

masculinity. Sex occupies their thoughts to a much less extent. But, like the tremendously virile, they are naturally polygamous. Only these two classes of males, together with ultra-androgynes and a small proportion of the mildly androgynous, sow wild oats, beginning in their later teens and ending usually in their later twenties. Prior to settling down in marriage, the ultra-virile secretly do not care a fig for the sexual mandates of Christian society. But for the sake of appearances, they hypocritically chime in with the regnant note and openly condemn in the harshest terms the least infraction of the conventions by another than themselves. After marriage, however, their infidelities are few and far between. Perhaps a score in a life-time, as compared with a thousand upward for the tremendously virile.

The ultra-virile make excellent husbands and divorce is rare. The wife, however, while herself occupying first place in the husband's affections, has much cause for jealousy.

While the ultra-virile do not regularly choose an occupation free from prosaic toil and ministering to love of sport and adventure, they are usually averse to intellectual pursuits, favoring the manual. If possessing unusual brain power, the ultra-virile man heads some engineering or construction enterprise. The ultra-virile build our railroads, great bridges, leviathans, and sky-scrapers. A handful are distinguished by a knack for political leadership and have contributed the vast majority of such leaders.

Both the tremendously and the ultra-virile tend to excel in physique and comeliness. Some athletes, however, are only mildly virile. "Virility" refers only to sexual power. More than the ordinary erotic ardor, however, usually goes hand in hand with *brawn*, just as intellectual tastes and spirituality do with *brain*. With the evolution of the race in culture, erotic ardor, together with the animal side of man's nature in general, is declining. The goal for which the race is headed is the minimum of sexual consciousness, coitus for procreation only, just enough offspring to keep the number of the human race on earth stationary, lengthened life, and ever increasing expansion of the intellectual in man at the expense of the physical. With this evolution, the proportion of sterile bisexuals will also increase.

The fighting forces of a nation are almost entirely made up of the two more virile classes, although together constituting only about twenty-five per cent of the total manhood of civilized nations. It is dangerous for the world's peace when these two classes get control of a great nation's government. Of the five classes of males being described, these two alone love war and seek occasion for it.

(3) The MILDLY VIRILE constitute, among so-called "Christian" nations, about seventy-five per cent of all males.[1] Only on rare occasions do thoughts about sexual congress enter their minds. That is, if married, they desire it only about once a fortnight or so, and up to the date of marriage, the incentive is so weak that they never gratify it. Thus up to the bridal night, this class three have usually been as chaste as their better halves. They have usually never indulged even in masturbation, while the generality of classes one and two have indulged frequently from around the age of ten to the period in which opportunities *cum femina* or *cum androgyna* become plentiful. In the mildly virile man's ignorance of the force of sex in classes one and two, however, he has been known to be obsessed with the delusion that sex in himself is strongly developed. The mildly virile always marry, although a few postpone it until much past thirty. Subsequently they have at most only negligible desires to drink water at a strange cistern. They are content to go to their graves having been absolutely faithful to the lawful wife, or several successive ones, that God gave them. Divorce is almost unknown, since its cause, in nearly every case, is *de facto* polygamy in the husband, or his excessive demands on the frigid wife—two faults absent from the psyche of the mildly virile.

The sexual life of the latter flows on gently and smoothly. It is called humdrum by the tremendously virile, continuously wafted up and down in a dizzy fashion in the rapids at the center of the masculine river. But what the mildly virile miss of the "pep" of life is more than compensated by the blissful peace that characterizes their earthly journey.

Their abhorrence of androgynism is many times as intense as in the case of the more virile. While not a single mildly virile man would ever

---

1. A physician of wide experience who read the above before publication argued that in the United States, only five per cent are mildly virile. I stand unconvinced that my proportion is in error. The proportion surely differs with racial types and environment. The physician has always lived in New York City and practiced among liberal-minded, non-church, pleasure-loving people of Teutonic or Latin parentage. My own every-day associates, particularly in the village where I was brought up and which I still frequently visit, have been, almost entirely, ultra-puritan Anglo-Saxons. When I maintained their sexual temperance, the physician declared them hypocrites, whose secret practice is the same as "worldlings'." I have been intimately acquainted with hundreds of these male puritan church-devotees, and am convinced they are hypocrites solely in supposing their sexual moderation due to their own superior morals. Sex has naturally small place in their lives.

succumb to androgyne allurements, I have ascertained through many years' association with thousands of tremendously or ultra-virile that at least seventy-five per cent readily suffer capture providing their sexual needs are not already abundantly gratified. The chief reason for the bitter antagonism of the mildly virile is that they know androgynism only by hearsay. They have not, like the more virile—to whom alone androgynes gravitate—been eye-witnesses of the entirely innocent, innocuous, and even pitiable sexuality of these pseudo-men.

The mildly virile, constituting the vast majority of all males in "Christian" countries, seek to impose the dictates of their own sexual natures upon all men whatsoever. The sexual mandates of "Christian" society and of the New Testament express the sex feelings in part of the mildly virile, and in part of the anaphrodites. Whatever harmonizes with these feelings is right; whatever fails to, is "bestial."

The mildly virile are inclined toward the less strenuous occupations, as agriculture, manufacturing, and trade. They also include ninety-five per cent of intellectuals.

(4) The cold ANAPHRODITES are the particles that cling immovably to the banks of the masculine river.[2] They neither progress nor regress. They number about one-half of one per cent of all adult males. Like the ultra-androgynes, they have a horror of women from the sex point of view. But unlike the former, their minds are devoid of hero-worship and they shudder violently at the very thought of *any kind* of association grounded on sex differences. Their anaphroditism is either an after-effect of an illness in childhood or congenital.

For the most part, anaphrodites are intellectuals. The exquisite joys associated with courtship and marriage that they are predestined never to know are more than compensated by Providence in the way of extra allotment of intellectual enjoyment. Herbert Spencer is the shining example of anaphroditism of the nineteenth century.[3]

Since anaphrodites are not suffused with adoration for any type of human, the vast majority are the more inclined to lift their thoughts

---

2. Do not confuse with anaphrodites the excessively rare men who are attracted by female beauty and manners, marry, but then desire merely Platonic relations. Such are rather cases of impotence. The genuine anaphrodite never even courts a woman.

3. The author has always preferred to read biography to fiction. If his life is spared, he will write an extensive work on the sexuality of noted men and women. An unusually large proportion of geniuses have been either anaphrodites or androgynes. For example, Sir Isaac Newton and Immanuel Kant appear to have been anaphrodites.

to their Creator. Some great religious leaders have been anaphrodites. St. Paul, in his epistles, shows little patience even with normal sex phenomena. He advises that every man imitate his own absolute celibacy. "But if they can not contain, let them marry. For it is better to marry than to burn (to lust)."

It is impossible for the tremendously or the ultra-sexed to live up to the sexual ideals of an anaphrodite. And yet St. Paul's epistles bind them upon Christians. It is infinitely easier for an anaphrodite to be a saint than for the ultra-virile to be even decent. St. Paul's sex teachings constitute the greatest stumbling block of the church. They have caused the human race a world of woe. Belief in St. Paul's inerrancy makes it impossible to reconcile Christian ethics with the incontrovertible teachings of Nature. While, in respect to value to the human race, I give St. Paul's epistles first place among all published documents (the woe they have occasioned being, a thousand times over, outweighed by the light they have given man on the greatest questions that puzzle his brain) I must, particularly because of their false sex doctrines, deny their inerrancy. If inerrant, the human race ought to have ceased existence eighteen hundred years ago.

Jesus made no such blunders in his sex teaching. He was the only biblical teacher apparently to recognize the existence of androgynes without thundering against them. As "eunuchs from their mother's womb," he may of course have had in mind only anaphrodites. But apparently he was aware of the existence of androgynes, St. John the Divine, apparently his favorite disciple, having possessed the earmarks, particularly "softness" of disposition.

(5) ANDROGYNES are the eddies along the banks of the masculine river. Their movement is retrograde. They are instances of arrest of development. In the early fœtus sex is not apparent. Only later does differentiation begin. In more than ninety-nine out of a hundred humans, it is completed at puberty. But the individual androgyne or gynander remains, down to death, to a greater or less degree bisexual. Just as a mule is part horse and part donkey, so an androgyne or gynander is part man and part woman. To quote from Krafft Ebing: "They (androgynes) are neither man nor woman: a mixture of both; with secondary psychic and physical characteristics of the one as well as the other sex."[4]

---

4. I take no stock in the theory advanced by some medical writers that androgynism (generally termed male sexual inversion) is acquired and not congenital. The exceptional method of sexual expression can be **acquired** only by individuals congenitally on the very borderline between androgynes on the one hand and anaphrodites or mildly virile on

Androgynes tend to occupations having to do with art—in the widest sense of that word. They are extreme æsthetes. I quote from Edward Carpenter's *Love's Coming-of-Age* (published by Boni and Live-right) page 135, where he speaks of male urnings, called by myself "androgynes": "At the bottom lies the artist-nature, with the artist's sensibility and perception. Such a one is often a dreamer, of brooding reserved habits, often a musician, or a man of culture, . . . almost always with a peculiar inborn refinement. De Joux. . . says. . . : 'They are enthusiastic for poetry and music, are often eminently skilful in the fine arts, and are overcome with emotion and sympathy at the least sad occurrence. . . The nerve system of many an urning is the finest and the most complicated musical instrument in the service of the interior personality that can be imagined.'" (R. W's comment: An androgyne is usually a bundle of nerves.)

In my university course in æsthetics, the professor lamented that art tends to make its devotees immoral. He probably had in mind the

---

the other. The latest proponent of the "acquired" theory, Dr. P. M. Lichtenstein, in the August, 1921, issue of MEDICAL REVIEW OF REVIEWS, suggests that masturbation in boyhood may produce in adulthood a fairie or ultra-androgyne. In my physical prime, I was a fairie of extreme type. I never masturbated as a child or as an adult because of acute horror. My own pudenda never had any part in my sexual ardor—any more than had my vermiform appendix.

Dr. Lichtenstein's suggestion of the correction by parents of feminine predilections in small boys is futile. Those feminesque traits, when congenital, as I believe they always are in ultra-androgynes, can not be suppressed. Likewise his advice that the adolescent girl-boy seek the company of the gentle sex as a cure is as futile. In my teens, I forced myself to it, but it had not the least curative value.

Note Added in Galley: I just came across a scrap of a recent NEW YORK WORLD Sunday magazine, containing "**Glands That Govern Our Lives**", name of author missing. I quote: "The not uncommon phenomena of the smooth-faced man with a feminine voice and a figure resembling that of a woman, and of the deep-voiced, hairy-faced masculine woman, are produced by abnormalities in the development of these glands." Only in the third decade of the twentieth century is the comparatively new branch of medical science, **endocrinology** (the study of glands, particularly the ductless) coming forward to maintain the irresponsibility of "homosexuals" for their indiosyncrasy. It has also only just been brought into the limelight that the testicles are invigorating (as well as masculinizing) to the individual possessing them and the prime reason for man's being physically stronger than woman. I myself, for several years after castration at the age of twenty-seven, observed a marked diminution in my stamina. (For details, see my AUTOBIOGRAPHY OF AN ANDROGYNE.) My own testicles were abnormal judged by the fact that I, though always having intense horror of self-manustupration, suffered from acute spermatorrhea from the incidence of puberty up to castration, while I was totally devoid of the propensity natural to full-fledged adult males for emptying the seminal vesicles.

notorious frequency of homosexuality among æsthetes. But he got the cart before the horse. The æsthetes affected were born bisexual and their devotion to art was a consequence.

Androgynes are clearly of two types, each of which, the author estimates, constitutes in the United States about one out of every three hundred humans possessing the male primary determinants:[5] (a) The mildly androgynous, of whom Oscar Wilde is the best known of contemporaries; and (b) the ultra-androgynous, of whom the present writer is the most widely known of his generation.

(a) The anatomy of the mildly androgynous is not conspicuously feminine. Only a few feminine traits appear in the psyche. The mildly androgynous always mingle with full-fledged males and seek to pass as such themselves. As a cloak, they are prone to fabricate about excesses *cum femina*. But while secretly preferring homosexual romance, they are capable of espousing a woman and begetting children. Sexologists have therefore called them "psychic hermaphrodites."

(b) In ultra-androgynes alone, the physique is noticeably feminesque, and the psyche predominantly feminine. As a rule, they alone have a craze to decorate themselves in feminine finery and spread paint and

---

5. Other authorities make them more numerous. I quote from **Love's Coming of Age,** page 125: "Dr. Grabowsky. . . quotes figures. . . as high as one man in every 22, while Dr. Albert Moll (**Die Contraere Sexual-Empfindung,** chapter 3) gives estimates varying from one in every 50 to as low as one in every 500. These figures apply to such as are exclusively of the said nature (excluding the psychic hermaphrodites. Including the latter) the estimates must be greatly higher. . . Some late statistical inquiries (See **Statistische Untersuchungen,** Dr. M. Hirschfeld, Leipzig, 1904) yield 1.5 to 2 per cent as a probable ratio."

I myself have fixed upon the median of ratios I have read, as well as the frequency that has occurred to me as a result of a half-century's unusually intimate mingling with all social types in many nations, having possessed, at the time I lived in the foreign nations, some speaking ability in seven foreign languages. But the frequency is greater than I have given in the text rather than less. But the extreme German estimates are too high for the United States. It is my conclusion from intimate intercourse with the natives in many countries that the frequency of bisexuality per thousand is proportional to the density of population. Nature puts a break on over-population by increasing the proportion of sterile bisexuals. When a population is regularly underfed, the number of bisexuals born appears to increase. But that is not the only factor. Another law is that when a consanguineous multifamily (a group of families) multiplies with exceptional rapidity, bisexuals are born in that family even though the food supply is undiminished. The author believes the latter to be the reason he himself was born bisexual. It was because the generic womb (i. e., those of my grandmothers for several generations) had been overtaxed.

The ratio is probably much higher among the cultured—particularly art devotees—than among the "hoi polloi."

powder on their faces. They tend to avoid the society of full-fledged males except to display to a tremendously virile coterie—to whom they are generally incognito—their skill in female-impersonation.

Unless otherwise indicated I shall use the terms "androgyne" and "pseudo-man" only in reference to the ultra-androgynous. All my androgyne associates whom I shall portray in this book belong to this class, because with a few exceptions they alone are FEMALE-IMPERSONATORS. In my RIDDLE OF THE UNDERWORLD I describe some mild androgynes.

There exists vast diversity in the anatomy and psyche of androgynes— just as, from the standpoint of size and shape of the genitalia and sexual tastes, any two full-fledged males or any two full-fledged females differ more or less. In one androgyne, the only conspicuous external feminine stigma may be absence of beardal growth; in another, mammary glands; in another, the complete skeleton or the complete muscular system of the female. The one physical feminine stigma that is indispensable to the possession of a decidedly feminine psyche and the quasi-female method of sexual expression is the female variety of brain protoplasm. For there have probably lived naturally beardless men, males possessing milk glands or sissie voices, etc., who have nevertheless not been at all homosexual. But such are exceptions to the rule.

While an earmark of ultra-androgynism is sexual passivity, the mildly androgynous may be active pederasts or mutual onanists. Only in the case of ultra-androgynes are the individual's genitalia entirely divorced—as a rule—from the sexual life. For them, Nature has substituted other organs.

Ultra-androgynes are, by birth, practically identical with males castrated in early childhood, except that adult artificial eunuchs are usually overlarge. Adult ultra-androgynes tend merely to plumpness as a result of their dwarfed genitalia.

I have heard of ultra-androgynes, who, in their early twenties, on their physician's advice, married a *woman,* when Nature intended they should marry a man. All high-minded "homosexualists," soon after arrival at puberty, consult a medical man for a cure. From time immemorial it has been one of the profession's superstitions that marriage would cure homosexual tendencies. Some unsophisticated adolescent androgynes put faith in their physician's positive assurance that *marriage is a sure cure.* If, as a matter of conscience alone, the androgyne promises the physician to marry, he sometimes goes insane over the dread of it, or else commits suicide, either on the eve of marriage, or a few days afterward. But even if the marriage ceremony is performed, the consummation never takes place in the case of ultra-androgynes, and the wedded state proves very unhappy for both parties. At least in the case of the ultra-androgynes, such marriage possesses no curative value. Chronic and extreme homosexuality is congenital and incurable. It is monstrous to advise even a mild androgyne to marry, and thus contribute to propagating a line of unhappy and unwelcome bisexuals down through the centuries.

The two classes of androgynes do not mix well. Just as the full-fledged man is averse to attendance at a ladies' sewing-circle. Particularly the mildly androgynous fear suspicion of their secret if they associated with ultra-androgynes. Coteries of ultra-androgynes naturally form. Knowing their own nature, they readily recognize one another, although down to 1921 at least, the sexually full-fledged have usually been blind to the androgynism of daily associates, because never permitted to learn of their existence.

(6) PSEUDO-HERMAPHRODITES are humans possessing in part both the male and the female genitalia, or else organs so deformed that even sexologists are unable to determine the sex until puberty. In half such cases, the physician then pronounces the individual to belong to the sex other than that with which he or she has identified him or herself. As a rule, they subsequently live and clothe themselves per prescription. But some, accustomed to the dress and usages of their first sex, choose to identify themselves with it throughout life.

Pseudo-hermaphrodites are the limit toward which the ultra-androgynous approach by slight gradations. Their frequency is not greater than one in a million to ten million humans.

(7) FULL HUMAN HERMAPHRODITES—possessing both complete male and complete female genitalia—have never been encountered. There exists in medical annals, however, a pseudo-hermaphrodite who so nearly approached full hermaphrodism that at one period he-she claimed to have lived as husband and father, and at a later, as wife and mother. This reputed transposition is in accord with the observed phenomenon[6] of an individual's passing over from one sex class to another at the climacteric corresponding to menopause in woman.

---

6. See later chapter: THOUGHTS SUGGESTED BY THE HERMAPHRODITOI IN GENERAL.

EARL LIND

I have a theory that the sex class of an individual male depends on the size, but particularly the vigor, of his physical reproductive apparatus. I have ascertained such variety to be practically infinite, and psychicly as well as physically.

There exist no sharp dividing lines among the six classes of males. While the bulk of a particular class correspond closely to the description, there are individuals on each side of such mode who constitute slight gradations over to the next class. Thus each class gradually and almost imperceptibly shades off into the next. There exists indeed a sex scale along which all human beings can be theoretically arranged. At one pole stands the tremendously virile man—for example, the rough volunteer common soldier, as a rule intensely polygamous; at the other the petite, crybaby species of woman. Androgynes and gynanders occupy exactly the middle section, looking toward both the male and the female side.

It is quasi-instinctive with each sex class to scorn members of another class just because they happen to be built on a different plan. It is the same phenomenon prevalent in the religious domain in past centuries, when the Roman Catholic yearned to murder the Protestant and *vice versa*. Which intolerance the gradual conquest of human affairs by reason is pushing further and further into the background. But still in the twentieth century, reason is a nonentity in the domain of sex. There all is illogical instinct and bigotry. Each sex class still revels in calling the others bad names. The tremendously virile "fellow" bellows out at the mildly: "You milk-sop!" The latter calls back: "You rake!" The ultra-virile hisses through his teeth at the anaphrodite: "You dried tree!" The mildly virile points his finger at the androgyne: "Unclean! Unclean! Child of the devil! Monster!" And even if I do not say so here, the reader will conclude after finishing this book: The androgyne calls back at the mildly virile: "You hypocrite! You Pharisee!" For the outstanding earmark of the mildly virile is Phariseeism. They think they themselves are the only moral and God-fearing men in the world, and that all other men are sexually vile.

Is it right to chastise a horse because he prefers to munch hay out of a manger instead of walking into his owner's dining-room; throwing himself backwards into an enormous chair; squeezing with difficulty a spoon between his two front hoofs; and with it carrying to his mouth ice-cream and French pastry? The average man (who is of the mildly virile type) says that the latter is, for every creature, the superior method of taking nourishment, and insists on all others conforming to what is right in his own eyes. If they do not, he ostracizes and even imprisons and murders those who dare to offend his æsthetic sense.

In general, man is a free agent. But his sex class is imposed by Providence. Just as he is not responsible for the face he has to carry through life.

Why should not every human be at liberty to live out his life in the way Nature ordains for *him* so far as he does not thereby transgress against any one else?[7]

---

7. Bisexuality occurs also in animals and birds, but far less frequently than among humans. Perhaps this difference is due to the fact that the human male and female differ much less in respect to secondary sexual determinants than do most birds and animals. Several times in my life I have come across a newspaper item such as the following. I inquired of a poulterer, who informed me that he has had numerous hens that crowed and possessed secondary male determinants.

CROWS AND LAYS EGG. IS IT COCK OR HEN?
Copyright by **Press Publishing Co.** (NEW YORK WORLD), 1921
(Special cable despatch to the WORLD)

LONDON, Dec. 9.—A Buff Orpington cock at a poultry show in the agricultural hall at Islington has laid an egg. This bird began its career with all the attributes of a sure-enough hen. It laid eggs and cackled over them in time-honored fashion. Its head, plumage, and habits were all hen-like.

As it grew, its conformation underwent a subtle change. It began to grow a cock's comb, sprouted a cock's tail, developed spurs and crowed on appropriate occasions—but continued to lay eggs. When its owner exhibited it as a "cock-hen" and claimed despite its male affiliation, that it produced eggs, all the poultry fanciers derisively nicknamed it "Bluff Orpington."

One doubter offered to pay one hundred pounds if the bird laid an egg. It was watched day and night for the coming of the marvel, and yesterday duly presented its watchers with an excellent egg. . . Physiologists are dumbfounded.

III

Androgynes of Mythology and History

APOLLO is the pre-eminent androgyne god. He was always represented with a feminine face and coiffure, and therefore worshipped as the god of beauty.

In conformity with his semi-femininity, he was the *life-giving* and *light-giving* deity—both physical and figurative life and light. He was the leader of the muses—the spirits presiding over all human inspiration in the fine arts.

The artistic instinct—the poetic temperament, "sentimentality" in its highest sense—goes hand in hand with a rounding-off of the sharp corners of masculinity. Artistic or poetic decades have been conspicuous because of a semi-slumbering of fundamental masculine traits, that is, the instinctive relish for wrangling and war. The sterner sex has temporarily laid aside its primal *fighting* function ordained by Nature and become to some degree effeminate.

As a rule, abstract beauty's devotees—"æsthetes" in the highest sense, that is: poets, novelists, painters, sculptors, and superior musicians—have been characterized by more or less effeminacy. They have been particularly prone to homosexuality. While among full-fledged males, the proportion that has achieved proficiency in one of the fine arts is something like one in a thousand, among androgynes (the two varieties combined), it has been one in about twenty. I will later point out that the pinnacle in poetry, sculpture, and painting has been achieved by androgynes.

But the feminesque Apollo was the god not only of beauty, but of *adolescence*—the period of life during which human beauty is at its culmination. He possessed eternal youth. He is even referred to as "the boy god." Adoration of him sprang out of man's delight in the semi-womansouled and quasi-woman-bodied stripling just before arrival at puberty.

And ultra-androgynes remain—to a large extent—in that pre-puberty period down to thirty-five. Their development has been arrested. Full-fledged male associates absolutely ignorant of the existence of androgynism have described—in the author's hearing—androgynes even close to fifty years old as "still mere boys."

But an adolescent androgyne or boy god was also worshipped by the Semite nations (other than the Jews) under the name Ablu, and by the Celts under the name Maponus.

Philologists will recognize that "Apollo," "Ablu," "Maponus," and "boy" are descended from the same vocable in the language used by the Asiatic tribe from which most of the civilized nations of the ancient and modern world derive. *B* is only a strengthened *p*; the liquid *l* has often been transmuted into the kindred *n*; and the diphthong *oy* indicates the elision of a liquid. We have here etymological evidence that an adolescent-androgyne deity was worshipped before the dawn of history.

Today, among some primitive races, as the aborigines of America, androgynes are the central feature of the most sacred rites.

HERMAPHRODITOS stands second among androgyne gods. The myth is that "he-she" was originally a full-fledged human adolescent and an entirely separate nymph in the full flower of feminine charm. The nymph, falling in love, besought Zeus that the adolescent and herself might be forever amalgamated. Excepting the pudenda, the body remained that of the nymph. The psyche became a compound of the masculine and the feminine. This myth was a poetic recognition of the existence, at the very dawn of history, of androgynes such as exist today.

A picture or statue of Hermaphroditos adorned nearly every Greek and Roman home of the better class. This was because the ancients held the androgyne in honor as the super-human—man and woman in one individual.

GANYMEDE ranks third.[1] Originally a human adolescent of extraordinary feminesque beauty, Zeus snatched him up into the heavenly zone and conferred immortality that the feminesque youth might be his cup-bearer. The latter's statues represent him with a mademoiselle's chevelure, hips, and legs, but with male breasts and pudenda. The fact

---

1. "Catamite" is the Latin, as well as modern, corruption of the vocable "Ganymede." For the relation between Jupiter and Ganymede, see Dr. Wm. Lee Howard's **Pederasty vs. Prostitution** in **Journal of the American Medical Association,** May 15, 1897. Also Plato's **Phædo**. Greek literature in general is suffused with pederasty. I read Greek six years in "prep" and university. My observation is that androgyne scholars have a penchant for that language and drift into teaching it. Prior to the twentieth century, the Greek and Latin masterpieces—in all "preps" and colleges read unexpurgated because the sexually full-fledged have not generally understood the homosexual descriptions—were the only publications affording androgynes an inkling of the secrets of their sex life.

that the father-god of the classic world entered into this most intimate union partly explains why the androgyne was held in honor by the Greeks and Romans.

SOCRATES is the earliest historic character whom sexologists have declared an androgyne. For centuries, a common designation of male homosexuality has been "Socratic love." In Plato's "Dialogues," Socrates is the teacher. His remarks of extreme affection to his youthful disciples are sickening even to me, though an androgyne myself. Present-day scholars who close their eyes to the facts of androgynism, who cling to mediæval sex ideas, and hence hold homosexuality to result from deep-eyed moral depravity, have denounced Socrates as the greatest moral leper that ever lived. But from Socrates' own generation down through the nineteenth century, he was universally recognized as the greatest saint of the classic world.

That Socrates was a married man and father and wore a beard does not disprove the sexologists' claim. The mildly androgynous—psychic hermaphrodites, like Oscar Wilde—occasionally marry and procreate; chiefly for social reasons, not from the sexual incentive. Secondly, the razor was practically unknown in Socrates' generation. Even today, some of the less extreme androgynes wear a full beard because of horror of a razor.

One of the three charges on which Socrates was condemned to death was that he was "a corruptor of youth;" the identic charge that landed Oscar Wilde in prison. But neither of these geniuses ever corrupted any youth. The prevalent idea that the association of an older androgyne with a sexually full-fledged younger man corrupts the latter is absolutely groundless. The androgyne only benefits, in several ways, the adolescent whom he loves far more than a father loves an only son. Socrates' two most brilliant disciples, Plato and Xenophon, wrote books, still extant, one of the purposes of which was defence of Socrates from the charge mentioned.

PLATO, the St. Paul of the pagan classic world—as was its Jesus (Socrates)—was an androgyne. His voluminous "Dialogues"—one of the world's two score of literary masterpieces—are permeated with homosexuality. In the *Symposium*, Plato confesses himself a homosexualist. In his day, homosexuality was not regarded a disgrace any more than heterosexuality. The charge against Socrates was largely a pretext, the politicians having to give some plausible reason for ridding themselves of him.

Plato's falsetto voice—a common characteristic of androgynes—is commented on in writings of his day still extant. He never married nor procreated.

ALEXANDER THE GREAT has been adjudged by sexologists an androgyne of the mild type. He was the first prominent Greek to dispense with hirsute decorations. The probability is that he was naturally beardless. But in imitation of the genius and leader of their generation, all the men who wished to be somebody started to shave clean. Knowledge of the razor first became common in Greece because Alexander the Great happened to be congenitally beardless!

As a monarch, Alexander was compelled to espouse a woman. But he spent nearly all his married life absent from his legal spouse, and was incapable of procreation. All the evidence is that his real soulmate was a young warrior of his entourage. The two were inseparable. His strange affection for other young men of his entourage is remarked by contemporaries. He bewailed the death of favorites in battle as only a wife can mourn a husband.

Androgynes, because they possess the feminine psyche in greater or less degree, are generally very much opposed to war. But it is possible for a less extreme androgyne—of the psychic hermaphrodite type—to be a great general when the leadership of armies is *thrust* upon him. Genius occurs far oftener in connection with androgynism than with full-fledged masculinity. The rare keenness of mind of an androgyne like Alexander would enable him to plan successful campaigns. But his feminine cowardice would always keep him far from the battle-front, where there was no danger of a hair of his head ever being touched. And that is what happened with Alexander. Above all things else, he was a sybarite.

Androgynes, though never mixing in a fight themselves, are particularly attracted toward the war-loving "hero." Much more than half of my own associates during my female-impersonation sprees belonged to a profession whose object was to kill their fellow man. For almost twenty years of my "youngmanhood," I was an habitué of barracks, etc., and a worshipper of swords and rifles, although I would have been horrified if required to take them into my own hands. I have known other androgynes whose female-impersonation sprees were staged before professional common soldiers. A young androgyne acquaintance actually enlisted in the hospital corps in the war with Germany because he wished to be surrounded continually with warriors—the type of manhood which androgynes in general most servilely worship. Walt Whitman is celebrated for his work among the wounded in America's War of the Rebellion. I read in a medical journal that during the World War, a problem with the Italian army heads was to debar androgynes, who were said to demoralize the army because of their cowardice and seductive influence on their sexually full-fledged comrades. I heard of an androgyne who received a dishonorable discharge from the American conscript army because wrongly judged to be the incarnation of deepdyed moral depravity.

Perhaps the reason why Alexander and the next mild androgyne to be described were two out of the three greatest generals and conquerors of history was their craze to pass practically all their adult lives surrounded by warriors!

JULIUS CÆSAR has been adjudged by sexologists an androgyne of the mild type. He married, as social custom demanded of aristocratic Romans, but spent nearly all his wedded life absent from his legal spouse. His offspring is *said* to have consisted only of a single daughter. History *says* he had a son by Cleopatra. But this is doubtful because that queen was every man's wife. But even if Cæsar had offspring, he would merely be proved a psychic hermaphrodite.

Cæsar was always clean-shaven, if not naturally beardless. He even had his body depilated—as is customary today with "fairies." Like the latter also, he was, in dress, notoriously fussy and feminine—in order to prove attractive to his lieutenants. He was an instinctive female-impersonator. His entourage were accustomed to refer to him as "the queen." Of all historic characters, Cæsar excels in respect to the sensational stories of homosexual excesses found in contemporary authors still extant.

Cæsar was a great conqueror merely because circumstances, largely beyond his control, placed him at the head of an army. As in the case of Alexander, Cæsar's genius enabled him to plan successful campaigns. Others, however, had to expose life and limb, while he kept himself safe in the rear passing his days and nights as an extreme voluptuary.

MICHELANGELO, with the renaissance of civilization after the Dark Ages, heads the list of the mildly androgynous. He never married or was known to have a mistress. He left behind many hitherto unpublished homosexual sonnets of such merit that his nephew-executor gave them to the world after radical expurgation. Angelo's statues and paintings are pre-eminent in their consummate, although sensual, outlines of the nude adult male, the principal subject of his art. His statues of the nude youthful Bacchus, Cupid, and David of his middle twenties point the direction of his sexuality. Before thirty he also produced the picture, "The Battle of Cascina," 288 square feet crowded with nude male figures. His favorite Greek sculpture was a statue of Hercules.

RAPHAEL was an ultra-androgyne. He was always beardless (probably natural) and boylike in appearance. Instead of choosing a Roman mademoiselle to be mistress of his mansion in the then most aristocratic residence district of the world, he took two young men to live with him as "sons",—a common practice with well-to-do twentieth century androgynes.

The SHAKESPEARE-AUTHOR was an androgyne. The proof lies in the numerous homosexual passages of his sonnets. The authorship of the Shakespeare literature is still undetermined after close to three hundred publications on this question. If Providence grants me time, I will finally prove beyond the shadow of a doubt, by the homosexual argument original with myself, that Francis Bacon was the Shakespeare-author. I give below an outline of my proposed thesis.

The young actor, Shakespeare, was a tremendously virile male, but estranged from his wife and living apart during most of his married life. Bacon was an androgyne several years older than Shakespeare. He married only in middle life and solely for money. He was a great statesman, but sorely in need of money to meet his extravagant tastes. Apparently he was incapable of procreation. Both men lived in London, and were at least acquaintances, during the dozen years which saw the creation of the Shakespeare literature.

Bacon was the foremost scholar and one of the foremost statesmen of his generation. He and the Shakespeare-author are recognized today as two out of the three greatest intellects which have ever blossomed forth in England—even by those who deny the identity of the two, and hand the palm of Shakespeare-author to the obscure actor, Shakespeare.

Numerous literateurs believe that evidence exists that the incomparable Bacon's fad was writing plays, the theatre in his day being comparatively a new craze (that is, for modern times)—as are the "movies" in the first quarter of the twentieth century. It would then have been regarded as incongruous for the dignified statesman, Bacon, to write plays as for an expresident of the United States today to write scenarios for the "movies." Through covering his authorship, Bacon was spared the jests of his upper-crust entourage.

Whatever credit, too, the plays had, Bacon would wish his adored soul-mate to reap—just as the present writer has sacrificed his own interests fundamentally that his soul-mate might be benefited. But if Bacon had thought the Shakespeare literature would survive his own generation, he would doubtless, on his deathbed, have confessed himself its author. But even for many years after his death, everybody considered it would be forgotten by man as soon as the shredded leaves of the first printing were thrown into the fire place.

Another reason why Bacon would never confess his authorship is that in his age the law condemned to burial *alive* any one guilty of such homosexual sentiments as he was constrained, by passion, to express in the "Shakespeare" sonnets.

Francis Bacon published extensively under his own name. He published extensively—as a large body of literateurs believe—under the name of "William Shakespeare." Just as the present writer has quite a number of publications under his legal name, and a number under the name "Ralph Werther—Jennie June." And no one suspects the identity of the two present-day authors.

The actual Shakespeare—behind whose skirts Bacon hid—was, down to his death, only an obscure actor, not known personally to any writer of his own generation except (by supposition) Bacon. The actor Shakespeare has achieved immortality through having been Bacon's soul-mate.

Walt Whitman stands foremost among American androgynes. But he was of the mild type. Many passages of *Leaves of Grass* and *Drumtaps* exist as proof. He never married, although closely pursued by even wealthy women desiring him as husband. In middle age he spent his hours for recreation in the society of adolescents—as I was informed by Whitman's so-called "adopted son". That is, he courted them, as a normal man courts a woman. Chance made me intimate with the "adopted son" in his seventies. All three of us happened to belong to New York City.

Surely we androgynes, who for two thousand years have been despised, hunted down, and crushed under the heel of normal men because they have misunderstood biblical condemnations of homosexuality, have no reason to be ashamed of our heritage. America's foremost poet; the world's greatest sculptor subsequently to Athens' golden age; the two greatest ethicists and two out of the three greatest intellects of ancient Greece and Rome; two out of the three greatest conquerors of history; the greatest painter of all ages; and—to cap the climax—the greatest intellect that the English-speaking world ever produced and the greatest literary genius of all time (these two distinctions united in Francis Bacon)—ALL WERE ANDROGYNES.[2]

---

2. For twenty-five years, the author has combed the medical press for information on androgynism. This chapter is the fruit. I made no notes, never expecting to publish the results. At the present writing, I lack the necessary month for research to the end of making a complete list of my sources. For Socrates, see Plato's **Symposium** and **Phædo,** Xenophon's **Symposium,** and Haller's **Die Rede des Sokrates in Platon's Symposium**. For Plato, see his **Dialogues,** particularly the **Symposium**; Grote's **Plato;** Ellis's **Sexual Inversion,** page 229; **The Sexuality of Plato** in **Journal of Urology and Sexology**, 1916, page 201. For Cæsar, see Dr. Wm. Lee Howard's **Pederasty vs. Prostitution** in **Journal of the American Medical Association,** May 15, 1897, and Suetonius' **Lives of the Cæsars,** written about A. D. 120. The latter work is a revelation of the pederasty with which the best Roman society was honeycombed. I believe conditions are about the same today in all civilizations above the barbarous, although in Christian nations one has not been permitted to publish the facts. They are really not horrible, nor portentous of ruin for society; merely **imagined** to be so. They are not really conducive to the detriment of society, and have existed practically as now throughout history. It is all because Nature has created the phenomenon of androgynism, really beneficent to society, but sorely misjudged by writers grossly ignorant of the phenomenon. Its final investigation in the twentieth century can do no hurt; only a world of good.

For Michelangelo, see his Sonnets and his biography by J. A. Symonds. For the Shakespeare-Author, see his Sonnets and Oscar Wilde's **The Portrait of Mr. W. H.,** published in **Blackwood's** in 1889, as well as that same article expanded in a monograph published by Mitchell Kennerly in 1921. For Whitman, see his **Leaves of Grass** and **Drumtaps.**

Mrs. Havelock Ellis, in her **New Horizons in Love and Life,** says: "Inversion (sexual) and genius have a sort of affinity. They certainly both tend to belong to the neurotic group." (R. W's comment: As a rule both androgynes and gynanders, but particularly the former, are bundles of nerves.)

The valuable popular exposition of the philosophy of sex, Edward Carpenter's **Love's Coming-of-Age** (published by Boni and Liveright) did not come to my attention until after THE FEMALE-IMPERSONATORS was written. The following are excerpts from the chapter, **The Intermediate Sex,** the bracketed words being my own: Page 124: "Charles G. Leland ("Hans Breitmann") in his book, **The Alternate Sex** (1904), insists much on the frequent combination of the characteristics of both sexes in remarkable men and women, and has a chapter on "The Female Mind in Man," and another on "The Male Intellect in

And to you full-fledged males I say: "What God hath cleansed (through endowment with sublime talents) call not ye 'Unclean!'"

Woman." (I once read the statement in a medical journal, name not recalled: "Homosexualists are particularly common among authors.")

Page 139: "The instinctive artistic nature of the male of this class (urnings or androgynes), his sensitive spirit, his wavelike emotional temperament, combined with hardihood of intellect and body. . . may be said to give them. . . through their double nature, command of life in all its phases, and a certain freemasonry of the secrets of the two sexes which may well favor their function as reconcilers (of the full-fledged males with the full-fledged females) and interpreters (of human nature, particularly from the standpoint of sex). Certainly it is remarkable that some of the world's greatest leaders and artists have been dowered either wholly or in part with the Uranian temperament (that is, either ultra-androgynes or ultragynanders or else psychic hermaphrodites)—as in the cases of Michael Angelo, Shakespeare, Marlowe, Alexander the Great, Julius Cæsar, or, among women, Christine of Sweden, Sappho the poetess, and others."

It is noteworthy that tremendously virile males—who alone, as a rule, have been intimate with the extreme type of androgyne—have named him "fairie" in English-speaking countries and "petit-jesus" (Little Jesus) in France, largely because of his having, innate, the disposition of an angel; while the most common scientific term for androgynes in general has been "urning", from Greek **ouranos**, meaning "heavenly being." The originator of the term "urning", however, was himself a bisexual, K. H. Ulrichs, an Austrian, the originator, about 1880, of the scientific study of sexual intermediates, and author of several published papers on the theme.

A lesser historic character than those listed in my text, Lord Cornbury, cousin of Queen Anne and colonial governor of New York, had the fad of attiring himself in feminine finery for a stroll on the capital city's principal promenade. One of the most prominent judges (now deceased) of the Atlantic coast was declared to me, by a citizen of his own town, to be a psychic hermaphrodite. An official once high up in the government at Washington was declared to me, by a citizen of his native place, to be an androgyne. One of the greatest factors in world politics today is merely a grown-up **infant** and an androgyne, though at the same time a genius.

IV

MAN IS A PASSIONAL, RATHER THAN A RATIONAL, BEING

Twentieth-century psychologists are coming around to the view that even the leaders of thought are governed by instinct and *mores* rather than reason. Even for intellectuals, truth is what is intuitive or what satisfies their prejudices and instincts. Still in the twentieth century, the leaders of thought bow down before intellectual idols, although other than those overthrown by Francis Bacon. Still today—as in the generation of Roger Bacon (13th century)—conservatives yearn to imprison, or even burn at the stake, those in whom a purer reason than their own operates.

My own is thus a Herculean task: To be an intellectual iconoclast. To break down the last remnant of cultured man's savage, criminal instincts and *mores*. But, like Roger Bacon, I may comfort myself with the thought that my views are centuries in advance of my time; but, like him, I am therefore bitterly persecuted.[1]

"Away with any one who attempts to bring out the truth about sex!" cry the conservatives. "Crucify him! Crucify him! Sex is a theme too disgusting for discussion!"

In the university I took an extended course of lectures on physiology. But not a word was said about sex. The professor would not have thus befouled his mouth, nor corrupted the morals of his students. Martin's *Human Body,* the standard text-book of the time, had to be published in two editions: (1) That which treated of human sexuality as viewed in the Dark Ages, and (2) that which imagined the *genus homo* to be asexual.

---

1. A confidant who read these paragraphs commented in substance: "'Physician, heal thyself!' Your book shows that you yourself are governed by instinct and prejudice. 'Those that live in glass houses should not throw stones.' Therefore omit these paragraphs."

If I am governed by instinct and prejudice, I am conscious of being ruled only by reason. Perhaps those who advocate the suppression of intermediates without investigation equally feel they are governed by pure reason. Granted that both they and myself are ruled by instinct and prejudice and that it is impossible for mankind to exercise pure reason, nevertheless intermediates should finally have their day in court. They number 700,000 in continental United States alone, including some of the brightest minds and most useful members of society.

One presumed male out of every three hundred belongs to the *third sex,* strictly speaking. That is, the ultra-androgynes—the pseudo-men who possess only undersized and non-functional male pudenda, whose body otherwise tends toward feminesqueness, and whose psyche, predilections, tastes, gestures, and postures remind one of a female.

The third sex is a commonplace topic in the Underworld, which comprises about one-tenth the population of "Christian" lands. The Underworlders, however, generally fail to understand the cause of the effeminacy. The nine-tenths of the unlearned who have never entered a more immoral place than a "movie" theatre are almost entirely ignorant of the third sex. What hazy ideas they have are criminally incorrect. And except for a handful of sexologists, the learned still cling to views handed down from the Dark Ages.

In the seventeenth century, when a cyclone demolished a hamlet or an epidemic broke out, a council of physicians, lawyers, and clergymen was called to determine which semi-bearded old hag had *wished* the catastrophe upon the community. After prayer for divine guidance and an exhortation by a parson that the Bible taught that witches ought to be ferreted out, the high-brows would seek to determine who of the several bags of bone known to all of them presented the most loathsome appearance, and who should therefore be burned at the stake as the *witch* responsible for the catastrophe—as the necessary human sacrifice to appease the anger of the Unseen Powers. For even down to the twentieth century there survives in Christendom the pagan superstition of the necessity of a human sacrifice now and then.

But in the twentieth century, leaders of thought have evolved from the belief in witchcraft. They must look elsewhere than to semi-bearded hags for their sacrificial victims on whom to load the sins of mankind, and the blame for the decline and fall of nations. Since, next to hags, they consider sexual cripples as the most loathsome of humans, they make the latter the scape-goats of present-day society. While they no longer burn them at the stake or bury them alive (as provided in old European law) they are permitted by twentieth century statutes to imprison inoffensive androgynes for twenty years. And these archaic statutes are still frequently enforced. Only a few months ago I read of a Boston clergyman who was sentenced to prison on the testimony of a young exsoldier. But today these statutes serve chiefly as ground for extensive blackmail of Nature's step-children, hardly one of whom, if belonging to the middle or upper class, but has had to pay out considerable sums, occasionally running into the thousands.

Instead of imprisonment, public opinion has generally substituted banishment of the disclosed androgyne forever from all he loves.

During the few months of composing this book, the New York papers have told of the abrupt flight to parts unknown of three intellectual leaders in their communities, two just over the city line and the third within a hundred miles. They had to flee, not because they had done the least real harm (all three were pastors of churches) but because of the mediæval ignorance and bitter hatred that their communities immediately manifested toward a "man" (reputedly) all of a sudden disclosed to be a "monster" (though in reality a harmless and pitiable sexual cripple). The populace, ignorant that he had probably practiced a thousand times more self-denial than any one of themselves, but had at last been able to withstand Nature's demands no longer, chased him out of his community for good and all with the feeling that he was the lowest scoundrel that ever contaminated it.

I admit that these unfortunates did show bad judgment in remaining in the ministry when they knew they were afflicted with a powerful instinct abhorred by the sexually full-fledged, and they showed the worst kind of judgment in having recourse to boys under puberty. But they were in a tight place, and besides felt that they were doing no one any harm. For the androgyne generally comes at last to the view that what Nature demands can be no sin and, if properly fulfilled, no transgression against any human.

The newspaper devotee runs across a similar item every once in a while, and nearly always the "monster" is a clergyman or a teacher. But the abhorred penchant (fellatio) is, of course, not peculiar to these professions. Simply their high ethical standing, and the common fancy that they should therefore be proof against what is incorrectly regarded as the worst of vices, attract greater attention, and give news value to the occasional disclosures.

But it is probable that among the occupations, those two, together with all having to do with art of any kind, have the largest proportions of androgynes. As a rule, male bisexuals are goody-goody boys who develop into ultra-religious adolescents. They are enthusiastic to better the race morally and spiritually. The robes commonly worn by clergymen are also a powerful drawing card, since androgynes yearn for apparel that conceals that they are bipeds. Thus quite a number who were born intellectual and whose sexual ardor, during adolescence, is comparatively weak, gravitate into the two professions standing highest ethically and religiously. When making his choice, the adolescent is filled with religious fervor and possessed of a strong determination to crucify his "homosexual" tendencies. The androgyne already yielding would never put on "the cloth," although he would go into pedagogy. But the puritan-minded regards these tendencies as his "besetting sin" and fights them for years in the strenuous manner described in my own AUTOBIOGRAPHY OF AN ANDROGYNE. Throughout his teens, and perhaps even his twenties, he never expects to be overmastered. But later in life many a one of these sexual cripples who have put on "the cloth" disgrace it notwithstanding his prior unparalleled mental struggles against Nature's behests.

Or if coming out victor in the lifelong struggle, the pitiable woman-man lives down to death under the obsession (due to misinterpreted biblical texts) that the gratification of his unusual instinct is the most heinous of sins, and spends all his days, in which God meant that he should rejoice, in mourning over his sexual ardor (for which he does not realize he is irresponsible), in crucifying his body continuously, with its affections and lusts (as commanded by the anaphrodite, St. Paul), and is thereby, throughout adult life, en the borderline of insanity. I have heard sermons from such clergymen and was moved to pity as they were shedding tears in the pulpit and rendering themselves unpopular, both with their fellow preachers who are sexually full-fledged and with the laity, because their aspect was always that of tragedy. I advise that all such melancholiacs immediately ask that they be honorably deposed from the ministry. As a result, their lives would be happy and satisfying.

The vast majority of preachers are manly. I have a higher respect for that profession than for any other. If it had not been for my androgynism, I would have myself entered it. It would be well for the Church authorities to question, as to their sexuality, all candidates for beginning a theological course, and in the kindest manner advise adolescents in the least bisexual to choose some other profession because of the public's misunderstanding of this phenomenon. Sexual conduct is not primarily a voluntary matter or an ethical question, but rooted in anatomy, physiology, and psychology. The androgyne who yearns to preach the Gospel can do so through the printed word. Because of St. Paul's sex teaching (that of an anaphrodite) the profession of "the cloth" is rightly open only to anaphrodites and the mildly virile. The more virile are likewise excluded because it is next to impossible for them to abstain from adultery.

Why are androgynes so hated? Primarily because the leaders of thought have always identified them with the men of ancient Sodom (mistakenly, because the Sodomites were full-fledged males) and historians have mistakenly (because they never met androgynes personally and were taught in their boyhood to hate them with all their heart, soul, mind, and strength) laid upon them all the blame for the decline and fall of nations, and declared that therefore effeminacy or androgynism is a type of moral depravity to be crushed mercilessly. Better that some thousands of androgynes be deprived of life, liberty, and the pursuit of happiness than that the general welfare of the nation be imperilled! Androgynes—they argue—are unavoidably the scapegoats of the race.

I answer: In the first place, such imperilment is only a *figment of the imagination*. This superstition can be disposed of by merely asking to what extent the welfare of humanity was imperiled by the sex functioning of the arch-androgynes listed in chapter III? In the second place, androgynism is not moral depravity or degeneracy. I myself—an extreme type of androgyne—spring from the most puritan stock. I was brought up to consider that on Sunday, reading anything but Christian doctrine or walking a hundred feet for mere pleasure were heinous sins. In addition to springing from the most puritan stock, both my paternal and maternal stock are of unusually strong build. A paternal and also a maternal uncle were professional athletes. A brother was the champion athlete of my native village. My stock and early environment are indeed the last that any one would pick out as likely to bring into the world a homosexual or androgyne as a result of moral degradation.[2] My androgynism has, however, made me myself rather lilliputian. With one exception, I grew up to be the smallest man of my paternal and maternal families.

It is not necessary to crush androgynes in order to guard against the spread of effeminacy. Effeminacy, in the sense of androgynism,

---

2. My own case indicates that Nature creates androgynes and gynanders as a brake on too rapid multiplication. Both paternal and maternal stock have averaged eight children to a marriage. It seems that Nature wishes to preserve to as many of her children as possible the joys of courtship. Often, instead of making cold anaphrodites or female icebergs out of the men and women not needed to perpetuate the race, she brings into the world androgynes or gynanders—as a rule, sterile.

does not spread by example. It is entirely congenital. Only a physical male born with quasi-feminine predilections would adopt the role of a female after becoming adult. An androgyne's predilections and practices are regarded with such repugnance by all full-fledged males that none would stoop to them unless constrained by instinct.

Why imprison and murder the androgyne any more than the deaf-mute? The former is no more abnormal than the latter; no more degenerate; no more depraved. It is unfortunate that the human race is handicapped with either of these defective classes. But the androgyne deserves only pity, the same as the deaf-mute.

Effeminacy in an entirely different sense, and a kind that spreads rapidly through example, is the actual cause of the decline and fall of nations; in the sense of the weakening of the moral fibre of the males of the upper crust or ruling class through their having grown overfond of ease and pleasure and lost their joy in industry and justifiable fighting. A neighboring nation of superior moral fibre is quick to learn of such effemination and subjugates the decadent one. But these *effeminates'* fondness for the gentle sex has in no way declined. Generally it has greatly augmented. Witness the decline and fall of the Greek, Roman, and Turkish empires.

Where has androgynism been more prevalent than formerly among the American aborigines? Probably because the tribes were constantly underfed. Whenever a male arrived at puberty, the weapons of the warrior and the cooking vessels of the squaw were ceremoniously placed before him that he might choose his future social status. A not inconsiderable number of adolescents (because congenital androgynes) always chose the culinary utensils and passed the rest of their lives as squaws, the hair of the beard being plucked out as fast as it showed itself, and the costume being that of the female sex. Surely savage tribes continuously on the war-path can not be accused of degenerative effeminacy!

About one-third the soul-mates of androgynes who have come under my observation have been voluntary common soldiers or blue-jackets. I am far from being the only androgyne who has gravitated toward the "supreme men" whose voluntary profession has as its aim the killing of their fellow man. Androgynism appears to go hand in hand with militarism rather than *vice versa*. Havelock Ellis says that homosexuality is particularly common among the Sikhs, the most military of the Hindustan races.

It is more likely that the emergence of androgynism is a sign of national health. The ultra-brilliant Age of Pericles surpassed all other periods in the recognition and influence of androgynism, which promotes art and general culture. The androgyne, being a combination of man and woman in a single individual, has a wider view of life than the full-fledged man or woman. He possesses, in a measure, the mental qualities peculiar to each sex. That is why the Shakespeare-Author knew both the masculine and the feminine mind better than any other writer. Such duality is the reason artistic genius crops out far more frequently among androgynes than among the sexually full-fledged. The amalgamated man-woman nature gets nearest to sentiment and emotion—to the soul of art.[3]

Why do cultured androgynes carefully conceal their quasi-feminine sexual predilections? Why did Angelo not publish any of his homosexual sonnets? Why did Raphael not proclaim on the housetops the happenings in his house at night? Androgynes hide their sexual predilections and practices, not because of consciousness of personal degeneracy, but because grossly misunderstood by the sexually full-fledged. By exception, Oscar Wilde was open and above board, and was therefore shut up in prison.

Only bigoted pseudo-scientists have pronounced androgynes degenerates. Only mediæval medicine, not modern medicine. Androgynism is merely an instance of arrested development; or possibly of atavism—an attempt on the part of Nature to return to the original hermaphrodism of man's early antecedents. The androgyne who follows the dictates of Nature is not a whit more degenerate morally than the full-fledged man who marries. It is only the fallible *mores* which make the full-fledged think that a person with apparently male pudenda who impersonates a female is infinitely below themselves morally. Were Socrates, Plato, Angelo, Raphael, and Francis Bacon monsters of depravity? Ought the Shakespeare-Author to have been buried alive by his hare-brained fellow citizens before he had a chance to pen a line?

The chief charge against androgynes is that they are guilty of "the awful crime of race suicide." But it is the fault of Nature alone that the

---

3. I wrote this paragraph, so much like that quoted (at close of preceding chapter) from Carpenter's **Love's Coming of Age,** before I had heard of the existence of the book named.

ultra-androgyne is incapable of doing his part in the perpetuation of the race.

The cultured androgyne, knowing his irresistible instincts are harmless to his soul-mate, is unable to discern in them any transgression against ethics or against God.

But a very small proportion of adult androgynes have been guilty of a lamentable transgression because finding themselves in a tight place: that is, recourse to boys under puberty. The prudery of full-fledged men has hitherto prohibited androgynes from scientific knowledge of themselves. Until thirty years ago, American and British public opinion would not tolerate the publication of the facts about androgynism even for circulation among the medical profession. Havelock Ellis's *Sexual Inversion*, the earliest published book in the English language on androgynism, was promptly suppressed by the British government thirty years ago. I myself had to bend the knee for eighteen years to medical publishers before my AUTOBIOGRAPHY OF AN ANDROGYNE was fed into the printing-press in 1918.

Thus, because full-fledged men have interdicted to cultured androgynes the means of understanding themselves and knowledge of how they ought to pass their lives, some—particularly those who have achieved places of honor, because androgynes of lower rank do not need to be so crafty in hiding their terrible secret from the heartless world— have ultimately been revealed guilty of recourse to the immature (because they could not screw up their courage to disclose their abnormality to an older and wiser male). But on account of the tyranny of the full-fledged, these erring androgynes merit mercy. Their offences have probably not been at all harmful to the immature. They are merely asserted to be so by men unable to accept any scientific results except those inculcated by mediæval savants. But this one offence of androgynes will be a thing of the past when they are permitted recourse to books which explain the riddle of their lives, and when full-fledged men read such books in order that they may do justice to Nature's step-children.

As already stated, ultra-androgynes, having a woman's psyche, are goody-goodies. Indeed goody-goodiness may be regarded as their most marked characteristic. For this reason, in France, they are called "little Jesuses" (*petits jesus*) notwithstanding that the more extreme are public female-impersonators in resorts of ill repute. Ultra-androgynes are incapable of doing any real harm. If all the human race were as harmless, this world would be a far better place in which to live.

The cultured androgyne is a desirable citizen and a desirable member of any circle. While ultra-androgynism makes its victims physically weak—like a woman—it has no deteriorating effect morally or mentally. The usual charge of gross immorality is merely a relic of mediæval bigotry.

It matters not, however, that androgynes are absolutely innocuous practically and ethically. Do they not offend the *æsthetic* sense of the majority of mankind? What better cause for grinding them under one's heel?

And this bitter persecution that has been the lot of some androgynes has rendered them misanthropes. Not their androgynism *per se*. A mildly androgynous acquaintance—an intellectual giant of the highest moral character except for his irresponsible and innocuous passive pederasty—is, as a result of society's shutting him up in prison for the five years of his intellectual prime, a chronic and bitter reviler of the Church. Because zealous churchmen were responsible for the wrecking of his life through their misunderstanding of the biblical teaching on homosexuality.

But in general we androgynes, possessing the long-suffering feminine psyche, are resigned to being ground to powder by the hypocritical world. It is better to suffer than to inflict suffering. Though the world despise and ostracise us, the All-Knowing is still our refuge, and another life awaits us where conditions will be more just. The bigoted and pharisaical judges and juries who have haled hundreds of innocent androgynes off to prison should remember the Old Testament doctrine: "'Vengeance is mine!' saith Jehovah." Those who incarcerate the innocent in this world will in the next have to serve time in the darkest dungeons of a just God.

PART II
HOW THE AUTHOR CAME TO BE A
FEMALE-IMPERSONATOR

(PART TWO summarizes my pre-nineteen life and my physical and mental traits for those not reading my AUTOBIOGRAPHY OF AN ANDROGYNE. Particularly for details of purely medical interest, the scientist is referred to that work, since the present volume is designed primarily for the general reader. PART TWO, however, presents many facts not in mind when I wrote the earlier work over twenty years ago.)

I

Reveries Suggested by My Infancy

Connecticut, famous for its wooden nutmegs and other freak products, gave to the world, in 1874, one of its half-dozen most widely known girl-boys.

My mother has said that I was the greatest crybaby of her eleven children. I have really never outgrown this characteristic. Still in my late forties, I occasionally weep bitterly for a whole hour.

Up to my eighth birthday, timidity made me reluctant to leave my mother's side to play with other children. Sticking very close to "mother" as a child, and extraordinary devotion to her when adult are common earmarks of androgynism. I have known of no other reputed male so devoted to his mother, even down to his late forties, as I. My mother is still, by a kind Providence, spared to me. I frequently weep bitterly at the thought of her dying and can not imagine living when she is in the grave. I knew an androgyne who, in his sixties, died from grief a few days after the death of his mother around ninety.

In my early childhood, only one other person attracted me in a comparable fashion—a neighbor's burly boy, F'ank, five years older than myself. All my life I have seen him at least several times a year, since he has remained a close friend down to the time when we both count about half-a-century of life. His influence is still strong, although sexual relations ceased when I was seven. He was one of the most amorous of boys. From my third to seventh year, he sought me several times a week. Perhaps he also embraced every chance for heterosexual relations—common among the children under twelve in the "best set" of the village, among whom I was privileged to be brought up. And yet all these contaminated youngsters—excepting myself—turned out fairly virtuous adults. The ultra-amorous and active pederast F'ank became, when adult, exclusively heterosexual and quite promiscuous, being of the tremendously virile type. But around thirty, he settled down into absolute monogamy. He, however, never had a child. At past fifty, he stands at perfection in health, strength, and morality.

I say they "turned out"! That is, so far as I ever heard. But they would all have said of me that I passed through my adult life a cold anaphrodite! One can never know! Some might secretly have been addicted to venery as much as I. But they betrayed no external sign. Neither have I.

But while all those who indulged in "nastiness" before reaching their teens grew up, so far as I was able to observe, into men and women above reproach, two of "my set"—those who were "kids" at the same time within a radius of five hundred feet of my own paternal roof, the several homosexualist schoolmates elsewhere described having lived outside that radius—the two that had been most carefully brought up and shielded by their mother from corruption by other children, almost the only two that were sexually unblemished as children, "went to the bad" immediately on arrival at puberty. They were brother and sister—the only children of a wealthy, pious couple. The brother became a chronic dypsomaniac and roué. The sister, a beautiful and brilliant girl who had enjoyed a college education, died before thirty as a result of excesses in her chosen profession of *fille de joie* in New York City. The mother died of a broken heart in her early forties. The father, previously active in church work, became despondent on seeing both his children "go to the bad," took to drink, and died a sot.

Debauchery was born in these two children, for they had never missed Bible school up to their middle teens. They were unusually innocent prior to puberty. But religious teaching failed to convince them. They thought the "goody-goodies" were trying to rob them of the pleasures of life through false representations. I believe both could have been saved from shipwreck of life if, at puberty, a book, scientific, not goody-goody, could have been put into their hands, demonstrating that alcoholic and venereal excesses bring on ruin and often early death. Children inclined to dissipation on arrival at puberty are far more likely to heed the pronouncements of a physician than of a Bible school teacher.

In that same immediate puritan circle in my childhood's village, I have lately observed a similar case in the *next* generation. I have known well a certain gentleman of my own age since we were boys together. He is of the tremendously virile type and sowed his wild oats as hardly another young blood in the village. But in his middle twenties he was "soundly converted" in a puritan church (to which I myself belonged) and married one of its purest daughters. In his subsequent life, he attained rare success financially and socially. He has had only two children—both girls around twenty years of age at the date of writing. I know the family intimately. I have direct information that both girls are "fast going to the bad" (notwithstanding they have always been under only puritan influences) and that the father has "backslidden," evidently being no longer able to restrain his *de facto* polygamous instincts. The purest of wives is heartbroken and on the borderline of insanity.

Every one says the girls and their father are wilfully depraved and their puritan community has already begun to treat them as outcasts. *I say* the girls inherited their craze for venery from their father, in whom likewise it was inborn. He is a noble man in every other respect. All three are largely irresponsible. They are, by birth, not fitted for the puritan society in which they were brought up. Under present social ideas and usages, the only outlet for the girls is prostitution and the consequent early loss of health soon terminating in death. But their only fault is nymphomania. If society had some way by which it could bring about the satisfaction of these needs of these cultured girls, the latter could be saved from the shipwreck of life and be useful members of their community. In my own life I have proved that Christian conversion and absorption in the teachings of the Bible can not save one from innate nymphomania. I could suggest a means of salvation for these girls, but dare not. If only the leaders of thought did not prescribe an identic sex life for every daughter of Eve, although Nature has created them with such diversity along these lines! If only the leaders of thought permitted *real* sexual problems (as well as namby-pamby) to be investigated, as all other phenomena are searched out to the very bottom! If only the leaders of thought permitted the truth to be told about sex instead of continuing to propagate the hypocrisies and fabrications regnant down from the Dark Ages!

I have read statements of puritans of the dreadful results that will follow the common sex relations of children under twelve in city tenements. I have spent a large part of my life in rural districts as well as in great cities. My observations are that conditions are the same among children of both types of environment. Numerous youngsters receive their sex initiation before twelve. But, unless carried to excess, it does not seem to have any bad influence, particularly after they become adults. The probability is that the same practice has ruled among small children for thousands of years. It is Nature.

And the context moves me to remark: It turned out that of my several hundred schoolmates (prior to the university) I achieved in adult life the highest success. Not as a business man or money-maker, in which line I did not excel. Not in art or politics. But in the following fields, both individually and combined: Intellectual and general cultural development; enjoyment of (but not adeptness in) all species of art; breadth and depth of life and knowledge of human nature; enjoyment of the society of my fellow humans, particularly sexual opposites; and, last but not least, fame, or, as some would prefer to have me say, notoriety. For I feel that I, as an extreme type of the bisexual, am doomed to live in the minds of savants for scores of years after every one of my hundreds of schoolmates, and my other hundreds of university associates, are eternally forgotten.

(**Note Added in Galley:** I omitted to mention that I have also far excelled in suffering inflicted by man and in sorrow—which two items together have about counterbalanced the advantages enumerated.)

But I have achieved this last element (terrestrial immortality) of the highest success in life denied to all my wide circles of childhood and adolescence through my "going to the bad"—as the saying is. But though that was the fate marked out for me by the Architect of the Universe, I was actually able to restrain my "evil" propensities so as not to make shipwreck of life. My girl-boy intimate described in the early part of the second chapter following did make, decidedly, shipwreck of his life, as have many other girl-boys. My salvation lay in practicing *relatively*[1] extreme temperance in the indulgence of the sexual propensities except

---

1. For me it was extreme temperance, considering my natural sexual ardor. For most people it would have been gross intemperance. Extreme temperance might be defined as the denial of six-sevenths of one's strong fleshly desires. That is what it was with me. Professional fairies commonly indulge more than ten times as often per year as I did. But as a result, they go early to the grave.

during my Bowery period described in my AUTOBIOGRAPHY OF AN ANDROGYNE and RIDDLE OF THE UNDERWORLD. Extreme temperance in indulgence of any fleshly appetite is, for all humanity, the sole means of salvation from the shipwreck of earthly life. Overindulgence of any appetite defeats its own end.

Thus while nearly all other girl-boys are doomed to be forgotten by mankind a few years after their bodies return "dust to dust," I myself am—I feel—destined to live in the memory of savants primarily because of my extensive self-restraint, and secondarily because of my excelling the other girl-boys in innate brain-power.

It was F'ank who initiated me, at two, in the mysteries which gullible parents think children do not learn before puberty. But down to twelve, I considered all species of sex relations as the monopoly of naughty children. All adults had of course outgrown such depths of nastiness.

Down to my present age of close to half-a-century, F'ank has been the hero in half my many sexual dreams. After I reached seven, we ceased to be confidential. I therefore never confessed to him that his influence prior to my seventh year almost wrecked my adult life— probably consigning me to an irresponsible, intensive fairie career— and a thousand times made me wish, because a slave to fellatio, that I were dead. For I firmly believe that girl-boys, if not repeatedly seduced before puberty, will, as adults, have only weak and controllable desires for the sexual functioning ordained by Nature for their type. While they are commonly fellators or else pathics *congenitally,* only oft repeated seduction in early childhood makes them, after puberty, irresponsible psychic nymphomaniacs who recruit the ranks of fairies. But for those repeatedly seduced in early childhood, the penchant is truly irresistible in adulthood and would be followed regardless of all legal penalties. Just as most men would steal a loaf of bread if their only means of salvation from death through hunger.

Not too often repeated homosexual acts on the part of a small child, however, are not likely to make him an adult pervert. An *innate* tendency is practically indispensable. Early experiences along innate lines merely strengthen a congenital bias, just as the author became an intensive adult fairie as a result—I am inclined to believe—of my intense fairieship from three to six.

While I believe sexual relations of children under twelve when not often repeated will not render them particularly lustful as adults, an *intensive* sex life of a small child—as in my own case—is likely to render him or her extremely intemperate sexually after puberty. Mothers should therefore keep a watchful eye over the whereabouts and associates of the "angel child," and not allow it in secluded cosy nooks with older children. A careful watch should be kept over nurse-girls. Children under twelve, and even under six, need chaperons almost as much as those just past puberty.

Parents should take pains that the "angel child" regards them as confidants, sharers of its every secret. If this had happened in my own case, I might have been spared a world of woe after puberty. To preserve the frankness of the "angel child," not even a mild rebuke should ever be administered for its sexual lapses; but kind persuasion alone, and care that the child does not again come into exciting surroundings.

My own parents and teachers never vouchsafed the least sex knowledge. I once asked where babies came from. Doctors found them in the street gutters and brought them to people's houses. Instinct and older boys were my only instructors. Parents, teachers, but preferably the school physician, should begin with children of six a clean initiation into these mysteries—absorbing even to youngsters of that tender age—to replace the hitherto regnant nasty one wrought by child lore handed down, from mouth to mouth, through the centuries, and characterized by unprintable words, in uttering, seeing, and hearing which numerous children seem to take delight.

Or is the subject of sex irreformable and hopeless? Is it really the crying shame of the human race?

From my third to seventh year, F'ank and I were drawn toward one another. I yearned to recline in his arms. "F'ank," I once said, "I'm not af'aid on your lap. But I'm af'aid nearly always. I'm af'aid, when I get as big as papa, hair'll grow on my cheeks, like on his. How could I ever use a horrible wazor, like him! I hope I'll die before I get big!"

I was destined to be a sort of pet with others of the more stalwart boys. It was because I retained my babyishness—like an idiot—at least down to the age of seven, and was, besides, girlish. I commonly felt myself a little girl and told playmates to call me Jennie. They have remarked that I was "more girl than boy." Adults, however, were blind to my bisexuality. They ridiculed me for carrying a doll in my arms when I took a walk; etc. Because I was the only child of my set thus violently crossed, I was the most unhappy. Taunts sometimes drove me to throw myself on the floor, bang my head, and exclaim: "I wish I were dead!"

But, on the whole, my early childhood was happy. With F'ank I would play "papa and mamma." He would "go to business," while I took care of the dolls; etc. I made and laundered their wardrobes. One day a sudden shower surprised me. Gazing at the ill-fated wash on the line, I sobbed: "Oh it yains! It yains! And my c'ose 'll get wet!"

The day of thoroughgoing disillusionment came early in my seventh year. It was the style for boys to wear skirts up to that age. How I loved them! And I never expected to clothe myself otherwise. Even down to my middle forties, I have always felt more at home in skirts.

Then I wasn't to be allowed to go through life as a girl and a woman? I was up against the choice of spending the rest of life in my bedroom, or drawing on a pair of the utterly loathed breeches. At first it was the same as if I had to go on the street in my underclothes. I would dodge behind a tree when an acquaintance hove in sight. How poignantly I missed petticoats as a screen for my shameful nether limbs! Not to mention the deprivation of the pleasure of feeling them dangling about my knees.

II

School Days

*F*irst year: How terrible the aspect of the big brick academy! How awe-inspiring the smell of the newly varnished floor on the first day of my school life! How my heart jumped to my throat whenever I caught the cold, stern eye of the school-marm piercing through my own little self! How bold and bad and rough all the boys were! Why must I sit with them and enter by their door when I so longed to be with the gentle and soft-voiced girls?

And could I ever bring myself to see what was on the other side of the sign: "For boys only"? What right had *I* there? For I already recognized I was really not a boy! At that age I gloated over being a *girl-boy*.

There was thus provision for the comfort of the boys. There was provision for the comfort of the girls. But architects have never thought to make provision for the *girl-boys*!

The first week I suffered terribly rather than invade the retreat barred to all but boys. Then an unprintable experience right at my desk afforded the room a good laugh and sent me home for dry clothing. I now preferred the horror of the retreat to being laughed at and sent home. But I made a virtue of haste and watched for a moment when no other boy was out.

Second year: I sat on a rear seat with a boy whom I stared at and touched because of the softness and radiance of his hair, the rich red of his cheeks, and his sturdy build. Now and then we kissed when no one was looking. But once a loud smack reverberated just after the near-sighted school-marm had requested such stillness that one could hear a pin drop. As she had never been kissed by a person of the opposite sex, she considered a smack the unpardonable sin. My hero-boy took his whipping with a cynical smile. But I wept for a half-hour.

Third year: I was caught in an immeasurably worse impropriety[1] under a desk. The teacher thought my parents ought to know. Violently angry, my father hammered my body with the heel of a boot. In a dozen

---

1. Fellatio.

years, not one of my numerous brothers and sisters (although I was the only goody-goody one) suffered such a thrashing. All the rest of my home life, father treated me the worst of all, notwithstanding I far excelled in school-work. What a trial to have a *girl-boy* son? Why had I ever been born? Subsequently there existed a lifelong coolness between father and me.

Fourth year: (A typical spring afternoon.) After school, the west playground was thronged with boys. I alone hastened directly to the street, embarrassed as a little girl alone with two hundred boys. One calls out: "Ralph, hurry to the girls' yard where you belong!" Another: "Ralph, your legs are as shapely as a girl's. You would make a goodlooking girl!" A third throws his arms around me and exclaims: "Kissing you is as good as kissing a girl!"

My embarrassment prevented my relishing these attentions at the moment. But I always gloated over them after I got to bed.

I had not quite reached the gate when a ball rolled to my feet and the players shouted for it. With beet-red face on account of what I knew would be said, I gave the ball an awkward toss. "Hah hah hah! You throw just like a girl! Miss Nancy!"

Often I went around Robin Hood's barn to avoid this particular embarrassment.

Arrived in the girls' yard, I felt as if freed from captivity and in my proper element. Shyness and fright gave way to gleefulness. Moreover, I cared only for the less strenuous games of the gentle sex.

Several boys mounted the high fence in order to tease me. "Ralph, I promise you my sister's doll carriage to push to school!" . . . "Heigh, Miss Werther, have you finished the mitten I saw you knitting?" . . . "Say, Ralph, give me a kiss, will you?"

While with girls, I liked nothing better than such bantering. I outgirled them in our reaction to the boys' teasing. We finally succeeded in provoking the boys to chase us—my wish all along. To be chased by boys was the highest of childhood's pleasures.

I was always the ringleader of my girl clique, never reflecting on its unnaturalness. They never regarded me as a normal boy—only a "girl-boy." We would even discuss our boy favorites.

Fifth year: My parents thought that if I were shut up closely with boys and away from even the sight of girls, I would be cured of my effeminacy. Thus my fifth to eleventh years of school life were staged at a boys' "prep" several miles from my home village and numbering about a hundred students. But I was only a day-pupil except during my senior year.

The first week, it was an ordeal on a par with being forced into breeches. I was in a state of chronic fright. When addressed, my reply was inaudible six feet away. But after becoming well-acquainted with class-mates, I have seated myself on their laps right in the school-room. For they appeared demigods.

They would run a hand up my arm. "Your skin is softer than velvet. And your pencils look as if you had chewed them off with your teeth. And what makes you scream when a fellow merely touches you? Ralph, you certainly ought to have been born a girl! You will never make a man!"

On holidays I would run off to the house of a girl friend. With several of the gentle sex, I would play hide-and-seek in remote nooks, as hay-mows. Later I would exchange clothing with one, and we would seek boy acquaintances that I might display my skill in female-impersonation.

Adult intimates would point the finger of scorn in vain. To pass life as far as possible like a girl was the very essence of existence, for which I was willing to sacrifice everything else.

The instinctive manner of coasting is a criterion of psychic sex. Every boy of my set, excepting myself, rode bellyflops—too strenuous for the soft-muscled and timid girls. As I possessed their physical and psychic softness, I also coasted upright.

In ascending the hill, I kept with the girls. I enjoyed talking about only their interests. As the boys passed, they would call out: "Girl-boy! Mollie Coddle!"

One afternoon, two snow forts were built fifty feet apart. All the boys, excepting myself, took their stand bravely behind the breastworks and rained snowballs on the defenders of the opposite fort. The girls were almost prostrate in the deep snow behind—out of danger of being hit in the face—packing snowballs for the throwers. And I, GIRL-BOYWISE, did as they, the eternal impropriety never dawning on me.

But one of the girls cried out: "Why are you not throwing snowballs with the boys? Afraid of getting hit, are you? Why don't you put on petticoats?"

After I retired that night, I had not yet recovered from my speechless chagrin. "Why was it that I was not taking a boy's place in life? Why did I sit upright when coasting? Why did I feel more at home in girls' attire? Why did the boys tease me just as they did the girls? Could it be that I was *a girl imprisoned in the body of a boy?*

"How could I face manhood? Are men under compulsion to go and vote? But how could I push my way into the crowd of rough men always hanging (at that period) around the polling places?

"How terrible to be a boy! Couldn't I take papa's razor and in a minute rid myself of the excrescence? A razor ought to be sharp enough to do the job! O God, change my body this moment by a miracle! Turn me into a girl!" I sobbed.

One day, being a goody-goody, I had felt it my duty to tell the teacher on a mischievous boy. As I left the school for my train, I was seized violently. "If you were a big, strong fellow like us, we would give you a good thrashing! We'll only see if we can lift you off the ground by your hair. The more you cry, the better we like it. Keep your hands down! Slap! Slap! Slap! And stop carrying your books on your arm like a girl!"

When they let go their grip, I started off on a run, only one boy pursuing and shouting out threats. I shall now reveal the girl-boy's patented secret for getting out of a predicament. I sprinted to the porch of the first house, gave the door-bell several violent jerks, and shrieked for help.

Sixth year: I was absorbed in fashioning a doll's dress. An older sister angrily exclaimed: "Why don't you get out on the ball-field like all other boys? I hate effeminate boys! Mother, I'm afraid Ralph is not normal!"

At the moment I felt ashamed ever to look my disgusted sister in the face again. So ashamed that I wanted to kill myself. (One of my girl-boy playmates, because bitterly persecuted on account of his effeminacy, actually committed suicide at twelve by swallowing rat poison.) "I not normal? What did my sister mean? Could she have had in mind my queer habit of sitting on the boys' laps? I was the only boy that acted so queerly. I had not realized it could be described as 'abnormal.'"

On another occasion, I was, with two brothers, skirting a creek on the way to the swimming-hole. We came to a row of stepping-stones. My brothers trotted across several times. But I lacked the courage even to set foot on the first.

We found several "shavers" in the swimming-hole. My two brothers joined them. But I liked only to recline on the bank and feast my eyes. I would as soon have stripped before boys as would a little girl. I only got a sight of the swimming-hole because I had brothers.

For the first time it occurred to a "shaver" to strip and duck me. My brothers were ashamed of my being a girl-boy and thought it would contribute toward making a man of me.

"Stop your screeching, Ralph! You've got to be stripped so we can see if you are a real boy! Stop your scratching, or we'll give you a black eye! . . . Now let's dip him under to stop his yelling! . . . You can't come around the swimming-hole any more unless you get into the water with the rest of us! . . . Cry-baby! Cry-baby! You're a hopeless case! . . . Clear out of here!"

I half-way dressed and ran off in terror. Their driving home the fact that I was a hopeless sexual cripple brought on such melancholia as I had never before experienced. I repeatedly blubbered out as I ran: "I want to die! I want to die!"

III

AN ANDROGYNE'S YOUTH

It was not until my sixteenth year that I came to a full realization that I am a male in name only. I had always recognized my girllikeness and wished Nature had created me a female. At the same time I had, during my early teens, sometimes reflected that I would outgrow all my feminine predilections and be a normal man. But at fifteen my bust development made me think that perhaps God at last was answering my fervent prayers, around the age of nine, to be changed into a physical girl. For I was already one psychicly.

In my middle teens, my desire changed radically, due chiefly to my having just become a God-intoxicated youth, with the work of a missionary in China as my goal. I now prayed far more intensely for full-fledged manhood than I ever had for physical femininity.

Superficially and according to man-made law, ultra-androgynes are men. According to the unabridged dictionary, they are neither men nor women. That is, they are capable neither of begetting nor conceiving. But in respect to mind and feelings, in respect to their protoplasm—and thus essentially—they are women.

Being neither male nor female, with whom do androgynes associate? Up to the dawning of puberty, pronounced specimens—like myself—gravitate toward the gentle sex. As soon as the sexual life is fully developed, the vast majority (not happening to be overconscientious and ultra-puritan) give that sex the widest berth and lean on the bosoms of the ultra or tremendously virile of their acquaintance. But they never join in the sports of the sturdy sex. For in athletics, they are as awkward as girls, and besides lack the necessary physique.

But Nature happened to make *me* over-conscientious, and my training was ultra-puritan. While, after I entered my teens, I was ashamed longer to make myself one with girl acquaintances, and besides was violently repelled by our both approaching the full-flower of our sexuality, my now looking upon my attraction towards youths as the most heinous of sins, together with my aversion from masculine interests, forbade association with boys outside the schoolroom. Thus from the age of thirteen to eighteen, I endured an almost companionless existence outside the home, the schoolroom, and the church edifice. I did occasionally take a walk with an androgyne of my own age, goody-goodiness, education, and social standing. He, however, was not religious or of puritan parentage, and was even then extensively promiscuous with the economically better class of the village's youthful "sports."

I myself turned away in deep shame from the propositions of tremendously virile youths, although secretly I would rather have yielded than do anything else at all. At middle life, I have had doubts as to whether I did the right thing in resisting. I believe my health and happiness were tremendously impaired by my ultra-puritan views which made me obstinate before Nature's behests. On the other hand, through yielding I would have lost my reputation and probably been barred from "prep" and university. I was expelled from the latter as soon as the faculty learned that I lived according to Nature's behests. The university training is, of course, worth erotic pleasures ten-thousand times over. But during the first two years of my college course, my health and happiness (as recounted in my AUTOBIOGRAPHY OF AN ANDROGYNE) were sorely wrecked by abstinence. Does the wrong not after all lie in the groundless intolerance of "prep" and university for androgynes who obey Nature's demands, and fill, in an unobtrusive manner, the niche in the universe for which the Great Architect predestined them?

Thus being excluded from the pastimes of both the recognized sexes and from their joint social intercourse—on account of my belonging to a third and outcast sex—I found my only recreation from an ultra-studious college-preparatory life in long walks on country roads, during which I often brooded because Providence had consigned me to membership in the third sex. From the age of thirteen to eighteen, I endured the most melancholy existence I have ever heard or read of.[1]

---

1. Particularly during my teens, I have worried and grieved a thousand times as much as the average individual. I say for the solace of fellow melancholiacs who retain their reason that at my present age of forty-seven, I show not the least sign of thinning or whitening hair. But this may be due to my being an ultra-androgyne, a subspecies blessed with perennial youth. Strangely also in my own case intense grief (except the agonies in my Garden of Gethsemane, for which see close of this chapter) has seemed to put physical strength into my usually weak body. I feel also that it sharpens my wits and adds to my wisdom and literary ability. "There's not an ill wind but blows some good."

At the age of forty-seven my conviction is that great sorrows, after the lapse of a score of years, are recognized to have been blessings in disguise. My life experience has demonstrated that "there is a Providence that shapes our ends, rough-hew them as we

Can the reader conjure up any worse fate for a *youth* than to make the startling discovery that he, though extremely conscientious and offenceless, is a type of sexual cripple that has always been regarded by the sexually full-fledged—because of their ignorance and Phariseeism—as the lowest of the low, a monster of wickedness, and an outcast from society?

Can the reader conjure up any worse fate for a *girl*—and a very high-strung one—than for Nature to disguise her as a boy, and foreordain that *she* should be brought up as a boy and be, at school, office, etc., always shut up with the sterner sex?

Can the reader conjure up any worse fate for a *girl* than to be doomed to pass through life incarnated in a male body? How grief-provoking for a mademoiselle to be cursed with a slight growth of hair on lip or cheeks! Only a trifling male stigma! How much more heart-rending for a mademoiselle to possess the male physique to such an extent that even all physicians (except a handful of sexologists) with their present lack of knowledge—or rather their closing their eyes to all evidence—would declare *her* a male, and prescribe that *she* should in life fill the latter role.

Such was my chronic burden almost throughout my teens. (Subsequently, with the exception of brief spells of melancholia, I became reconciled to my fate.) And such is the burden imposed by Nature on one youth out of every three hundred in every social set of every country in the world. But because of my intellectuality, high-class environment, and extreme androgynism, my grief was exceptionally

---

will." My life experience has demonstrated that the biblical teachings about human life are in general true, and that either the Christian or Jewish religion is practically necessary to save from despair and suicide men and women foreordained to drain the cup of anguish to the dregs. My personal faith in Christian doctrine, and my habit, instilled in infancy, of "taking everything to God in prayer," have saved me from suicide a thousand times and made the deepest of sorrows tolerable.

The upshot of my very exceptional life experience is: (1) "Praise God from whom all blessings flow;" and (2) Even pain, sorrow, and death are blessings in disguise. The heart of the universe is beneficent.

As I have had an unusual religious experience, one of the numerous books I plan to write, if my life is spared, will be entitled: MY SPIRITUAL AUTOBIOGRAPHY. I have made many discoveries in religion and ethics which I long to proclaim to the world. As already stated, I have always been ultra-religious and a deep student of the Bible. Another book I plan to write will be entitled: THE BIBLE AND THE SEXUAL INSTINCT. In the latter I will seek to demolish the Church's chief stumbling-block. As already stated, I was cut out for a preacher.

intense. I do not believe the mildly androgynous are melancholy during their teens. They have not yet become conscious that they are abnormal.

My chronic lamentation during my seventeenth to nineteenth years was: "Miserable wretch! Miserable wretch! Miserable wretch! That's all I am! I was born with a deformed nature, despicable in the eyes of all people! I am a soft effeminate youth who is wanted nowhere! I am ashamed to look any one in the face! I feel like putting an end to my life, or else losing myself, to all who know who I am, in a distant city where I could live according to my queer nature. I have nothing to live for! I may be disgraced, disgrace my family, be compelled to flee, be disowned by my parents, be cursed and be despised throughout the land!"

An older sister frequently vented her spite on me because of her disgust at my effeminacy. The Sunday school picnic in my seventeenth year led up to one of the greatest sorrows of my youth. "You little coward!" my sister the next day began. "Even eight-year-old George has more pluck! I was so mortified to see you the only boy to refuse to pick up the rifle in the shooting contest! The others could hardly wait their turn. And today you do look like a freak in that pink ruffled shirt! And with your hair banged! Trying to doll yourself up as much like a girl as you can, are you?"

"I am, too, so ashamed of your bangs, Ralph!" my mother chimed in. "They make you look as if you didn't know anything!"

"Mother, make him go to C's party next Wednesday. He stays away from all gatherings of young people. He will grow up a boor."

"I would rather be thrashed than go to any party! I do not like to pay gallantries to women!"

"You will never make a man unless you do, son. I insist that you go to C's party."

Wednesday evening arrived, and with two score youngsters, I was lounging in C's parlors. My older sister had managed to have me escort a girl. Unfortunate female, to be attended by one of her own sex whom Nature had disguised as a man!

It was extreme torture to have to go into society and put myself forward as a gallant. Accordingly I grasped the first opportunity to escape to the garden. I could look into the brilliantly lighted drawing-rooms filled with the youthful merry-makers. The spectacle moved me to tears.

"To think that Providence permits to all young people excepting myself the joys of love and courtship! Because if I followed my inclinations along these lines, people would call me a monster and I would be a pariah![2]

"I wish I might get away from the world and live as a hermit! Then I would in a way be unsexed, and would be so regarded by the world.

"People see that I am an effeminate youth! An effeminate youth! And my sister has often expressed her disgust for that type! Who can like them?

"I feel that there is nothing which can henceforth give me interest in life! I feel so mortified that I am a girl-boy! Oh it looks as if there were no God!"

---

2. After my conversion at fifteen, I fought against my sexual attraction toward schoolmates as few others have struggled against the ruling passion. I was no longer a coquette, although desiring as much as ever to be such. My passion for loud apparel, however, was not suppressed since I did not recognize in it any sin.

At fifteen I developed into a religious prodigy. Until my debut as a quasi-public female-impersonator at nineteen, I, though the most melancholy person of my community, was active in church work. During these four years, I attended seven religious services a week (exclusive of college chapel every morning during two of these years) and from fifteen to seventeen, spent two hours a day in private devotions in addition. As early as fifteen, I was the leader of prayer meetings. I preached from the pulpit a dozen times at nineteen—a few months before I relinquished all Church work because instinct drove me to female-impersonation. All the ultra-pious of my ultra-puritan entourage predicted for me a great career as a herald of Christianity— to which vocation I had already at fifteen dedicated my life.

Thus as early as fifteen, I was frequently called upon to lead the congregation in extemporaneous prayer. Usually my key-note (for my private prayers as well) was my life's motto, which I adopted at fifteen:

> *"My times are in Thy hand,*
> *Whatever they may be;*
> *Pleasing or painful,*
> *Dark or bright,*
> *As best may seem to Thee!"*

Tears would course down my cheeks and my voice tremble with emotion. I never failed to remember that I had the greatest need of all for the rest for which I pleaded and which Jesus has promised to give "the oppressed and heavy laden."

After service, all other youths escorted a girl home and lingered over the gate for blissful conversation. But I had the habit of making my solitary way to a desolate abandoned graveyard whose latest headstone was set up in the twenties of the nineteenth century.

Behold my Garden of Gethsemane, where not merely once, but once each week, I would throw myself on a grass-covered grave, writhe in an agony of moans, and even shriek. All my muscles seemed to be rigid, and my fists were clinched. I would dig my fingernails into my palms, and throw my arms about wildly.

"Change my nature, O God," I would cry. "This very moment. By a miracle. Give me the mind and powers of a man.

"Am I being 'tried by fire,' as the Bible predicts for God's children? Are others so tried by fire as I have been nearly all my life?"

(After half-a-century of rare opportunities to learn human nature, I have ascertained that I was tried worse than any one else I have heard of—that is, by torture of sexual desire that must *not* be gratified, and practically was not from seven to eighteen, inclusive. I was tried by fire a hundred times as hot as the average person ever knows. Probably so hot because of my intense fairie-ism from two to six. I believe I have, for years together, resisted lust many times as intense as the average person ever knows.)

"I am experiencing the enslaving power of sin. I now know how to sympathize with poor drunkards and harlots. I will flog and starve myself in order to conquer my flesh. (I actually fasted and flagellated myself to ascertain the effect in deadening my amorousness but found these religious exercises useless.)

"I feel tonight that I can never become a preacher of the Gospel. I feel that I must give up all plans for a noble career, and that maybe I shall come to a disgraceful end!

"Oh that all instinct would die in me! It makes my life miserable. How gladly would I be free from all desire so that I could make a name for myself in the world! An extreme girl-boy can hardly become a scholar and a preacher.

"Is it my divinely appointed task to learn the lesson of resignation in affliction? To feel myself crushed to earth by the Almighty Hand? Like Isaac, to be tried in order to see whether I am willing to be slain in my youth—in my own case morally?"[3]

After an hour of bitter tears and heart-broken pleadings to the Architect of the universe, I would be in a state of mental and physical collapse for twenty-four hours. Can the reader wonder that, weighed down by such a burden, I repeatedly meditated suicide during these

---

3. I had in mind possible predestination to be a **fille de joie**—the career which haunted me, off and on, every year of my life after my second, even years before I heard of the existence of such **filles**. I had already had an intensive five years career (third to seventh years). Another foreshadowing (that of my actual career from my twenty-sixth to fortieth years) was a common dream, from about my ninth to fourteenth years, of being chased through streets and fields by youthful soldiers, who would finally catch me, and great terror would result. The dream occurred so often that in my waking hours I resolved, the next time I had that dream, to tell the soldier boldly: "I am not afraid of you, because this is only a dream!" Repeatedly in my dreams did I tell that to the soldier who had grabbed me, but he replied (as I dreamt): "You are mistaken. This is not a dream. It is the real thing!" And then I would become as terrified as ever. My dream would always end a second or two after being grabbed, and generally I would wake up as if from a night-mare.

four terrible years? And I realize now—at middle age—that I had to suffer these four years of melancholia only because of cultured man's misunderstanding of androgynism, prohibition of any one's inquiring into the facts, and bitter persecution of androgynes.[4]

Events have proved that it was the policy of the All-Wise and All-Good not to answer my prayers, notwithstanding their almost unexampled earnestness and repetition. The Eternal foresaw that it was to the best interests both of the human race and of myself that I should leave to others the coveted work of preaching the Gospel to the heathen and spend my physical prime in New York's Underworld as an avocational female-impersonator. That was the cross that God willed that I should bear. The role of female-impersonator is the niche in the universe that its Architect had created me to fill.

In middle life I have often thought that Providence mercifully spared me from suicide—the fate of so many youthful androgynes as a result of the world's persecution—and foreordained my career of female-impersonator that I might, through publishing the present trilogy, remove the veil of ignorance and prejudice as regards androgynism that now blinds the cultured, and occasions terrible persecution to Nature's inoffensive step-children, who number one out of every two hundred inmates of our state prisons, having been incarcerated merely on the ground of homosexuality.

---

4. Anglo-Saxon leaders of thought have hitherto been of the opinion that the domain of sex is **"terra interdicta,"** just as those of Roger Bacon's time (priests and monks exclusively) would have believed it sacrilege to use a telescope or microscope—"to see what God meant man should never see." Roger, although having invented these instruments, did not dare tell his generation because the leaders of thought would have burnt him alive for invading **terra interdicta.**

IV

I Grow into The Fairie Boy

At sixteen, I entered a college in New York City. I alone was responsible for the scene of my university training. I had frequently visited New York and wished to reside there. But I had then no intention of ever yielding to my detested instincts for female-impersonation. I had not realized that residence in a great city would make temptation far stronger than in a village. My being fated to make my home in New York almost throughout my adulthood has had a tremendous influence on my life, particularly from nineteen to thirty-one.

My father gave me every educational advantage because in the fairly large "prep" that I attended from my tenth to sixteenth years, I attained the highest scholarship in the history of the school. In an address to the students, the principal named me as the youthful scholar to be patterned after by the other boys (! ! !).

I know I shall be accused of exaggerated ego for the way I talk about myself in this and the next chapter. But seven articles have been published about myself in medical journals, exclusive of numerous reviews of my Autobiography of an Androgyne. How many people can go into a library, call for magazines, and gaze at pictures of themselves within their covers? How many people have had a three-volume autobiography published? With such a record, I suspect that I am either insane or else one of the half-dozen most remarkable sexual curiosities of my generation. On the latter chance, I am moved to leave on record a full account of both my inner and outer rare life experience.

As to bragging about my intellect, my experience of half-a-century is that in general, Providence makes compensations in the lives of men so that as they, one by one, pass on to the next world, all have fared equally as concerns Heaven-sent boons and the opposite. As a counterweight to having created me a bitterly persecuted sexual cripple (for His inscrutable but surely wise ends) the Architect of the universe endowed me with a brain of such capacity as found in only one out of twenty-five university graduates. I wrote stories at eight. At thirteen I was confident I would become an author and my name be chiselled on the walls of fame.[1]

My college associates commented on my feminesqueness and infantilism. I perceived that I was looked upon as a curiosity.

I am a curiosity in that while throughout life remaining a species of moron,[2] certain cerebral lobes have nevertheless progressed to a high development enabling me to graduate from a university almost at the head of my class notwithstanding my general psychic infantilism and my suffering from acute spermatorrhea and (during my freshman and sophomore years) acute melancholia. If my physical health had been as good as that of the three men who outstripped me, I might have led my university class.

I am a curiosity in that down to twenty-five, I was a fair specimen of physical infantilism or lilli-putianism. I was said to possess the skull and facial lines of an infant. Down to twenty-five, I never weighed more than 110 pounds on a height of five feet five. Nearly all my brothers and uncles have been six-footers.

I am a curiosity in that I possess the light female osseous structure. Even before I began to develop adipose tissue after twenty-five, I would float on fresh water without moving a muscle, my observation being that the slim normal boy must vibrate his hands.

I am a curiosity in that form of skeleton and contour of body are mostly feminine, particularly the bust.

Not until the age of nineteen, when I went successively to two medical college professors and implored them to make me a complete male, did I learn that practically all the tissues of my body are of characteristically feminine texture. My muscles, judged by their weakness and my using them in general woman-fashion, are those of a female. The beardal growth is normally male except that it could never reach the length of an eighth of an inch and has no stiffness. If I had not shaved or eradicated the beard, I would have been, after seventeen, one of the dog-faced boys of the circus. Although the hair cells seem as dense as on my scalp, I could never have exhibited virile whiskers.

---

1. However, as described in detail in my AUTOBIOGRAPHY OF AN ANDROGYNE, the congenital extraordinarily keen edge on my intellect was progressively and permanently dulled from the age of sixteen to twenty-three by emissions during sleep twice a week. It is necessary to add that I always had acute horror of self-abuse.

2. An adult who never surpasses the mentality of a child of twelve.

Another feminine resemblance is that at the age of half-a-century, I show not the least tendency to baldness.

Several of my college associates coddled and babied me. They would throw an arm around me and cry: "Child!" They would hold me on their laps. With the three ultra-virile with whom I became most intimate and confidential, I would often in private throw myself into their arms and pillow my head on their bosoms, while they would exclaim: "Lovesick boy!" They never betrayed my strange conduct to others or appeared less friendly. Only one of the three made greater advances than I myself— the only one belonging to the tremendously virile class. What chiefly kept me from even hinting at extremes was fear of expulsion in case it should become generally known. But I was also strongly influenced by the dictates of society and the teaching of the Bible—as I then erroneously understood the latter.[3]

"You still possess the real childlike naiveté," students have remarked. "And you possess childlike features to harmonize with your decidedly childlike manner of going about things. You are certainly THE BOY WHO NEVER GREW TO BE A MAN."

"I like to watch you because of your childlike grimaces. That is why the fellows are continually teasing you; because it is just like teasing a child or a girl. You react with a sort of pleased childlike pride at being the object of attention."

"Your voice, though hoarse, has a feminine timbre. It possesses the penetrating and carrying power of a child's voice. It often breaks and changes, sometimes in the middle of a sentence. From being masculine, it suddenly changes timbre and becomes decidedly feminine, passing over from a bass to a treble. Your voice is sentimental, bland, caressing. It is the kind of voice a dying woman would choose to hear."

"I never saw the chevelure (as they shoved their fingers through it) so fine and silklike in any one else who wore trousers. Your hands (as they would hold them) are as soft and hairless as those of a girl. And

3. One of my three confidants achieved the highest success in life of any student in college with me—one of the highest political offices in the United States. Down to forty, I confided my homosexual adventures, although after we graduated, our personal relations were never closer than shaking hands. Within two years of his **honorable** name's appearing in absolutely every newspaper of the Union, he permitted me to receive mail addressed to one of my aliases (used only by those who knew I was an androgyne) in his care. At the time I did not realize the favor I was asking—the risk to his reputation that he unselfishly took. Ungrounded scandals sometimes arise when a full-fledged man does favors for an androgyne.

you have the arms of a woman (when my sleeves were rolled back). And you blush just like a woman. And you sob like her. I never saw tears run down the cheeks of any other man as he sat in the class-room."

I have jokingly replied with a smile at my classmate's mystification: "You do not know but what I *am* a woman!" But I shrank from any serious disclosure of the secrets of my sex, such a mystery to many of my every-day associates.

If I live to old age, I intend to call the present trilogy to the attention of some of my associates of early years who have indicated great curiosity to know the secrets of my sex life. I have permitted only three friends (of course the closest) who know me under my legal name to read my AUTOBIOGRAPHY OF AN ANDROGYNE, and one of the three dropped me from his friendship. Men are so biassed on the subject of sex that I can not let my friends read the secrets of my life until I reach an independent old age when they can not make me suffer much on account of my androgynism.

In college, I was compelled to exercise in the "gym." I hid my form. It was a terrible ordeal to have to strip before the physical director, who remarked: "Your figure is feminine." Apparently he did not suspect the sexuality that was bound up with that figure. If military drill had been required—as in 1917—I would have quit the university.[4]

Since nineteen my yearning for skirts has been in part met by habitually wearing about my home an ornamental dressing-gown. Thus clad, I have often gazed in a mirror, imagining myself a complete female. I have taken pleasure in hearing the gown rustle, like a silk dress; in feeling it strike against my legs; and in holding up the front in ascending the stairs.

THE FAIRIE BOY was my nickname from nineteen to thirty-one outside my every-day circle. And outside I was far more widely known. Inside I had the reputation of being an insignificant, puritan, unpractical bookworm and Mollie Coddle who knew nothing of life

---

4. Some androgynes of a less extreme type, however, tolerate militaries. I know of two who served in the World War—because they wanted, every day and hour, to be surrounded by adored young Mars. But if they ever got to the front, they would probably malinger. I know of another androgyne who was so afraid of being drafted that he took a hatchet and chopped off two fingers of his right hand. In the World War, I was subject to draft under the latest law. I had planned to escape by claiming that I was **not a man**, the law specifying that sex alone as liable.

and human nature. Outside I achieved wide notoriety as an amateur actor—or, properly speaking, actress.

That the distinction, among the sons of Adam, of being THE FAIRIE BOY came to me, is nothing for which I can take credit to myself. It was merely because Providence had made me, as an adult, physically as well as psychicly, one-third man, one-third woman, and one-third infant. Providence endowed me with a "small-boy" aspect, the subject of comment in my every-day circle down to my early forties; freshness of complexion down to thirty; innocent expression of features and marvellous absence of animality (in appearance only); cry-baby mentality; eternal childlikeness even in my professional life; and slender, lithe, and lilliputian figure down to twenty-five.

THE FAIRIE BOY! To be frank—I am proud of the pretty nickname. This Providential distinction is part of my compensation for my almost unparalleled sufferings from persecution at present inseparable from the lot of an ultra-androgyne.

THE BOY WHO NEVER GREW TO BE A MAN

For the most part, the present chapter covers my twenty-sixth to thirty-second years, during which my most descriptive nickname was THE SOLDIERS' FRIEND. For I was foreordained to a sort of army life for many years, detailed in my AUTOBIOGRAPHY OF AN ANDROGYNE, but omitted in the present volume. Here I limit myself to some related personal description.

PHYSIQUE AND PSYCHE: My career as avocational female-impersonator during the second half-dozen years of my physical prime was even more remarkable than during the first (outlined in PART THREE). My quasi-public career as female-impersonator ended at thirty-one—at its very zenith—because I deemed myself too old longer to play the part of "French doll-baby," and because the instinct thereto progressively weakened from the age of thirty. My being able to play that part down to thirty-one was possible only because Nature had endowed me with the proper physique and psyche, already described. Less extreme androgynes lack the qualifications, while practically all the extreme (commonly known as "fairies", "fags", or "brownies") lack the necessary good sense, modesty, temperance, and high grade of general morality that were mine because of my puritan childhood and youth and university education.

The proneness of the eternal feminine greatly to understate her age made me in my twenty-sixth year, when impersonating a doll-baby, pass as twenty-one, and in my fortieth, as twenty-eight. An unmarried female, as long as she has hopes of lassoing a husband, never gets beyond the lingering years of twenty-eight or twenty-nine.

SIMULTANEOUS "MALE" PROFESSIONAL LIFE: In my twenties, thirties, and forties, I have worked hard in three successive learned professions. At nineteen I had already relinquished my amateur work of preacher of the Gospel on being forced by Nature into the avocation of female-impersonator. Simultaneously with my satisfying my frivolous and coquettish instincts of French doll-baby, I also met the demands of my male intellectual spirit by doing brain work of a high order. My three successive professions have seemingly been adopted by chance, although during "boyhood" I manifested special aptitude for all three, besides that of preacher. I did not choose them. They were only makeshifts after I was barred from my choice: preaching the Gospel. I can not name them lest I disclose my identity.

I have achieved the average professional success. But my extreme effeminacy and both facial and psychic infantilism have prevented employers meting out the full advancement that past work merited. Men less capable than myself have been promoted over me because my chiefs had the impression that I was merely "a grown-up child"—that is, moron-like, although as a matter of fact I possessed the intellectual qualifications.

Office associates have now and then commented in my hearing on my feminesqueness notwithstanding they have not usually entertained the least idea that from nineteen to thirty-one, I impersonated, an average of one evening a week, a French doll-baby. Some remarks, however, even down to my middle forties, indicated that some suspected the truth about my sexual life. But I never betrayed that life to any of my business associates excepting three or four confidants, who—I must explain— were mere Platonic friends. I was too much ashamed to ape the woman before those acquainted with my intellectual accomplishments. The following are samples of remarks of office associates:

"Good morning, Baby!"

"Grinning kid!"

"You look like a frightened bunny!" (While being teased. I was always the favorite subject for teasing by full-fledged males. In school, university, and office (the latter down to my middle forties only) they teased me as they would a girl. Moreover, my face expresses my emotions in an uncommon manner.)

"Your breasts are certainly beauts! You must be half woman!"

"Look, Ralph, Ed is throwing kisses at you!"

"Ralph, I was just going to ask you for a kiss!"

"Ralph, you are nothing but a child half-a-century old!" (When impressed by my childish grimaces and childlike way of going about everything.)

"Say, Ralph, won't you favor me with the recipe for perennial youth? I never saw such a contrast between apparent and actual age!" (During my early forties.)

"Ralph, you are a tub of mush! You look like a fat *frau* in the last stage of pregnancy!" (The reader will pardon the vulgarity occasioned by my wish to give the exact words used by an office associate to describe my figure after the age of forty-three.)

Nearly all my professional life has been under my legal name. It has been completely apart from my avocation of female-impersonator. I have sometimes thought I might be an instance of the dual personality recognized by psychologists. Only, while living out either side of my own duality, I have always had a complete memory of the other side and recognized the oneness of my ego in my two widely opposed careers.

In my middle twenties, I lived under *three* names and personalities. I worked seven hours a day for a legal journal as "Earl Lind." Because under that name I had called on its editor to persuade him to publish my Autobiography of an Androgyne, representing myself as merely its author's agent. The editor was in his sixties, and happening just then to need an assistant, immediately hired me, never questioning the truthfulness of my representations as to who I was. He was at the time also one of the leading criminal lawyers in New York City. He employed me in all sorts of confidential capacities and let me into many of the secrets of his clients. Of course I would never have proved false to his trust, even though he never knew who I really was and where I lived. I attended court with him as his clerk. I learned all the intricacies of establishing a false alibi for a wealthy androgyne whom he represented in a case originating in blackmail by an adolescent. I was his assistant while he was defending a client from prosecution by Anthony Comstock, when the latter gentleman was personally acquainted with me under the name of "Earl Lind," and knew I was trying to get the Autobiography of an Androgyne published, which he had already interdicted.

Thus I was, in a sense, a court employee of New York City, while at the same time one of its greatest criminals—according to a statute that is a legacy from the Dark Ages.

Simultaneously with my career as lawyer's clerk, I taught school five evenings a week under my legal name, and every Saturday evening took up my avocation of female-impersonator under the name of "Jennie June."

Though I passed as three separate personalities within the same week, they had—poor things—to share the identic body alternately.

Necessity of Aliases: I have used five: Raphael Werther, Ralph Werther, Earl Lind, Jennie June, and Pussie. When I began my double life, I told the Underworld my legal name was Raphael Werther. I named myself after "the Prince of Painters," because he was the greatest ultra-androgyne who ever lived. He was my idol—my ideal. I wished him to pass through the earthly life all over again in my body. I further named myself after "the Prince of Amatory Melancholiacs" since I was myself such during my teens. Werther was Gœthe himself, the most brilliant and most versatile man, "the Prince of Men," born subsequently to the Shakespeare-Author (Francis Bacon).

As for the genesis of my first feminine name, I chose "Jennie" at four. I have always considered it the most feminine of names. When I began my double life, I appended "June." I adopted that surname because of its beautiful associations, as well as because of the repetition of the *j* and *n*. I have always considered "Jennie June" as the most exquisite of names: the poetic name; the magic name; the "divine" name (in the sense that we speak of the "divine" or "godlike" human form). I later substituted the feminine "Pussie" because so nicknamed, much to my delight, by the tremendously virile.

I later adopted "Earl" primarily because it rhymes with "girl", the creature of enchantment that I longed to be, and secondarily because it arouses noble ideas. I adopted "Lind" after Jennie Lind, one of my models.

Perhaps these fancies about names are proof of insanity. A medical reviewer of my Autobiography of an Androgyne, who devoted only five minutes to the 70,000 words, declared me "clearly insane."

When I transferred my female-impersonations from Mulberry Street to the Fourteenth Street Rialto, incredulity occasioned my transliterating the fancy "Raphael" to prosaic "Ralph."

As a result of my 1905 court-martial making the names "Ralph Werther" and "Jennie June" known to some army heads, I found it advisable, when in 1907 renewing my kind of army life for seven years, to choose new masculine and feminine names. I feared it might become known to the army heads that the fairie "Jennie June" had transferred "her" stage for female-impersonations to a distant military post. Hence the substitutions of "Earl Lind" and "Pussie."

On a single day I have had to sign myself with four different names. Always after writing my signature, I must review it painstakingly to make sure I have put down the proper one. Only once I have made a mistake. In receipting for a registered letter addressed "Earl Lind, General Delivery," I signed my legal name. To the clerk's inquiry I replied that I had been authorized by Lind. He sent word to Lind for written authorization, which was promptly despatched.

I have had to acquire two entirely distinct handwritings—the second for my numerous love letters.[1] None were ever written more mushy than those of "Jennie June" and I guarded against their ever being traceable to the intellectual and puritan "Ralph Werther" (by which name I refer to my every-day self in my books). I have often, within an hour, written letters in the two different hands.

CONFIDANTS: Throughout the three decades of my double life, I have, outside several physicians, disclosed it only to nine confidants of my every-day circle. One expressed his amazement that I should disclose it at all, affirming that even my best friend would be likely to get me thrown out of my economic and social position. All my lay confidants, however, proved helpful and compassionate excepting one, who, while never disclosing my secret, dropped me from his friendship, although we had been the very closest of Platonic friends. One physician brought about my expulsion from the university and made me a Bowery outcast and fairie.

Because of the terrible persecutions inflicted by the criminally-minded "saints" who happened to be born sexually full-fledged, hardly a single cultured androgyne ever betrays his bisexuality to a single confidant of his every-day circle excepting the tremendously virile bachelor whom he may have chosen as soulmate. I am an exception in outspokenness. Decades ago I rose above the prudery and bias with which most leaders of thought are today bound hand and foot. I desire that men interested in the improvement of the human race, and in the question of justice to all classes, have the opportunity of getting at the facts concerning the atypic and atavic types with whom I have been intimately thrown through having been foreordained to pass a large part of my life in the Underworld.

---

1. Non-mushy specimens are given in my AUTOBIOGRAPHY OF AN ANDROGYNE. Its editor killed the mushy.

PART III
THE FAIRIE BOY

I

FEMALE-IMPERSONATION

In PART THREE, I shall outline what kind of adult career is the natural sequel of the childhood and adolescence described in PART TWO; what kind of adult career is bound up with the physique and psyche with which I am endowed. I shall disclose what Providence had in store for the youthful religious prodigy of the Connecticut hills—the delicate, lilliputian, chicken-hearted girl-boy—after he had been swallowed up in New York's millions.

Since ultra-androgynes are, in a sense, instances of dual personality—a male soul and a female soul inhabiting the same brain and body—it is natural for them to live a double-life.

Moreover, as the "classy," hypocritical, and bigoted Overworld considers a bisexual as monster and outcast, I was *driven* to a career in the democratic, frank, and liberal-minded Underworld. While my male soul was a leader in scholarship at the university uptown, my female soul, one evening a week, flaunted itself as a French doll-baby in the shadowy haunts of night life downtown.

Since my student and subsequent professional career were prosaic, I leave them almost unmentioned throughout PART THREE. I, however, always gave them first place in my life. But I here confine myself to what I experienced and learned while impersonating a French doll-baby because it constitutes something novel to most readers.

Indeed PARTS THREE, FOUR, and FIVE portray the social life and diversions of the most cultured New York coterie of THE THIRD SEX during the last decade of the nineteenth century. For, while little has yet been published about instinctive female-impersonators because of the prudery of the sexually full-fledged, they form (necessarily *sub rosa*) quite a large class of society—about one out of every three hundred physical males. During the last decade of the nineteenth century, the Fourteenth Street Rialto was their chief stamping-ground in the New York metropolitan district. I became acquainted with them because during the decade indicated, I was myself in my prime as a female-impersonator in two out of the three principal bright-light quarters of the metropolitan district.

(There exists also A FOURTH SEX, the gynanders. But experience has not qualified me to describe them in detail. That task awaits some brave, high-minded, and brilliant *physical* female. See, however, chapter on GYNANDERS in my RIDDLE OF THE UNDERWORLD.)

The Overworld has enjoined complete silence about female-impersonators because of their thoroughly false view that any adolescent adopting the role mus*t* do so from moral depravity. They argue: "If I myself adopted the role, it could only be through unspeakable depravity. Ergo, the same is true for every male." They overlook the fact that Nature did not make all anatomical males of like passions. What would be moral depravity for one is not for another.

Instinctive female-impersonators are sexual cripples from their mother's womb. They had no choice in the matter. Thus they merit pity rather than scorn. Further, since their impersonations occasion no detriment to any one, but are a source of much entertainment to their sexually full-fledged associates, they are a positive ethical good. All beneficent talents that the Creator has distributed among mankind must have been meant for use—not for strangling.

As to the ethical question, I myself, who from the age of nineteen to thirty-one had an intensive career as fairie—female-impersonator, can truthfully state, on arrival in my late forties, that I was not once, during that career, guilty of an irreligious or unethical act—excepting alone that I seriously impaired my own health. But it is doubtful whether the impairment was permanent. In my late forties, my physical vigor is not at a lower level compared with males of my own age than it was during my childhood. My health has always been delicate.

Numerous wives and mothers suffer in health from the sex passion as much as I. If my having had my health wrecked by it proves it immoral for me and to be legally repressed, then the yielding to it by wedded pairs is equally immoral and to be interdicted. If it be objected that the human race is perpetuated by the latter, I answer that this consideration would only permit to married couples a sex-union when offspring was the object—that is, for a cultured couple, from one to three times throughout their married life.

In the description of my own physique and psyche, I have indicated the general characteristics of the extreme type of androgynes foreordained to become quasi-public female-impersonators. But the outstanding feminesque physical stigmata of each "fairie" (as they are commonly called in the United States) tend to be *sui generis*. In one it is natural beardlessness alone. In another, the possession of female breasts alone. In a third, the female skeletal shape, particularly an over-long spine, short legs, and broad pelvis. In a fourth, natural soprano voice. Etc.

Whoever has beheld an instinctive female-impersonator when keyed up, must confess that this type are *born* actors—or "actresses," as they prefer to be called. Their histrionic skill is not primarily the result of practice or instruction.

Their audiences have marvelled because the impersonators' faces are devoid of any sign of beardal hair. Usually the beard is eradicated. It is allowed to grow for a full week in seclusion. By means of a mask of depilatory wax, every hair is then pulled out by the roots, the outer portion having become embedded, like hair in wall-plaster. For three weeks, the face is as glabrous as a baby's. Then the week's seclusion and the final excruciatingly painful yank of the wax mask all over again. The process has no permanent effect, either good or bad.

All the impersonators adopt a fancy feminine name, as Pansy, Daisy, and Lily. Often the names of living star actresses are adopted and "dragged into the mud," as people say. For while the career of a female-impersonator is a purely physiological and psychological phenomenon, it is incorrectly regarded as deep-dyed immorality.

All impersonators belonging to the middle and upper classes also choose a masculine alias, represented in the Underworld to be their legal name. They do not wish to risk disgrace to their family name. Moreover, on their sprees in the bright-light districts, they are careful to wear nothing containing their everyday initials.

Except for a few weeks, I myself was only an avocational impersonator. I gave to it only three hours a week, as compared with 109 waking hours to my student (or later, professional) life. I did not adopt the avocation until near the close of my sophomore year. Almost throughout the preceding twenty-four months, however, I had fought violently against almost irresistible tendencies to disappear for an evening in the Underworld on a female-impersonation spree. But my ultra-puritan education had injected into me such a moral horror of female-impersonation that I was able to resist the tendencies for two whole years after the date that Nature ordained them to begin.

The "French doll-baby" spirit had dwelt in my brain since birth. Throughout my life down to nineteen, it had manifested itself strongly, although after fourteen I had struggled to crucify it. At nineteen, it refused longer to be suppressed. I (the puritan, bookworm spirit in me) had to arrange a compromise. I promised to yield my physical and mental powers to it only one evening each week. And the doll-baby spirit was satisfied. Previously I had been the most melancholy person in the university. But dating from the compromise, my life flowed on peacefully and blissfully. Only occasionally—moments while suffused with ambition to make a name for myself in the intellectual and philanthropic world—would I turn against the doll-baby spirit with abhorrence, and ask myself how I could ever give place to it.

For the serious work of life, I realized that I must practically strangle the feminine side of my duality outside the three hours a week during which I conceded to it full possession of my personality. While at my every-day tasks, I sought to forget the doll-baby spirit that dwelt in my brain side by side with the scholar spirit.

II

A Typical Female-Impersonation Spree

The one evening a week on which I (the scholar-spirit) surrendered, I called "going on a female-impersonation spree." The typical spree did not occur until the December (1894) of my senior year. I had become somewhat adept in the art of impersonation through a year's apprenticeship in the Mulberry Street Italian quarter. As that training has been detailed in my AUTOBIOGRAPHY OF AN ANDROGYNE and THE RIDDLE OF THE UNDERWORLD, I omit it here.

On the afternoon preceding a spree, I would be overwhelmed with dread and melancholia. I dreaded disclosure, which I realized would mean expulsion from the university because of the full-fledged man's horror of a sexual cripple. I dreaded possible disfigurement by blows— or even murder—by one of the numerous prudes who detest extreme effeminacy in a male (supposed). I was melancholy because about to embark on something that my puritan training had impressed me as in the highest degree disgraceful, and that I secretly wished I did not have to undertake. But to be contented and even happy for the following week and to guarantee that tranquillity necessary for the best scholarly success, the weekly spree was unavoidable.

Only a handful of upper-class female-impersonators adopt feminine attire for street wear. For myself (being a university student, and subsequently an honored member of a learned profession) it was too risky. I merely kept some feminine finery locked up in my room for occasional decoration of my person while I gazed in the mirror. But during the eighteen months that my sprees were staged in the Fourteenth Street Rialto and the six years on or near military reservations in New York's suburbs, my attire was as fancy and flashy as a youth dare adopt. Fairies are extreme dressers and excessively vain. To strange adolescents whom I passed on the street I proclaimed myself as a female-impersonator through always wearing white kids and large red neck-bow with fringed ends hanging down over my lapels.

I would set out from my lodgings with the feelings of a soldier entering a terrific battle from which he realizes he may never return. As the car carried me farther and farther from where I staged the puritan student life and nearer and nearer to where I staged the "French doll-baby" life, my overwhelming melancholia would gradually give way to a sense of gladness that in a few minutes I would find myself again on "Jennie June's" stamping-ground. I had left at home all my masculinity (a very poor variety). The innate feminine, strangled for a week in order that I might climb, round by round, the ladder to an honored place in the learned world, now held complete sway.

During the last decade of the 19th century, the Fourteenth Street Rialto ranked second only to the "Tenderloin" as an amusement center in the entire metropolitan district. While it still holds the same rank in 1921, its present night life is only a shadow of what it was. A quarter of a century ago, New York was wide-open, whereas for more than a decade, the lid has been down tight. Promenading the Rialto on an evening of 1921, the pedestrian would conclude that no such phenomenon as sex attraction existed. But during the period that I was an habitué, the Fourteenth Street Rialto was as gay as European bright-light districts, which I was fated to explore.

The Rialto is confined principally between Third Avenue and Broadway. While I was an habitué, theatres, museums for men only, drinking palaces, gambling joints, and worse abounded.

On pleasant evenings, when the sidewalks were thronged with smartly dressed adolescent pleasure seekers, I would promenade—up and down, up and down—until I chanced to meet a coterie of young bloods who invited me to join them. Our evenings would be spent in pool-rooms, gambling joints, beer gardens of ill repute, or worse resorts. Nature made me proof against the vices I there witnessed. My only weakness was the craze for female-impersonation. My greatest joy was to flaunt myself as a bisexual before those who did not know my identity. I realized that every soul among my Rialto associates was turning his or her back on the Creator. But I was always determined to give Him first place in my affections. However, for fear of bringing reproach on religion if *I* made myself its representative—*I*, a misunderstood female-impersonator, whom even the Underworld in general regarded as one of the most impious of humans—I never mentioned the theme except under extraordinary circumstances.

If the weather were bad, I would immediately enter a beer garden and call for sarsaparilla. I would consume it in driblets while watching for the opportunity to join some tremendously virile bachelors out for a lark.

On the typical evening I have chosen to describe of my many passed in the Rialto, I happened to run across several youthful Lotharios waiting in front of a theatre for something "to turn up". Only one adolescent "male" out of three thousand in New York City adopts the role of quasi-public female-impersonator. A Rialto habitué therefore does not often run up against one. Judging by my own experience, a female-impersonator proves an attraction of the first order for young bloods having time hanging heavy on their hands. Thus this coterie—as many others have done—called out jubilantly on catching sight of me: "Hello Jennie June!" . . . "Hello sweetheart! That is what you want us to call you, isn't it?" . . . "Let me introduce you to Mr. A and Mr. B. They have never met a female-impersonator, and are dead anxious to see you take off a girl."

"And you are Jennie June, are you?" A and B exclaimed. "We have heard a lot about you and longed to meet you."

"Bon soir, messieurs," I replied. I had a liking for addressing chance-met beaux in a foreign tongue. I happened to be the foremost linguist among the university students.

"Bon soir, Jennie, bon soir!"

"Meine sehr geliebten junge Herren, wie geht's bei Ihnen?" I continued with a twinkle in my eye.

"Ganz gut," sounded the reply. New York is a Babel. On an hour's promenade in the Rialto, conversation in a score of languages would impinge on one's ear. Bright young men brought up in a New York foreign colony acquire a score of the commonest expressions in several languages.

"I miei amici, siete amati da me," I next declared in a third language.

"Pee-an-gou, savez? We don't understand Dago, Jennie. Tell us in American how much you love us."

I reply in Spanish: "Esto es lo mejor que podemos hacer. Hablemos ingles."

"Bert, Jennie seems to be a bright fellow—or girl—doesn't she? All these impersonators seem to be brainy. Jennie, I don't know whether to call you a fellow or a girl. Which is proper?"

"Girl, of course," I replied with a smile.

"Well, fellows, Jennie' June is part *he* and part *she*. *He* wears trousers, but *she* has breasts just like a woman and wants us fellows to regard her as a girl."

"Well, Jennie, if you are a girl, why do you wear breeches? And why don't you let your hair grow long?"

"Because I have the misfortune to be only part girl. I am only a girl incarnated in a boy's body. But besides my girl's mind, my entire body is shaped very much like a girl's and I possess her bone and muscular systems. Because I am part boy, the law prohibits to me my natural or instinctive apparel. But you will be so kind as to overlook my not appearing before you in gown and picture hat, won't you? I will make up for that lack by outwomaning woman in my actions. It is my nature to give up all I have, and do all I can, for the entertainment of *heroes*—as you manly fellows seem to be."

"Jennie, let's walk around to the ladies' parlor of the Hotel Comfort[1] and have a few drinks."

We arrived in an artistically furnished room 25 feet by 75. At one side was a bar from which waiters continuously carried drinks to the fifty-odd couples seated around the small ornamental tables which occupied most of the floor. Nearly all the patrons were under thirty, and absolutely all, highfliers sexually. The vast bulk merely smoked, drank, and "chinned." Only a few were playing cards for money. All were refined and orderly. I have never circulated among more delightful people than I met frequently at the Hotel Comfort.

I had become well acquainted with the proprietor and all his employees. For more than a year the "hotel" was substantially the home of my feminine personality, "Jennie June." But this refined and luxurious "hotel" would have tolerated only a cultured and outwardly modest female-impersonator. Most examples of that biological sport were far below the standards of the Hotel Comfort, and would have been barred. But I was looked upon as a personality likely to attract a pecuniarily desirable class of patronage.

My five companions and I spent an hour sipping beverages.

(While during my twelve years as quasi-public female-impersonator, my companions always drank intoxicants, I always called for non-alcoholics. The latter's price was double in order to discourage the consumption of temperance drinks. I had been brought up to loathe alcoholics, and during my twelve years intimacy with heavy drinkers, came to a more and more rational loathing.

---

1. Substitute for the real name of the pseudo-hotel.

Alcoholics are by far the greatest curse of the Caucasian race. I have had almost unequalled opportunities for studying venereal diseases. My twelve years of having roués and *filles de joies* for bosom friends taught me that the presence of alcohol in the blood is the *sine qua non* of venereal disease. Perhaps my greatest contribution to the betterment and happiness of humanity is the epigram original with myself : No Alcohol, No Venereal Disease. But it is necessary to be a Total Abstainer. Mere moderation does not confer immunity. The total abstainer may possibly contract venereal disease, but it is sure to be benign, almost negligible, and inflicting no permanent injury. Dr. Robert W. Shufeldt, who as army surgeon had extensive experience in the treatment of venereal disease, wrote in the Journal of Urology and Sexology, 1917, page 458: "In my opinion, alcohol bears the responsibility more than any other single agent—indeed more than all the others put together—for ensuring venereal infection.")

"Jennie, why not take a cocktail instead of a lemonade? We want to warm you up. Then you will give us some of your recitations and songs. Won't you drink a few cocktails for my sake?"

"I would not put the poison into my system for anybody! I do not need that kind of stimulant. You know what kind I need to get warmed up to declaiming and singing!

> "*I am a-thirst, but not for wine;*
> *The stimulant I long for is divine;*
> *Poured only from your eyes in mine!*
>
> *I am a-cold, and lagging lame;*
> *Life creeps along my chilled frame;*
> *Your love will fan it into flame.*
>
> *I am a-hungered, but the bread I want;*
> *The food that e'er my thoughts doth haunt;*
> *Is your sweet speech, for which I pant!*"[2]

"If that is all the stimulant you need, Jennie, it can easily be supplied."

---

2. Decades ago I read in a newspaper this imperfectly remembered lyric. Name of poet not published.

We were the merriest party in the parlor. The attentions of my beaux were having their usual effect. To achieve my best success at female-impersonation, the stimulus of an appreciative and responsive audience of youthful Lotharios was necessary. Our hilarity was more and more attracting the eyes and ears of all other guests. Some recognized me as a female-impersonator. Calls began to reach me: "O you Jennie June, give us an impersonation of a prima donna!" The old-timers were remarking to new patrons of the "hostelry": "The little fellow with the red bow is a fairie!"

Hypnotized by the adulation of those whom I looked upon as demigods, as well as by the well-disposed attention of the other hundred-odd guests attracted by my unique, yet fairly modest, behavior, I broke into the "Old Oaken Bucket"—a song affording unusual opportunity to display my masculine-feminine tones: below middle A, baritone; from A upward, alto; with an occasional soprano and tenor modulation thrown in just to excite wonder. I fancy my singing voice is unusual in its variety of possible modulation as a result of my body being both male and female. In my singing voice particularly, these two elements are ever striving for the upper hand. One stanza each of several songs then in vogue followed: "After the Ball Was Over"; "Sweet Rosy O'Grady"; "Just Tell Them That You Saw Me"; etc.

Next I recited a dialogue, my naturally bland, sentimental, and caressing voice now aping a cry-baby mademoiselle, and now a stern, hoarse-voiced he-man. Now I burlesqued feminine airs and cadences; and now strove after the most virile and dare-devil effects.

I was, while the focus for all eyes, conscious only of the joy of being alive and in the midst of an admiring group. I experienced a feeling of exultation that for a brief spell I was looked upon under my real character—a bisexual. I was intoxicated with delight because emancipated—though only for a few moments—from a hated dissimulation and disguise, and enabled to be myself. Assuredly another personality than that of my every-day book-worm self was in possession of my body and faculties. I realized I was the same *I* who was one of the leaders in scholarship at the university. At the same time, I realized I was doing things incongruous with that position.

At midnight, I bade my convives a reluctant adieu. Before boarding an elevated train, I turned several corners abruptly and hid in the first dark doorway to make sure of not being dogged. But no Rialto associate ever did. After alighting from the train, I adopted the same strategy, to make assurance doubly sure.[3]

Arrived in my room, I first dropped to my knees to thank Providence for restoration to my every-day world. I rejoiced that the ordeal of a female-impersonation spree was over for a week. But the following days, while resting my mind for a moment from hard study, I gloated over the memory of my latest associations, as a member of the gentle sex, with the tremendously virile type of adolescent.

---

3. I was dogged only three times in my many years of leading a double life: (1) Several Stuyvesant Square clubmen succeeded, unbeknown to me, in boarding the same elevated train. I discovered them only after I had descended to the street. My refusal to proceed to my lodgings so incensed them that they disfigured my face with blows. (2) I was dogged again by several other Stuyvesant Square clubmen. I discovered them before I boarded the train. Again my refusal to proceed angered them to giving me a beating. (They beat me because they had been taught that androgynes are monsters of depravity. All were around twenty years old.) (3) I was dogged in 1918 by a ruffian of twenty-two, with whom I had talked confidentially, but finally forsook because my usual test had shown him untrustworthy. He followed me for more than a mile, although I turned several corners suddenly and stood in a doorway and watched. But he had reckoned on my doing just that, and in some mysterious way guarded against my discovering him. He was evidently a super-crafty criminal. On straight stretches of street, I looked back half-a-dozen times, but saw nothing of him. (Because he had always taken the opposite side of the street and kept such a distance behind I could not recognize him, while his own eyesight carried further than mine.) When I arrived at my goal (fortunately this time an amusement resort and not my home), he gave me one of the surprises of my life by coming up to me. I fled from him in irrational terror.

Note.—See "Memories" in Part VIII.

III

The Gambler

"Where is my wandering boy tonight—
The boy of my tenderest care,
The boy that was once my joy and light,
The child of my love and prayer?"

In chapter III I shall portray one of the most remarkable of the Adonises that I met during my 18-months Rialto career, to which the present PART THREE is devoted, and in chapter IV, the most remarkable youthful Hercules. Other Adonises of the Rialto are protrayed in my RIDDLE OF THE UNDERWORLD. The remainder of the present book, to the end of Part V, will describe some of the most remarkable ultra-androgynes (female-impersonators) that I met in the Rialto. For a description of my most noteworthy "fallen angel" confidants, I refer to my RIDDLE, and to my fourth book, now in preparation, SUSA, which gives the entire life of the Queen of the Rialto of the middle of the last decade of the nineteenth century. As I was fated to become the most widely known female-impersonator of the Rialto, Susa was the most widely known vampire. Two detested and cordially loathed types, but actually not a hundredth as bad as they had the name of being!

Numerous Rialto pals were adolescent professional gamblers. Because of that, I have chosen to devote an entire chapter to a characterization of the type. More than that, the young blood forming the subject of the present chapter was my "No. 1" friend among the couple of hundred Lotharios with whom I mingled in the Rialto. He became my favorite because he was the most elegantly dressed—and close to the handsomest—adolescent I ever met. Above all, he possessed the most genial disposition.

Has the reader ever remarked that just that kind of disposition generally goes hand in hand with deceit and hypocrisy? Later—to my bitterest sorrow—the hero-boy now being described was discovered to be the greatest hypocrite I ever met. In January, 1895, I made his acquaintance. For half-a-year he manifested the greatest affection—all feigned as I later found. When he had wrung me dry, he—entirely unexpectedly—flourished a loaded revolver around my head, and cried: "If you ever speak to me again, or even come into the same room, I will put a bullet through your head!"

This *quondam* soul-mate had such a craze for acquiring money—generally by foul means—as I have never witnessed in another. He made it a condition of our spending a couple of hours together that I put into his palm a five-dollar bill. But though I could get plenty of other company of his type gratis, I was so fascinated with *him* that I never gave a second thought to the self-sacrifice that such gifts demanded during my student days. While promenading the streets with *him*, I would, every other minute, glance into his face, reflecting: "The handsomest and best dressed young fellow of the Rialto is MINE." While we were seated in a theatre together, I would often gaze into *his* face instead of at the players, reflecting: "New York's Beau Brummel is MY SOULMATE." For no soft hair, no rosebud cheeks in a male, no arched eyebrows—ever surpassed those of the Adonis now being described. *He* was *perfection* in face, head, and body. *He* was *perfection* in dress. *He* was *perfection* in disposition—ONLY HE WAS ULTRA-DECEITFUL.

Note.—See "Recollection" in Part VIII.

BUDDIE McDONALD! Whom for over twenty-five years I have not seen or had news of! I am here addressing you because it is the only possible way to get through a message. If these lines should ever fall under your eyes, and you should, in this chapter, recognize yourself—somewhat covered in order to hide our identities—I wish to tell you that I have through the years always granted you first place in my heart after my mother alone, and if we could ever run across one another, I still stand ready to enslave myself to you, notwithstanding you doubtless have lost (because age deals no differently with you than with all other sons and daughters of Adam) nearly all your litheness and charm. But I still love you for what you were in your earlier twenties. Throughout a quarter of a century I have been longing and waiting for a chance encounter with you. Many times have I eyed every man passed in New York's crowds hoping to recognize your face. Nothing would I like better than to spend my declining years knit to your genial personality and heroic, grand-aired spirit. I freely pardon your past treachery—though it almost drove me insane—if only you would condescend to let my soul be knit to yours until death do us part!

B UDDIE McDONALD! The most precious of all names! If it were my idol's legal name, I would not disclose it. It was the alias he used in the Rialto and the only name I knew him by.

Buddie told me that he was born and brought up on a farm near Lake Ontario. His people were Methodists. He had always gone to Sunday school and Epworth league, because his parents required it. For he was a black sheep by birth—the only one in his little rural community. When nineteen, the seventeen-year daughter of a neighbor appeared with her parents before a justice of the peace. Buddie lived with his child-wife only three days and then stole away for parts unknown. What pangs the poor girl must have suffered thus to lose a genuine Adonis—in beauty one man out of a thousand—to the arms of the demimonde! She had doubtless been comforting herself and congratulating herself that she had won for life as her helpmeet the most bewitching young blood of the community. And after just three days to be forever left in the lurch!

"Buddie McDonald" immediately bobbed up in the Rialto under that alias. In the Rialto! At that time one of the two chief amusement and gambling centers of the Western Continent, the magnet for the black sheep of pious families all over the United States. He immediately adopted the profession of card sharper, being endowed with the peculiar mentality necessary.

While we were pals, he was twenty-two—just a year older than myself. From ten to midnight one evening each week, I dogged him in one of the half-dozen gambling joints among which he divided his "working" hours.

I was too much of a goody-goody ever to gamble myself. I would merely sit for hours as spectator. It was intense pleasure merely to have under my eyes the type of adolescent that sows wild oats.

Among my associates in the Rialto resorts were youthful actors playing at the several theatres, racetrack book-makers, wealthy adolescents who spent their evenings sipping gross pleasures, and high-fliers of the feminine persuasion—at that date as thick in the Rialto as flies in summer around an open jug of molasses.

I was now in my third year of leading a double life. My every-day circle was without suspicion. Outside my one evening per week in the Rialto, I led a most industrious student life, even winning prizes. I had already been awarded the bachelor's degree *cum laude* and was in my first year of graduate study. Of course I had never revealed to any Rialto associate that I was a university student. I was known there merely as "Jennie June," while the few who took the trouble to inquire my legal name never questioned "Ralph Werther." And my three most intimate Lothario friends of the Rialto were too busy evenings—Martin and Paul,[1] chasing chippies, and Buddie, victimizing youthful greenhorns—to investigate where I spent my time while not in the Rialto. They have each asked me where I lived. I gave a fictitious address, hoping they would not investigate. And they never did. And my three most intimate androgyne friends—Roland Reeves, Eunice, and Phyllis—were, like myself, living a double life incognito, and thus were the more inclined to respect my disinclination to refer to my every-day life.

To the university circle I thus continued the "innocent" from whose view Heaven had mercifully shut off the seamy side of life, particularly the Underworld. They declared they never saw any one with such weak sexuality! But I actually knew a thousand times as much about passion and crime as any one of them. Some complained because I "never associated with men and learned human nature"! But I secretly knew human nature far better than any of them. They thought that my feminine predilections and lack of worldly wisdom (seeming) were due to my being a recluse! And I was a recluse so far as concerned university social affairs. For I elected to take my diversions as a mademoiselle—not as a gallant.

BUT TO RETURN TO BUDDIE: I have picked out for description that one of my numerous evenings spent in part with him which best illustrates his character and our relations. Afternoons and evenings he hung around fashionable hotel lobbies and exhibition halls to scrape acquaintance with moderately wealthy and sportily inclined Reubs making their first trip to New York. With his unmatched geniality and hypocrisy, he was decidedly successful in getting a line aboard some "sport" from upstate, and taking him in tow. For with Buddie, it was "Brother, this" and "Brother, that". A large proportion of the Reubs whom Buddie condescended to buttonhole congratulated themselves doubtless on their good luck in happening on such a friendly New Yorker—a gentleman of leisure and a big roll of yellow backs (which Buddie always took pains to wave before the eyes of Reubs, a manoeuvre tending to hypnotise them) who condescended to show them the sights of the metropolis, and, above all, take them where they *could quadruple and quintuple their funds in a single evening*. The passion for enrichment by a stroke of luck is, after woman and wine, the chief pitfall for "he-

---

1. Martin and Paul are depicted in THE RIDDLE OF THE UNDERWORLD.

EARL LIND

men." An appeal to this craze in Reubs ambitious to be "sports" has good prospects of success for brainy metropolitan prestidigitators.

On Buddie's and my entering into a solemn contract—very similar to a marriage bond—to be "best friends," he agreed to reserve one entire evening each week for me alone. But it was only the fourth that I had to sit in a Fourteenth Street restaurant for two long hours waiting in vain. I was wiping my tearbedimmed eyes four times a minute. Other diners probably thought I was experiencing some overwhelming bereavement.

At ten I made the rounds of the gambling joints frequented by my soul-mate. I finally caught sight of his wondrous blonde hair and peachlike cheeks in the very last—as always happens—of his half-dozen stamping-grounds. In the last decade of the nineteenth century, it was pre-eminently New York's Monte Carlo (which name I give it in this book). The walls were paneled in rosewood. Every six feet a heavy gilt-framed plate-glass mirror reached halfway to the 15-foot ceiling. The latter was painted with Cupids and Venuses, in all sorts of poses, amid fleecy clouds floating in such a blue sky as is actually beheld only in Italy. The myriads of crystal prisms pendent from the huge chandeliers emitted all the colors of the spectrum. The floor was mosaic—in such exquisite patterns that it seemed a sin to set foot on it. The ebony furniture was inlaid with mother-of-pearl in floral patterns.

I rushed to Buddie's side noiselessly because, with three other smartly dressed young bloods, he was absorbed in a game. I knelt beside my hero-boy with head against his arm.

When the hand was played out, Buddie, throwing at me the sweetest of smiles, addressed the only one of the four who was a stranger: "Mr. Myers, let me introduce Jennie June, the female-impersonator. I am used to her hanging around while we fellows are playing. Do not let her presence distract you. Jennie and I call each other 'Best Friend.' Perhaps you never before ran up against a person who is one-third man, one-third woman, and one-third infant. That explains why she nestles up against me so affectionately."

But Mr. Myers appeared to be unutterably shocked. Particularly since I was in male attire. He appeared incredulous. He had never even dreamed that a third sex exists.

After an hour Buddie said: "Jennie, take my keys, go to my room, and wait for me there. Because I will not get home until long after midnight."

On arrival he exclaimed: "Jennie, what do you think of your new friend, Mr. Abraham Myers, the Beau Brummel of Myersville upstate, who is enjoying his first visit to our village?"

"I think, Buddie, that before tonight he had never been in any place worse than a church social. His evening in the Monte Carlo must have been an eyeopener. Whenever my gaze fell on the poor innocent, the words of the Bible went through my head: 'He is led as a lamb to the slaughter! And as a sheep before her shearers is dumb, so he openeth not his mouth!' I am sorry my hero-boy stoops to take advantage of an unsophisticated Reub!"

While we ate our midnight lunch, Buddie confided his evening's adventure. I was always inquisitive about the ways and habits of the tremendously virile—how they looked upon the mystery we call "life"—and habitually put to my numerous soulmates a long list of questions in case they did not spontaneously overflow. But it is an earmark of crooks to be garrulous with their soulmates. The former are proud of their sharpwittedness and gloat in unburdening their minds to some one they think they can trust. Their characteristic bragging to confidants is one of the chief means by which many of them finally fall within the toils of the law.

Secondly, Buddie was my soulmate. At that date, we felt ourselves husband and wife. For I am myself fundamentally a woman, though possessing the male primary determinants. The relationship of knit souls—amalgamation of two separate personalities of opposite sex into One human being—I have discovered tends to mutual confidences. I had already several times been in Buddie's presence when he had an intended victim (always a Reub) in tow, and saw through everything even if he had not told me. If it be asked how I, pretending to be of high morals, could associate with sharpers, I answer: Love is Blind. In my subsequent Bowery period, described in my Autobiography of an Androgyne and The Riddle of the Underworld, I was knit into one being with youthful burglars, who, to whet my admiration for themselves, have entertained me with accounts of their burgling houses and demonstrated their truthfulness by exhibiting terrible scars from gunshot wounds suffered as they were fleeing from a burglary they had "made a mess of." I would never have thought of contributing in any way to bring them to justice; first, because I slavishly adored them, and secondly, because I knew I would be murdered if they should ever entertain the least suspicion that I would "peach."

Experience taught me, during my six years in New York's Underworld, that crooks are particularly prone to confess to a fairie intimate. For they considered fairies (under the legal ban of ten years' imprisonment in New York) far worse criminals and far worse defiers of the law than themselves. Fairies—they thought—would not dare "peach."

Fairies would serve as the best stool pigeons for ferreting out thieves, just as keen *filles de joie* are employed as detectives.

Buddie McDonald had already received many proofs that I idolized him and would never do anything to his detriment. True: five months later he did "shake" me definitely and emphatically. But this was because he had discovered he had wrung out of me all the money he could; he had become financially independent beyond his wildest dreams; and I had come to be a terrible bore through hanging around his room several times a week and demonstrating myself insatiable.

I summarize, as nearly as I can recollect, Buddie's account of the Abraham Myers adventure.

It was on account of my roping Abraham in, Jennie, that I had to cause you that terrible crying spell at the restaurant. But you will sure forgive me when you come to realize that it is not every afternoon that a fellow comes across a hundred-dollar wad on the floor of Madison Square Garden waiting for some bloke to pick her up.

While Abe and I were watching the poor devils spinning around the track, I slyly pumped out that he is the only son and hope of Jonathan Myers, owner of the knitting-mill that put Myersville on the map. Having once been a hayseed myself, Jennie, I know what pulls strong with them. So, to get a line aboard Abe, I first gave him an hour of soft soap. "Yes, brother, I spent the summer of 1892 up in Squeedunk in your part of the state. It sure is a garden of Eden. . . How did this year's potato crop pan out? . . . And I myself know everything from A to Z about breaking in a colt. I was raised on a farm up in New Hampshire."

After Abe showed he thought I am the best fellow ever and I had found him to be an easy mark, it was time to discuss money. "Money, brother! You have a little and you love it. If only a fellow has money, he can go everywhere and have everything. Wouldn't you like me to show where you can take your money, AND IN THE SHAKE OF A LAMB'S TAIL MAKE MORE MONEY OUT OF IT?"

Abraham right away bit hard. So I dropped the subject for an hour. I didn't want him to smell a rat. And my silence would all the more make him hanker after the magic place where one could see his dough swell five-fold at a sitting.

After the first hour of blarney, I asked Abe to let me show him some of the sights of the Tenderloin, which all red-blooded Reubs hanker to see. "I swan!" he exclaimed. "I never believed such charming and handsome ladies existed!" I next took him to the Waldorf to dine. Of course I did not let him pay out a cent. Only one red-blooded hay-seed out of a hundred will, at the last, balk at sitting down at the card table, where I can get every penny back with interest at 10,000 per cent. We sharpwitted fellows have to take those chances, Jennie.

As we swilled such grub as Abe had never even smelled of, he rubbernecked at the wonderful frescoes and stared at the polished marble columns which made the great dining-room like a forest. "This place is like what I have dreamed heaven to be!" he broke out over and over again. He was so soft! "You are awful good, Mr. McDonald, to bring me to see all these heavenly things. I never believed there lived such an awful good fellow!" . . . Hah-hah-hah, Jennie! He was clean daft!

But, Jennie, I would never humbug a friend that way. Specially you, because you and I are "best friends." You see, Jennie, Abe Myers was a stranger with a big wad. I was loading him with favors and pulling the wool over his eyes because my plan was to wring him dry before I let him get out of my hands. Such tricks are what we smarter straight men of Fourteenth Street are for. We have to live off the greenhorns. . .

Don't, don't begin to chew the rag, Jennie! My only sorrow is that I haven't enough dough. Abe Myers' old man has barrels full. Abe will not suffer more than a few hours on account of the eighty-odd bucks I wrung out of him.

At nine we boarded a car for Fourteenth Street. We went into the bar-room of the Monte Carlo and sent a few glasses of champagne chasing after the many already swallowed. The poor innocent said his head swam! Hah-hah! He acted bashful-like as if he had never before tasted a drop. But he was too scart of being set down as a sissie to balk at another, and still another, glass while I waited for Pedro and Tracy. For I had phoned them to meet me at the Monte Carlo at nine to milk a cow. For they are my regular partners, Jennie. They haven't the brains to get a line aboard a Reub, but know the ropes when I am at their elbow to give them their cue. We have an understanding that I will later make good their evening's losses, or take my share of the winnings that I throw into their hands. I guarantee that they will each be to the good by one-tenth of the night's clean-up; my share, for furnishing the brains and taking all the risk, being eight-tenths.

Of course we made it look as if Pedro and Tracy dropped in by chance. All three of us did our best to give Abraham the happiest hour of his life. When the time was ripe, I said: "Fellows, what do you say to a hand at cards?"

Pedro and Tracy seconded my motion. I watched Abe's face to learn what I could count on and how far I dared go. It looked awful sheepish, as you said, Jennie. But I must say for Abraham that he is red-blooded and would not back down in any manly undertaking. Like ninety-nine out of every hundred Reubs wanting to be sports, Abe Myers wouldn't balk even though he felt in his bones he was being led down to hell. But he barely lagged after us into the card-room. But this was probably on account of his Methodist bringing up, like my own. He could not possibly have thought we were plotting to fleece him. As we swilled grub in the Waldorf, I had given his hand a hearty shake when he told me he was a member of the Epworth League. I said I also was, as really when I lived back home. Besides all three of us had patted him on the back and lionized him. There were aristocrats all about. And the Monte Carlo is such a high-class joint, decorated like Vanderbilt's palace. Abe probably thought—like he said about the ceilings in the Waldorf: "Sure I ought not to mind the loss of a few bucks. It is worth that to see all this heavenly art, so much beyond anything I ever believed existed on earth. Besides Mr. McDonald has been awfully good! Spent a mint of money on me! He sure couldn't let any harm befall me!"

For, Jennie, just that is the secret of getting the best of strangers. Treat them just lovely until the moment comes to pluck out their feathers.

We were soon buried in faro, as you saw while with us, Jennie. I played the banker and the others staked their money against me upon the order in which the cards would lie as dealt from the pack. The play ran on for over two hours. We spoke hardly a word. First along we each staked a dollar on each layout. But later five. For the first hour—while you were watching, Jennie—I turned things Abe's way a little. I wanted to get him awfully interested. When the time came to throw things in the other direction, I had to send you home, Jennie, for fear you would make some remark about my sleight-of-hand that would put everything in bad. Of course if Abe had not been awful green at cards, he would have got wise too.

And, Jennie, I remind you this once for all time. The saying is: "Death to the traitor!" And I know that you love life better than death. See how easy it would be for me to grab your throat and in a few minutes you would be a goner without being able even to make a whisper. But I know you could never do anything but help along your "hero-boy."

After midnight, Jennie, there happened what I had been looking for. With trembling hands, Abe opened up his wallet to let us see the three one-dollar bills still lining it. He said awful plucky: "Fellows, I am almost at the end of my tether. I need this bit until I can get some dough from dad." I felt sorry for the poor kid, patted him on the back, and handed him ten dollars from my own wad. I said we would play till he won back his losses. But at last he balked. So I said: "Let's go to the bar-room and have a drink."

Pedro, Tracy, and myself spit out soft soap over our drinks for a few minutes. For some time I had seen that Abraham was awful worried. He now hardly opened his mouth except to answer a question. He looked as if he were all the time saying to himself: "I'll never get into another scrape like this again!" But he did not dare even breathe a whisper about us being sharpers. We were three against him alone, and even sweller dressed. Besides, being a stranger in New York, he lacked sense.

I judged it time to escort him to his hotel, because he needed some one to steady him. He looked a wreck. Because he was not used to champagne and all. We shook hands with Pedro and Tracy, and boarded a car for the Grand Union, where all the middle-class Reubs put up. Even when we were alone in front of his hotel, he did not have the nerve to call me down. I have fleeced Reubs who have given me a good punch in the mug when they got me alone. Abe must have thought I am straight.

I shook his hand good-night, patted him on the back for the last time, and said I would call this coming evening to give him a chance to win back his money. Of course I never expected to keep the engagement. I don't suppose Abe did either. As soon as he got inside his hotel, I sneaked away as fast as my legs would carry me. For a week, I shall have to keep away from the Monte Carlo.

IV

A Stuyvesant Square Pick-up

It is August, 1895—several weeks after Buddie McDonald had left me in the lurch, as he had his legal wife, and as he probably through life went on deserting quon*dam* soulmates when having no more use for them. Furthermore, during this single summer that I frequented the Rialto, I found it a barren stamping-ground for myself. Nearly all my Lotharios were of the moneyed class that go out of the city for the heated term, or at least while away their evenings at a shore resort in the suburbs. For I did not drift with solid business young men, but with those who sought an easy life. The book-makers were at Saratoga, the vaudeville artists at seaside theatres. Even professional gamblers preferred Saratoga or Long Branch during the months that fools with money to burn went to those places rather than to little old Fourteenth Street.

But in June I was fortunate in being introduced to some refined "young fellows" living near Stuyvesant Square, five minutes walk from the Rialto. Business or a slim pocketbook kept them in the city. I therefore formed the habit of staging my impersonation sprees in the Square—a park of about six acres. Within four weeks I had been introduced to several score young bloods—so many because all belonged to a neighboring club the talk of which I came to be on my advent because of my ultra-androgynism and female-impersonation. The majority liked to flirt with me an hour in the park as if I were a full-fledged mademoiselle. I was always clothed as a youth, although exceptionally loud, as fairies are wont. But the present work will pass over my relations with the Stuyvesant Square club-men because described in my AUTOBIOGRAPHY OF AN ANDROGYNE.

In that August occurred one of the most eventful evenings of my twelve years' career as overt female-impersonator. I had promenaded every path in the Square without running across any clubman—very unusual on a balmy evening. Therefore just before dark I seated myself next to the most attractive stranger in the park, where two thousand people were enjoying the cool of a scorching day. He looked to be twenty, was rather shabbily clad, but clean. It was not his features, but his powerful and well proportioned figure, that attracted me. His hair was red—a favorite color for neckties, but the very last I would choose for a beau's chevelure. His face, while well formed, was close to the very worst among the more than one thousand young bachelors with whom I have coquetted. His eyebrows and lashes were blonde and barely visible. His complexion resembled a sheet of faded pink muslin—a solid color all over, not rosebud or peachlike, as the lamented Buddie McDonald's. Particularly his cheeks were covered with pimples, common in redhaired men, so that one wonders how they shave. But because of his unapproached bone and muscular development visible even through his clothes, I did not like him a whit the less on account of his pigmentary defects.

For several months after that night, I fell in love, at first sight, with nearly every red-headed adolescent I ran across, particularly if his cheeks were covered with pimples.

In order to ascertain the trustworthiness, good-heartedness, and liberalmindedness of the Hercules, I first drew him out craftily by a long series of questions. Even people in my every-day world have given me the palm for inquisitiveness. I expected to put myself in the power of Hercules and needed to find out all about him. I was always ultra-wary about falling into a trap, as I already had several times in the Underworld. Androgynes are murdered every few months in New York merely because of intense hatred of effeminacy instilled by education in the breasts of full-fledged males.

I learned Hercules' entire history—providing what he narrated was true. To my joy he told me he had been reared in a village in the Mohawk valley. Through heart-to-heart talks with hundreds of strange young bloods in New York's Underworld I discovered that boyhood environment makes a vast difference in adult honesty and altruism. The country-bred adolescent manual-laborer is apt to be far less vile-mouthed and pugnacious, and far less likely to assault and rob one of Nature's step-children than a young-blood product of city slums.

Only after I had been able to form a favorable judgment of Hercules' disposition, I began to disclose, by my talk, that I was an androgyne. From my dress and mannerisms, however, any city-bred youth would have already judged my sexual status. Hercules later told me he had, but had feared saying something offensive. He said he had been impatient for me to declare myself.

The following conversation serves to illustrate and analyze the hero-worship of the androgyne. It is admittedly mushy. The question is whether the reader wants the mushy or the untrue. Ordinarily conversation with a sexual counterpart made me silly. All my flirtations were mushy. The following phraseology is very close to the actual except that I have semi-translated Harvey's dialect into ordinary English. Further, the reader must educate himself to judge justly even that with which, as he reads, he does not like to identify himself or make his own sentiment. For example, two confidential, Platonic literary friends told me that my original songs published in my AUTOBIOGRAPHY OF AN ANDROGYNE were "sickening." They could not sympathize with the androgyne sentiments and therefore the songs were "shoddy." Likewise the following conversation must be judged objectively and the reader's verdict be based on absolute reason, not on personal bias—not on the basis of the reader's ability to put himself in the place of the Hercules or myself. It is a conversation to be analyzed scientifically.

"Beau, see how much bigger your hands are than mine! And how horny the palms! I bet you would give a good account of yourself in a fight!"

"I've had lessons in pugilism. Besides I come from a strong-built family. Me father's piano-mover and me only brother steeple-Jack. Meself has worked as riveter on sky-scrapers."

"So you have wielded a sledge-hammer!" I exclaimed enthusiastically because of his more and more marvellous revelations.

"All day long while steel-worker's helper on the sky-scrapers."

"O you are such a wonderful young fellow! Wonderful alone in your being brave enough to mount the sky-scraper skeletons! And still more wonderful in possessing the muscle necessary for wielding a sledge-hammer all day! May I feel your biceps? I am anxious to have my hands on the very muscle that slung the sledge-hammer!"

"Anything at all!"

"O what a biceps! Like a tremendous boil protruding out of your arm except that it is hard as steel. Among the scores of Strong Hanses whose biceps I have been privileged to pinch, you are the muscular prodigy![1] You must be a terrible slugger! I pity your opponent! Only a pyramid of

1. In the summer of 1921 I twice saw moving pictures of Jack Dempsey arching his naked biceps. I was thirty feet away and his size was magnified at least twice. I carefully watched for comparison with Harvey Green. The protuberance was not equal to Harvey's, who was far from being approached by any of the scores of sluggers whose biceps I have pinched. I can never forget Harvey's mountains of biceps.

jelly after you got through with him! Do you know, Mr. Strong Hans, that I have fallen in love with your biceps?"

"That's a funny thin' ter fall in love with! But just feel me chest muscles and leg muscles."

"They are steel!" I cried in ecstacy. "Because of your being a muscular prodigy, I am driven beside myself in hero-worship! Do you know what the word 'worship' means? It means that I could prostrate myself with lips to your dirty shoes, and cry out, over and over again, forever, forever, your wonderful endowments! I could forever call you Sledge-hammer Wielder! Personification of Strength! Incarnation of Power! Man of Iron! Mighty Man of Valor! Mighty Man of Renown! Heaven wills that I, a poor weakling, bow low in adoration of a muscular prodigy!"

"You said it! I've got the build of a pugilist. But it's meself as needs ter go ter the dentist ter git me teeth filled and have n't the price."

"I'll attend to that. Because you are a rare find, Mr. Strong Hans! You are one young fellow out of ten thousand. I must n't lose track of you. Let me tell you the plans that have been going through my head since I met you. Nature has made it impossible for me ever to marry a woman. For I am myself really a girl whom Nature has disguised as a fellow. I only dress as a fellow because the law ignorantly requires it. Nature meant that I should go through life with a husband—not a wife, as ignorant society commands. For some years it has been my dream to take to live under the same roof, as long as God leaves me in this world, a young fellow who approaches my ideal. And you do as hardly another I ever met. And I want you to live with me as my husband. When you reach twenty-five, you may also marry a physical woman, and she will keep house for us. I shall always regard your and her children as my own. God has given me much above the average brain power, and I can earn money enough to support all. You will never have a care. You need never work unless you want to. For I will be your slave. Because you possess in by far the highest degree the bodily and mental endowment that are for me a magnet. You will be paying for all I do by merely allowing me to gaze at your marvellous build a few minutes every day.

"You—like every one else—probably think I am a very bad sort of person. But perhaps you will discover some counterbalancing good qualities. In reality my bad side is no worse than that (sexuality) of all other men. The virile call me 'Child of the Devil!' The pot has always liked to call the kettle black. A person always considers right and highminded whatever he himself is inclined to, and wrong and devilish whatever others are inclined to. Because people are thus in love with themselves and their own tendencies, they will not forgive my own bad side. Not because it is in any way harmful; merely because it is so exceptional.

"I have the means to support you from this evening on.[2] I guarantee you as good a start in life as young fellow ever had. Wouldn't you like to become a lawyer or physician? Then why not tell me your true name and address, lest I lose you? Because until I know you thoroughly, I can not reveal my own legal name and where I live. Because people misunderstand so terribly women-men like myself."

"Harvey Green, Eagle Hotel, Third Avenue."

"I detest 'Harvey' because two acquaintances of that name were such poor specimens of men. Since you are to be my own personal sledge-hammer-slinger, I change your name to 'Tom.' That is the most masculine of names, and because you are the most masculine of young fellows—indeed the Supreme Man—you must be decorated with it. For you appear to be even *more* than man. A wonderful visitant from some other world. A super-man!

"I am afraid, Tom, you may be only a dream. I am afraid you may be only an apparition with me a brief hour, then to return, like Lohengrin, to the heavenly realm where the hero is immeasurably beyond anything we have on earth.

"So from tonight on, your legal first name is 'Tom.' And after I have tried you out, you will take my own legal surname. But my pet name is 'Prince Wonderful!' Can you feel, Prince Wonderful, that you charm me as a serpent a bird that it creeps upon in order to swallow? I know I am doing something crazy in letting you swallow me; in turning my back on all my own pleasures and prospects in order that you may get more out of life. For I would rather be the instrument through which a demigod like yourself enjoys some good before my eyes than myself to enjoy it. It is crazy of me; but my instincts lead that way, and I have the will to act that way. Muscular prodigy! Sky-scraper dare-devil! Your prodigious strength and muscles cement me to you as with hoops of steel!"

We soon took a stroll of half-a-mile to the East River, to a neighborhood of gas-houses, closed factories, and storeyards. No one

---

2. I had graduated more than a year before and was earning a good salary during this summer vacation between my first and second post-graduate years.

ventured here after dark except homeless gutter-snipes in summer to sleep. I myself would not have ventured at night anywhere near these dingy and desolate blocks except under the protection of a Strong Hans.

On female-impersonation sprees in the Rialto and Stuyvesant Square, I was always richly clad and wore jewelry. While during my year's female-impersonation apprenticeship on Mulberry Street my pockets were rifled every night, I had not now for nearly a year suffered the theft of even a copper. And why should I entertain even the shadow of a suspicion of "Tom" whom I wholeheartedly accepted as an unsophisticated youth recently from the Mohawk valley and to whom I had pledged the usufruct of my fairly good earning capacity to enable him to live like a nabob? For more than an hour, on the park bench, he had demonstrated himself supergenial. He had seemed so glad and so grateful over what I had promised: To lift him from the slums to an honored professional career. The story of his life did contain some inconsistencies but I realized it only too late.

As soon as we arrived in an unlighted stone-yard and there was not another soul within hearing—at least we had seen no one for the last five hundred feet—Harvey Green suddenly changed to *just the opposite* of his supergenial and ultra-grateful mask. Only at the moment that he had me completely at his mercy did he disclose himself as a dyed-in-the-wool criminal—a fiend who would never give a second thought to having just committed a murder.

Since I had expected to take him under my own roof and acquaint him with my every-day professional personality, I had not gone to the extremes of frivolous female-impersonation customary before young bloods who would never meet me in every-day life. I had feared I would forfeit his respect. Thus I had bidden *him* call me "Ralph"—not "Jennie."

"Ralph, what a ya think when I say I've served time in Elmira Reformatory? I kin prove what kinder man I am! Reach your hand here and feel this terrible scar. And then reach it here and feel this other. Ralph, I got these scars from bein' shot while runnin' away after havin' made a mess of burglin' houses in villages. For it's better ter be shot than caught. And I did n't dare go ter any doctor. My pal dressed the wounds the best he could, and it hurt awful—I tell you! And both times the buggers bled and bled till I close ter croaked. But luck was with me; me guts escaped the pepperin'. And after I recovered from loss of blood and after the wounds began ter heal, I was as strong and husky as you see me tonight.

"But just tonight I happened ter be broke. I was just loafin' in the park waitin' for a sissie like you, Ralph, ter walk inter me trap, so I could git hold of some dough."

"Harvey," I could only stammer, being next to speechless because of surprise and terror, "I am stunned at what you say. I never believed you could so deceive me. Can I say nothing to bring you to your senses? Don't you realize you have ten thousand times more to gain by being my friend?"

"Ralph, did n't yez ever hear a bird in hand's worth two in bush? Besides I could never be friend ter feller of your nature, Ralph! My hand's agin' you, Ralph! Because I've a criminal record, Ralph, every man's hand's agin' me. And my hand's agin' every man. I'm a man without any heart. I'd as soon put a bullet through a bloke as look at him.

"No, Ralph, the burglar's life I've chosen kin alone afford the excitement I need. Up me sleeve, I did n't take the least stock in all your soft soap as we sat in the park. Your pet names and promises mean nothin' ter me at all! You sure must take me for a softy in me promisin' ter live with a feller like yourself! You're now goin' ter have a taste of what use I have for that kind of feller! Hand out your money! Hand out your money!"

As he spoke, he clutched a shoulder with one hand and clenched the other in my face. I handed over my wallet.

"Here! I'll relieve yez of that watch and chain. . . And off with that ring! . . . Now take off every stitch so I kin see if you've any concealed bills."

"You're welcome to all I have on me, Harvey, and I love you too much to prosecute. Only please, *please,* let me depart unharmed! I forgive everything! If only you will let me depart unharmed, I will immediately take you around to my room and put into your hand a hundred dollars I have locked in my desk."

"I could n't do that. It'd be too risky."

While we argued, I undressed meekly and in unspeakable terror. I realized I might be experiencing my last five minutes of life. I took as much time as possible in the hope that a watchman might chance along. But why a watchman in a store-yard of paving stones?

"I guess now I've got everythin' of value, though not as much as expected. You sneak, why did n't yez have more bills onter your carcass?"

On female-impersonation sprees in Stuyvesant Square, I carried less than ten dollars. But judging from my rich attire and not knowing I had set out from home just for such a spree, Harvey must doubtless have thought I had on me a big roll. The present is only one of the most remarkable of about two hundred adventures I have had with robbers, the thievishly inclined regularly preying on androgynes because knowing the latter are themselves outlaws and thus unable to complain to the police.

Incensed over the disappointing size of his haul, Harvey continued: "And now, you sneak, I've got yez at me mercy! There's not a man within hearin'! Shut your d—throat, or you'll be worse off yet! Hold down your hands from in front of your mug! Hold down your hands! You bastard! You cannibal! Your nature's so disgustin' that every rightminded man would agree your face oughter be used as a butcher's choppin' block! And it's me own great joy ter do the job!"

Only about so much of the fiend's ranting was I able to catch. After I had received several sledgehammer blows in the face, fallen to the ground, been kicked and stamped upon, I entirely lost consciousness. Even while I still heard his ranting, I hardly noticed any pain. I merely thought I was dying. I was fully reconciled, and prayed: "Father, into Thy hands I commend my spirit!"

The next thing of which I was conscious was violent retching—due to internal injuries. In his youthful verdancy, the fiend had probably thought he had finished me. But Providence overruled, as in a number of subsequent similar assaults when I was snatched from the very jaws of death, whereas every few months I see in the papers that some less fortunate androgyne has not lived to tell the tale.

I was at first puzzled as to whether I was waking up on the earthly plane or in another world. Until I fully recovered my senses, I lay inert. Then I slowly dressed and limped away, having to rest on the curb every five hundred feet. I searched out a street fountain to bathe my bloodstained face and try to counteract the swelling and discoloration. For, most of all, I feared arousing the suspicions of my every-day circle.

I then boarded a car for home, begging my fare. In its regular hiding place in a stone wall of a neighboring park, I obtained the key to the street door of my boarding house.[3] Fortunately without encountering anybody, I mounted the several flights of stairs and secured my room-key from its

---

3. On one spree, when I left the key in my pocket, it had been stolen out of meanness, necessitating the embarrassment, and risk of suspicion, of having to ring at midnight for admission.

hiding place. On arrival in my own snug harbor, the first thing I did—as always—was to fall to my knees and bless Providence for permitting me to see home again.

For several hours, I could not sleep. Every moment I felt as if I would lapse into insane raving. Every moment I besought God to show mercy on a persecuted outcast. I reflected on my lot: To go through life as a cordially hated bisexual. That was my cross, and I repeated over and over again—in my struggle to save myself from insanity—the identic prayer that I had at fifteen repeated over and over again on the night I had consecrated myself, and been consecrated by the brethren of the puritan church to which I then belonged, to be a preacher of the Gospel:

> *"Jesus, I my cross have taken,*
> *All to leave and follow Thee;*
> *Naked, poor, despised, forsaken,*
> *Thou from hence my all shalt be:*
> *Perish every fond ambition,*
> *All I've sought and hoped and known;*
> *Yet how rich is my condition,*
> *God and heaven are still my own!"*

Immediately following later similar assaults, I have had to have my wounds dressed by a physician before seeking my room, and on one occasion had to enter a hospital. But on this occasion I waited until the following morning to summon my physician. He made one significant remark: "It would be worse than useless for you to try to prosecute your assailant. The court would immediately turn around and prosecute you as a felon!"

For two weeks I had to keep to my room. Never in all my life have I seen such a swollen and discolored face; with one exception, and that exception died a few days later as a result of his terrible blows in the face. I told my landlady I had been in a fight defending a woman from her drunken husband. I telephoned my office that I was *slightly* indisposed. Thus emphasized so no business associate would call.[4]

---

4. In a later catastrophe, one did call. I was compelled to tell the truth, but he proved sympathetic and respected my confidences. He subsequently asked his physician about homosexuality and was informed it was deepest moral depravity and merited no sympathy. He himself happened to be one of the most broadminded of men. He remarked that physicians as a class are narrow-minded since most have not taken a liberal-arts course.

After two weeks, when my face had become somewhat presentable, I ventured to the office still retaining only a black eye. "In my room in the dark, I struck the edge of the eye-socket on a chair spindle." I doubt whether all believed me, but none proved so impolite as to ask embarrassing questions.[5]

---

5. In a later scrape, after being laid up for a week, I ventured to my large publishing office with practically no skin on my nose, that member having a week before been badly smashed. My physician had furnished me with the explanation that he had applied a mustard plaster for a cold and the nose resulted! But the better joke was that simultaneously another university-trained androgyne working in the same room was limping around with a crutch. He said he had been thrown off a horse, but I never doubted he had been crippled by some sexually full-fledged brute as a punishment for his androgynism.

B ut Harvey Green! I here address you in case your eyes should ever fall on these lines. I shall remember you to my dying day as occupying third or fourth place among the hundreds of hero-boys with whom Providence permitted me to commune. I never met your equal in strength and muscle. Whenever I think of you, the words, Supreme Man, come into my mind. If I ever run across and recognize you after the lapse of more than a quarter of a century, I shall merely step up behind—where your eyes can not recognize me—and call: "Supreme Man!" "Supreme Man!" Then, without yet seeing me, you will recognize "Ralph" to be behind you; because no one else has probably thought to call you "Supreme Man"; because no one else could ever have worshipped you as I!

Poor deluded youth that you were in 1895! I almost weep whenever I reflect what you have missed in life through your poor judgment in robbing, and even aiming to murder, your would-be benefactor. For a few dollars worth of trinkets and for the satisfaction of torturing effeminacy, you turned your back on benefits to which could be attributed a money value of at least ten thousand dollars. But I freely forgive. Like the soldiers who crucified the world's Savior, you did not know what you were doing.

V

Evenings at Paresis Hall

During the last decade of the nineteenth century, the headquarters for avocational female-impersonators of the upper and middle classes was "Paresis Hall," on Fourth Avenue several blocks south of Fourteenth Street. In front was a modest bar-room; behind, a small beer-garden. The two floors above were divided into small rooms for rent. In 1921 I visited the site, as well as that of the "Hotel" Comfort (the two Rialto resorts with which I was most intimately identified) in order to take photographs for publication in this book, but found both structures supplanted.

Paresis Hall bore almost the worst reputation of any resort of New York's Underworld. Preachers in New York pulpits of the decade would thunder Philippics against the "Hall," referring to it in bated breath as "Sodom!" They were laboring under a fundamental misapprehension. But even while I was an habitué, the church and the press carried on such a war against the resort that the "not-care-a-damn" politicians who ruled little old New York had finally to stage a spectacular raid. After this, the resort, though continuing in business (because of political influence), turned the cold shoulder on androgynes and tolerated the presence of none in feminine garb.

But there existed little justification for the police's "jumping on" the "Hall" as a sop to puritan sentiment. Culturally and ethically, its distinctive clientele ranked high. Their only offence—but such a grave one as to cause sexually full-fledged Pharisees to lift up their own rotten hands in holy horror—was, as indicated, female-impersonation during their evenings at the resort. A psychological and not an ethical phenomenon! For ethically the "Hall's" distinctive clientele were congenital goody-goodies, incapable (by disposition) of ever inflicting the least detriment on a single soul. They were of the type in the United States, by every-day associates totally ignorant of the secret sexual practices of Nature's step-children, denominated "innocents;" and in France, "little Jesuses" even though in that country their sexual character is an open book, since there the sexual appetite is regarded as no more shameworthy than the alimentary. But the "Hall's" distinctive clientele were bitterly hated, and finally scattered by the police, merely because of their congenital bisexuality. The sexually full-fledged were crying for blood (of innocents), as did the "unco' good" in the days of witch-burning. Bisexuals must be crushed—right or wrong! The subject does not permit investigation! The fact that it is race suicide justifies the denial of all mercy! Let Juggernaut's car crush out their lives!

It was Nathan's parable of the ewe lamb all over again. (Second Book of Samuel, chapter 12.) The full-fledged had innumerable opportunities for the satisfaction of their instincts. Androgynes had only "the Hall" with the exception of three or four slum resorts frequented by only the lowest class of bisexuals who had never known anything better than slum life.

Why deprive cultured androgynes of their solitary rendezvous in the New York metropolitan district and give *carte blanche* to the thousands of similar heterosexual resorts?

Paresis Hall was as innocuous as any sex resort. Its existence really brought not the least detriment to any one or to the social body as a whole. More than that: It was a necessary safety-valve to the social body. It is not in the power of every adult to settle down for life in the monogamous and monandrous love-nest ordained for all by our leaders of thought. For example: The existence of Paresis Hall was due chiefly to the fact that in about one out of every one-hundred-and-fifty presumed males, the internal testicular secretion has failed to be of the right consistency.

While in this book I use the resort's popular name, androgyne habitués always abhorred it, saying simply "the Hall." The full nickname arose in part because the numerous full-fledged male visitors—it was one of the "sights" for out-of-towners who hired a guide to take them through New York's Underworld—thought the bisexuals, who were its main feature, must be insane in stooping to female-impersonation. They understood "paresis" to be the general medical term for "insanity." The name also in part arose because in those days even the medical profession were obsessed with the superstition that a virile man's association with an androgyne induced paresis in the former, it not yet having been discovered that this type of insanity is a rare aftermath of syphilis.

By means of an introduction of the reader to several androgyne patrons of Paresis Hall, I aim to demonstrate that instinctive female-impersonation has no relation to brain lesions, dementia præcox, or other psychic disease. The prevalent diagnosis, by physicians, of androgynism as insanity is as rational as for a male alienist to pronounce all women insane because their psyche differs radically from his own. As already stated, androgynism is a mere matter of arrested development, due to imperfect internal testicular secretion, in the natural sex differentiation that begins in the early foetus and ends at puberty. This arrest has for its result an adult *homo* more or less bisexual—a sexual intermediate, whose existence the bigotry of the leaders of thought has hitherto prevented their recognizing.

At the university, the student is taught all about the anatomy of the frog, but the prevalent view among the leaders of thought that everything connected with sex is taboo has prevented even the *professors* of physiology from investigating androgynism, which touches the social body so intimately. They have turned their backs because "the subject leaves a bad taste in the mouth!"

You milk-and-water hypocrites! Is it nothing to you that innocent androgynes are pining in prison an aggregate of thousands of years, and being continually murdered by prudes, like Harvey Green, because you have taught them that no punishment is too bad for so-called "homosexuality"? For prudery is common to some ultra-criminals and to the leaders of thought.[1] In the sight of God, you latter, when deliberately refusing to hearken to the wailing of bitterly persecuted androgynes, are morally on a par with Harvey Green and the murderers of X, Y, and "Jimmie Q", the latter being three bisexuals whose cases are outlined at the close of this volume.

Paresis Hall was never my own headquarters. I visited it only now and then. I had too early become wedded to the "Hotel" Comfort. Moreover, I wandered more widely, and in some respects flaunted my androgynism to a greater extent, than any other female-impersonator of my day. I took greater chances than any other, except in the appearing in public places in feminine apparel, but was never arrested in the Rialto because always careful never to render myself liable. Never for a moment did I forget the possibility of being arrested. I was even hypersensitive in this matter. A common dream was that of being arrested. But this hypersensitiveness probably saved me, since others of my type were continuously being arrested and sent to the penitentiary. But the cultured androgyne is almost never caught by the police. Only those of poor mentality.

---

1. Prudery is one of the foremost earmarks of anaphrodites and the mildly virile, to which classes nearly all the leaders of thought belong. The trait is completely absent from the more virile, as well as androgynes. Some of the more virile, as Harvey Green, are prudes **only as to homosexuality** because taught that fellators ought to be killed.

On one of my earliest visits to Paresis Hall—about January, 1895—I seated myself alone at one of the tables. I had only recently learned that it was the androgyne headquarters—or "fairie" as it was called at the time. Since Nature had consigned me to that class, I was anxious to meet as many examples as possible. As I took my seat, I did not recognize a single acquaintance among the several score young bloods, soubrettes, and androgynes chatting and drinking in the beer-garden.

In a few minutes, three short, smooth-faced young men approached and introduced themselves as Roland Reeves, Manon Lescaut, and Prince Pansy—aliases, because few refined androgynes would be so rash as to betray their legal name in the Underworld. Not alone from their names, but also from their loud apparel, the timbre of their voices, their frail physique, and their feminesque mannerisms, I discerned they were androgynes. Indeed effeminacy stuck out all over Prince Pansy. Manon Lescaut's only conspicuous anatomical feminesqueness was extraordinary breadth of hips. While Reeves' trunk and legs were not so feminine, he excelled in womanly features, with such marine-blue eyes and pink-peony cheeks as any beholder regretted should be wasted on a member (?) of the sterner sex. Moreover, Reeves alone, of the two score ultra-androgynes that I at different times met at Paresis Hall, was naturally beardless.

While Roland, Manon, and the "Prince" looked to be between twenty and twenty-five, I later ascertained the first mentioned was thirty-seven. As already observed, perennial youth is an earmark of ultra-androgynism.

Roland was chief speaker. The essence of his remarks was something like the following: "Mr. Werther—or Jennie June, as doubtless you prefer to be addressed—I have seen you at the Hotel Comfort, but you were always engaged. A score of us have formed a little club, the Cercle Hermaphroditos. For we need to unite for defense against the world's bitter persecution of bisexuals. We care to admit only extreme types—such as like to doll themselves up in feminine finery. We sympathize with, but do not care to be intimate with, the mild types, some of whom you see here tonight even wearing a disgusting beard! Of course they do not wear it out of liking. They merely consider it a lesser evil than the horrible razor or excruciating wax-mask.

"We ourselves are in the detested trousers because having only just arrived. We keep our feminine wardrobe in lockers upstairs so that our every-day circles can not suspect us of female-impersonation. For they have such an irrational horror of it!"

On the basis of different visits to an upper room permanently rented by the CERCLE HERMAPHRODITOS, I am going to build up a typical hour's conversation in order to disclose into what channels the thoughts of ultra-androgynes run when half-a-score find themselves together. The reason for its unnatural ring is that I omit the nine-tenths that were prattle, retaining only the cream that I consider of scientific value.

It was about eight o'clock on an evening of April, 1895. Some of the hermaphroditoi were still in male apparel; some changing to feminine evening dress and busy with padding and the powder-puff; some in their completed evening toilette ready to descend to the beer-garden below to await a young-blood friend.

I do not recall that a single hermaphroditos was man enough to use tobacco, or even to spit. They affected foreign languages, particularly French. I recall one whose favorite method in beginning a conversation was: "Mes cheris, qu' est ce que c' est que vous savez de nouvelles?"

A second: "Have you observed the new styles? Very narrow skirts,[2] and very large hats. The material saved on the skirt goes into the chapeau."

"Nothing could be more beautiful," Angelo-Phyllis, the most effeminate of the hermaphroditoi, opined softly and sweetly, "than a feminine face framed in a picture hat set sidewise, with rim reaching below the shoulders. How I do like to stalk Fourteenth Street myself with such a chapeau![3] How the young fellows stare and throw remarks after me! I am glad the petite turbans are going into the rag-bag. And what low necks and short arms the new evening dresses are showing! And the material hardly more than cobweb! One could almost hide an up-to-date corsage in the fist."

"You seem, Phyllis, to be an expert on lingerie."

"My woman friends tell me I have the best eye for color effects they ever heard of. Millinery happens to be my business. A star actress whom I happen to know always asks me to accompany her to the modiste's. I

---

2. In the last decade of the nineteenth century also, there existed a feminine craze for skirts as narrow as a pant-leg. "Merry Widow" hats also had their day then. But in 1921 for the first time in Christendom, respectable women have been crazy to display their bare breasts, bare arms, and next-to-nude legs in the crowded streets. Respectable women have today adopted for street wear the garb, for exclusive brothel wear, of filles de joie of a quarter of a century ago.
3. See "**French Doll Baby**" in Part VIII.

must practically pick out all her robes, as well as hats—including the way they are to be made up. Just the sight of the artistic fabrics, as they are unrolled by the saleswoman, is an exquisite delight. My mind becomes crowded with emotions, and on the spur of the moment I could pen a lyric *sur les etoff es jolies* that any ladies' magazine would publish. . . The stupidity of some women! This actress has just divorced her husband and is looking around for a new alliance. If I happened to have been born a marrying man, I could make her my wife, although all the front-row bald-pates are crazy after her. She has given every hint—everything except an actual proposal. But if I did let her marry me, the morning following the bridal night, she would apply to the court for an annulment. She does not even suspect the existence of pseudo-men."

Another: "It is strange how often a girl falls in love with us women-men. I myself have had three proposals. Girls are particularly prone to fall in love with members of their own sex disguised as men. Of course we are really only girls ourselves whom Nature has disguised as men. Particularly, rather mannish women fall in love with us Mollie Coddles."

P hyllis: "That reminds me of a young heiress[4] whom I knew. Perhaps you read in the papers two years ago how a New York young woman disappeared, and the utmost efforts of the police were not rewarded with the least trace. She was of that mannish type. For months she was the pest of my life. I still have a big pack of letters and poems—all sickening—which she mailed me.

"I myself have no doubt of the fate of the poor girl. When the papers were full of rumors and hypotheses about her, I repeatedly wrote my theory to her father. When he ignored my letters, I gave the police my theory. They likewise thought it absurd and refused to investigate along the lines I suggested.

"When some mannish women find it impossible to marry an effeminate man, they adopt some petite cry-baby woman as their soul-mate. The papers stated that the last trace of Mollie Dale was her carrying away from O'Neil's several purchases. The latter immediately struck me as such alone as a gallant would buy to present his lady-love. When I told the police, they said: 'Absurd! Who ever heard of one woman being in love with another!'

"On leaving O'Neil's, Mollie Dale absolutely dropped out of sight for all time. It was as if the earth had suddenly yawned for her body and closed again so rapidly as to be unseen by the people nearby. Or as if she, absent-minded, had stepped into an open sewer man-hole and no one happened at the moment to have his eyes on the spot.

"My theory, hermaphroditoi, is that Mollie went right from O'Neil's to her cry-baby chum's. Probably within walking distance, because every soul in New York was asked through the newspapers over and over again if they had met on any public conveyance the morning of Mollie's dropping out of sight a young lady of her description, so detailed as to give even the pattern of her shoes, besides her much published photographs. Her disappearance was at the time the seven-days wonder of New York and every one was discussing it.

"The rule with men-women[5]—as with us women-men—is never to breathe to any one of their every-day circle a word about their sweethearts because of the misunderstanding and horror evidenced by

4. This anecdote deals with only one of a number of similar occurrences in New York. Gynanders, as well as androgynes, are doomed to suffer murder at the hands of hare-brained prudes because of the false teaching of the leaders of thought.
5. The scientific names "androgyne" and "gynander" evidence a blunder of their coiner. The order of their components is the reverse of their English colloquial equivalents.

people ignorant of psychology. As a rule the soul-mates of us better-class bisexuals belong to a much lower social stratum. Very likely Mollie's lived in one of the thousands of tumbledown tenements within walking distance of O'Neil's.

"According to my theory, hermaphroditoi—and I have seen a hundred times more of life than the average man, and possess some sense notwithstanding people not knowing me well set me down as only a high-grade idiot because of my outward frivolousness and an unfortunate infantile carriage—the cry-baby's husband or father had only just learned of what he, as well as ninety-nine out of every hundred men, mistakenly regarded as the horribly corrupting influence of the poor martyr Mollie on the hare-brained crybaby. Ignorant that men-women are victims of birth and that their so-called 'depravity' brings not the least harm to any one, and insanely angry with Mollie into the bargain, he that very morning bludgeoned her in his apartment. And he happened to succeed in disposing of the corpse.

"I thought of Mollie when last week the papers told about an unrecognizable female body, bent double, having been found in a trunk filled with salt that for two years had rested unclaimed in the trunk-room of the third-class Hotel X—just the type that a tenement-dweller would select to harbor such a trunk. The murderer was evidently a meat-packer, familiar with the processes of salting down.

"In such strange ways a continuous string of both men-women and women-men are being struck down in New York for no other reason than loathing for those born bisexual. And public opinion forbids the publication of the facts of bisexuality, which, if generally known, would put an end to these mysterious murders of innocents."

H ello, Mith Nighty!" several called as one of the tallest, oldest, and most brunette of the hermaphroditoi entered the Cercle's dressing-room. The androgyne who had adopted the name of a romantic woman had, during his twenties, before becoming thick-set, been a female-impersonator on the vaudeville stage.

"Mith Nighty!" one of the youngest hermaphroditoi shouted in a falsetto. "Queenie and I want you to coach us in female-impersonation. Next Friday at the Masked Ball we make our debut as public female-impersonators."

A senior: "The world would call our hobby insanity. But the explanation is that we were created psychic females, who yearn for the dress and role of that sex—to feel skirts flapping about our ankles—and nevertheless Nature has been so cruel as to incarnate our woman-souls in the abhorred male body."

Another: "But other than in us women-men, the male figure is infinitely more artistic than the female. The only disgusting thing in man is the beardal growth. I can tolerate in a beau a small moustache only, but prefer him clean-shaven. But feminine breasts are the very badge of beastliness! You, of course, excepted, Ralph-Jennie. The short, fat, knock-kneed feminine legs are monstrosities! If you"ll pardon me for saying it, Phyllis. On the other hand, the muscles of an athlete compel the attention."

Later it chanced that Roland Reeves and myself entered into a soft-spoken dialogue: "Ralph, do you know any woman-man whom we ought to get into the Cercle?"

"Four! But they do not realize anybody is wise outside the young athlete each has selected as chum. No one but another woman-man, or a full-fledged man who had read Krafft-Ebing,[6] would ever suspect them. Their public conduct is always the height of propriety. One of them even makes it a practice to boast of excesses *cum femina*—to ward off suspicion, for he has always shunned females as one would the plague. But on the basis of self-knowledge, we women-men easily recognize our own kind. I need only hear the voice and glimpse the features and figure.

"But none of the four ever visits the Underworld. They do not feel the need. Their being so fortunate as to have secured soul-mates among

---

6. Havelock Ellis's works on sex—the foremost in the English language—had not yet been published in 1895.

their every-day circle has proved their safety-valve. You, Roland, and I have simply been denied by Providence a hero-confidant from among our every-day circle. Moreover, we have been unwilling to risk betrayal to that circle. We are not hunting for high-figured blackmail and possibly years in prison.

"One is a university student. The college body refers to his ultra-virile room-mate and himself as "X and wife." But no user of the phrase ever dreams of its real significance, not knowing of the existence of intermediates. Of course they have heard of homosexuality, but think only the scum of mankind could be guilty. Impossible in the case of a high-minded intellectual!

"Here's Plum. Plumkin, you look as if you had lost your last friend!"

The 23-year Mollie Coddle sobbed: "Everything looks dark. Two days ago I was fired. I have hardly slept a wink since. I have hope for the future only in the grave. Some bigot denounced me to the boss. He called me into his private office. As this had never happened before, I guessed the reason. . ."

Plum outlined his conference. I have listened to several similar confessions. The following is a composite.

Plum: "I confess to being a woman-man and throw myself upon your mercy."

Fairsea: "That confession is sufficient, and proves you an undesirable person to have around!"

Plum: "It will be hard to find a new job, since I have been with you for five years and must depend on your recommendation."

Fairsea: "Knowing your nature, Plum, I could not recommend you *even to shovel coal into a furnace!*"

Plum: "But you have steadily advanced me for five years! Why should today's discovery make any difference in your opinion of my business ability?"

Fairsea with a sneer: "An invert ought to leave brain work for others! He ought to exhaust himself on a farm from sunrise to sunset so that the psychic movings would be next to non-existent. He should pass his life in the back woods; not in a city. He has no right in the front ranks of civilization where his abnormality is so out of place!"

Plum: "You mean that he should commit intellectual and social suicide in obedience to the aesthetic sense of Pharisees?"

Fairsea: "Certainly! The innate feelings and the conscience, as well as the Bible, teach that the invert has no rights! I myself have only deep-rooted contempt for him! Every fibre in my body, every cell in my tissues, cries out in loud protest against him! He is the lowest of the low! I dare say that at the bottom of your heart, Plum, you are thoroughly ashamed of the confession you made a moment ago?"

Plum: "By no means. I have learned to look upon bisexuality as a scientist and a philosopher. But you have just shown yourself to be still groping in the Dark Ages.

"No, Mr. Fairsea, I can hardly bring myself to be ashamed of the handiwork of God. A bisexual has no more reason than a full-fledged man or woman to be ashamed of his God-given sexuality.

"You appear, Mr. Fairsea, to be unable to get my point of view. All in my anatomy and psyche that you gloat in calling depraved and contemptible I have been used to since my early teens. If your views have any justification in science or ethics, I am unable to see it. Although it almost breaks my heart to be made an outcast and penniless by yourself, I prefer that lot, knowing I am in the right, than to be in the wrong even if sitting, as yourself, in the chair of president of the X—— Company.

"How do you define 'depraved', Mr. Fairsea? If in such a way as to exclude Socrates, Plato, Michael Angelo, and Raphael, then you exclude me also."

Fairsea: "But the phenomenon works against the multiplication of the human race. Nature, with this in view, instilled in all but the scum of mankind this utter disgust for the invert. To the end of the continued existence of the race, he must be condemned to a life of unsatisfied longing. For this reason he should be imprisoned for life, not for only ten or twenty years as the statutes now provide!

"We strictly segregate diphtheria and scarlet fever, Plum. Why should we not similarly quarantine against inversion?"

Plum: "Because there is a vast difference. Contagious disease, if not strictly segregated, would occasion death and acute suffering to many additional persons. WHEREAS THE BISEXUALS' BEING AT LIBERTY OCCASIONS NOT THE LEAST DETRIMENT TO ANY INDIVIDUAL, NOR TO THE RACE AS A WHOLE.

"A second reason: The quarantining of contagious disease is only a matter of shutting up a few persons for a few weeks in their own homes. It causes no serious privation or suffering. Whereas the segregation of bisexuals would affect for a lifetime tens of thousands of our most useful members of society. It would occasion, among these already accursed by Nature, additional intense mental suffering, despair, and suicide.

"Any one who can suggest the latter segregation is unable to see farther away than the end of his nose.

"And as to race suicide, Mr. Fairsea. You should be the very last to lecture anybody on that subject! You are the father of only two children and have put three wives under the sod through your beastly, excessive demands!

"Can it be that you shut your eyes to all evidence? Do ocular proofs count for nothing? Hasn't the human race survived the best decades of classic Greece? While the Greeks are acknowledged by all modern historians to have attained the highest development of mind and body ever known, they at the same time gave to the women-men who happened to be born among them—as among all races of all ages—an honorable place. And by far more place, both in their personal and social life, than in the case of any other nation of the ancient or modern world."

Fairsea: "But I had hoped that the human race had evolved above this phenomenon! I hate to believe it of the human race! Because the phenomenon lowers humanity down to the lowest levels of animal life! I——"

Plum: "So does eating!"

Fairsea: "I detest it! My disgust is innermost and deepseated! To begin now to show any mercy to the invert, after having for two thousand years confined him in dungeons, burned him at the stake, and buried him alive, would be a backward step in the evolution of the race!

"Plum, the invert is not fit to live with the rest of mankind! He should be shunned as the lepers of biblical times! If generously allowed outside prison walls, the law should at least ordain that the word 'Unclean' be branded in his forehead, and should compel him to cry: 'Unclean! Unclean!' as he walks the streets, lest his very brushing against decent people contaminate them!"

Plum: "All that is only bigotry and bias! Nearly every man's conduct is still governed by bias!"

Fairsea: "I even acknowledge that it is bias! For bias is justifiable in matters of sex! . . . You say that medical writers have declared inverts *irresponsible!* That declaration proves that they know nothing about them! You say inverts are assaulted and blackmailed! They deserve to be! It would be wrong for any one at all to show any leniency! Their existence ought to be made so intolerable as to drive them to lead their sexual life along the lines followed by all other men! Your case, Plum, fills me with such disgust that I could not rest knowing you were around the office!"

Roland brought the conversation to a close: "Mankind are so steeped in egotism! Whatever they are not personally inclined to is always horribly immoral! Whatever they are instinctively inclined to is always supremely right!

"Why not go to the root of the matter and take revenge on Nature, instead of her irresponsible and pitiable step-children? Nature alone is to blame for the existence of sexual cripples. Why not marshal every son and daughter of Adam for the work of honeycombing the entire crust of the earth with galleries to be filled with dynamite? And then set off the world-wide charge simultaneously so as to destroy all terrestrial Nature at one coup, humanity included. This would constitute man's sole *logical* vengeance on bisexuality.

"But Man is Truly a Passional, Rather Than a Rational, Being."

VI

Thoughts Suggested by the "Hermaphroditoi" in General

I associated with the hermaphroditoi less than a year. Paresis Hall then happened to be raided by the police and the hermaphroditoi—who happened to be the police's chief quarry—afterward gave the resort a wide berth for fear of arrest.

The hermaphroditoi numbered about a score. All were highly cultured ultra-androgynes varying in age from eighteen to forty. Half-a-score have given me their life-story. But the careers of only two were particularly tragic. I have therefore, in Parts Four and Five, detailed the life-stories of these two as nearly as I can remember, having of course taken no notes at the time.

In the lives of some hermaphroditoi, nothing particularly remarkable had ever transpired beyond their chronic female-impersonation sprees. For example, Roland Reeves, the most brilliant, was, in every act, moderate and sensible. He was of the type of cross-dressing androgyne that possesses little animality. He was by no means a coquette—as were most of the hermaphroditoi. People would say that he had more self-restraint and moral backbone than the coquettes. But my unusually wide observations have taught me that sexual moderation is as a rule due to weak instinct when not to lack of opportunity.

A prime regulator of the sexual intensity of the adult androgyne—as probably of all humans—consists of the influences toward sexual expression during childhood. My own adult career had its prototype in my intense fairie-ism from two until seven. Sexual impressions of early childhood have often a powerful influence down through middle life. In large measure they determine the course to be taken by the adult sexual life. Parents Can Not Be Too Watchful of the Secret Practices of Small Children, and of the Influence of Servants.

Androgynes, during childhood, are particularly prone to fall into bad habits (fellatio; or pathicism in pædicatio) because always confined with their sexual opposites. What would one expect of the chastity of a high-strung girl of twelve marooned for a summer on an island with merely a dozen ultra-virile youths? That is the identical situation of youthful androgynes.

As a rule, when an androgyne reaches the middle thirties, the instinct to dress and pose as a mademoiselle gradually becomes feeble. Age sobers many and they become practically asexual. I have observed the same thing in ultra-virile men during my twelve years career as their mignon. Their craze for the opposite sex is strongest from twenty to twenty-five (just at the time when Christian custom interdicts the propensity) after which it gradually declines. It is the same with animals. Poulterers cut off the heads of all but "adolescent" roosters. I have myself been a Guinea pig fancier. I discovered that the males gradually lose their virility at middle age.

Indeed I have observed that as androgynes approach fifty, they sometimes become more masculine than they ever were, and will even marry. It seems that in rare cases mild virility supplants sexual passivity as fifty is approached. On the other hand, I have heard of mildly virile men marrying in their twenties, begetting children, and only after reaching middle age, becoming somewhat sissified, acquiring *horror feminæ*, like ultra-androgynes, and finally seeking the latter's sexual role.

These changes in ultra-androgynes and in the mildly virile are like menopause in woman. There is a turning point in the sex life. The hitherto passive ultra-androgyne occasionally becomes active. The mildly virile occasionally develops a quasi-feminine leaning. The latter class were possibly mildly androgynous by birth, but the idiosyncrasies did not come to the front of the mental life until the climacteric corresponding to menopause.

In my AUTOBIOGRAPHY OF AN ANDROGYNE, I said nothing about my personal "menopause" because it came at about the close of my writing that book, and I did not recognize it as such until after the latter's publication. On page 197, I described how, at the age of forty-two, my weight, stripped, within six weeks, jumped from 133 to 160. For ten years, it had been stationary at 133. For the following five years, it has been stationary at 160. I now attribute the change to "menopause." Moreover, a few months after the increase in weight, I kept company with a young lady for half-a-year. I drifted into it almost unconsciously and involuntarily. I paid her gallantries immeasurably beyond any other incident of my life. I even regarded a Platonic marriage as a possibility, though not a probability.

But I was too extreme an androgyne, in addition to my having been castrated. The virility that occasionally for the first time surges up in ultra-androgynes at "the change of life" could not go very far with me. After six months, I renounced the pseudo-courtship entirely, with disgust at the feminine sex, but particularly with the young female who had done her best to rope me in as her husband. For she did most of the courting. I merely let myself almost fall into her trap.

Even in my twenty-second year—the period when I belonged to the Cercle Hermaphroditos—I had already written a brief AUTOBIOGRAPHY. But the bigotry of cultured man made me wait twenty-three years for publication. Already—because I happened to be an ultra-androgyne myself—I had selected androgynism as my special field in science and literature. I therefore desired to collect all the data possible, although not yet having acquired the habit of note-making.

In order to draw out atypic individuals—particularly androgynes—I made it a practice first to reveal my own secrets. This frankness generally led them to confide to me what they never breathed to another—people in general, and particularly cultured androgynes, having an absurd reluctance to discuss the sexual side of their lives. (Androgynes for fear of persecution and prosecution, not by reason of prudery.) And the human race has suffered so greatly as a result of this obsession!

When God created human nature, his handiwork was so horrible that mankind, as soon as they reached the stage of civilization, have thrown a blanket over their own nature, after the example of Shem and Japheth with their father Noah's drunken nakedness. Cultured man has interdicted human nature's coming out into the light of day because of its inexpressible ugliness.

E ven in the twentieth century in the English-speaking world, next to nothing is known about human sexuality. At least with the exception of a handful of sexologists. Each individual simply knows his own sexual life, refuses to divulge it because of its "nastiness," and is unable to overcome his shame to inquire whether other humans (men and women, respectively) are of like passions with himself. He assumes yes. But the truth of the matter is that on the sexual side of life, every individual is *sui generis*. And if a man or woman does chance to discover that an associate is different "from *me*," right away he or she is crazy to murder the associate for daring to be different! On no side of life is charity so much needed as on the sexual.

But Frank White (or Eunice)—whom, out of deference to the predilections of the general reader, I am going to let tell "his-her" own story in PART FOUR—needed, by exception, little urging to draw him out. He told me piecemeal. But I hand it on to my readers without a break. Moreover, I endeavor to reproduce his unconscious hifalutin, Johnsonese style of expression.

At the time he epitomized his life for me, Frank-Eunice (as he was known in the Underworld) was a comely blonde around forty, and five feet five tall. His physique was not noticeably feminine. He possessed merely a small-boy air and appearance, notwithstanding his hair was nearly white, though not thin. The beardal growth was sparse, always clean-shaven, and for special occasions, eradicated. The amative side of life ("erotic ardor", as he phrased it) was his only fault. In leisure hours he could talk of little else than modern exemplars of adolescent Adonis or Hercules. In this respect he was one of the two or three extreme hermaphroditoi.

PART IV
FRANK—EUNICE

I

Debut as Adult Female-Impersonator

Ralph, I was ushered into this mundane sphere in the year of our Lord 1854. I was a lucky dog to be brought up on the upper West Side a few blocks from Central Park (New York City). As a diminutive urchin, I dolled myself up in feminine habiliments at every opportunity. Eunice was my favorite playmate. I opined her appellation the most melodious that ever impinged upon my eardrums and regretted it was not mine personally. Whenever I flaunted myself in skirts, I adopted it.

In my early teens, father escorted me to a physician that the latter might query me concerning my feminine predilections and ridicule me out of same. Simultaneously father, through severe castigation, imposed a finis to female-impersonation in my own clique. I therefore commenced, during periods of special obsession to be a *puella,* the practice of perambulating the slums, first by daylight, and later after the shades of night had fallen. During these insensate peregrinations, there would swarm through my mind visions of flirtations with the ruffians around my age that I encountered. These "huskies" riveted my gaze. They fascinated me. But not until the fifth or sixth peregrination could I screw up courage to insinuate myself into the confidence of one of these magical intelligences.

I chanced for the first time to run across a Bowery bar-room, the "Pugilists' Haven," which, I had read in the papers, was the rendezvous of prize-fighters, gamblers, and gun-men (the most desperate type of gangster who will murder for pay). The press advocated its obliteration. Curious that just because of this reputation, I was immediately insane to enter. For it was unholy ground. I reflected: "In this lowest of dives, they may accept me as a *puella,* although superficially a boy." Because all early influences, Ralph, had made me opine that taking the part of a girl was the very lowest thing a boy could descend to. I further pondered: "Between the luxurious mansion of *pater familias* and this dingy dive, give me the latter! For here alone I might be able to pass as a *puella.* In my own cultured, Christian circle, female-impersonation is castigated. But would not the attitude of the offscouring of our mundane sphere—the Pugilists' Haven gunmen—be different?"

And how crazy I was to insinuate myself with the adolescent gunmen, whom I had only read about! The very supposition of their presence just within that latticed door attracted me as a potent magnet snatches steel filings to itself. I passed and repassed the dive, continuously imagining what would transpire if I should penetrate this unholy of unholies, and having delectable visions of every species of flirtation with the demigods who made the saloon their rendezvous.

I finally emboldened myself to thrust aside a leaf of the latticed portal. It was my first appearance inside a saloon, and I never had tasted any intoxicant. In my diffidence and ignorance of the proper course to pursue, I subsided into the first vacant fauteuil. For, on one side, against the wall, were rude, wooden fauteuils, almost all occupied by middle-aged cherry-nosed individuals. Extending the full length of the other side was a bar crowded with fast-looking younger men, each with a glass before him. Doubtless because of my verdancy, several commenced eyeing me, making remarks, and laughing. The nearest bartender immediately inquired: "Doll-baby, what'll yer have ter drink?"

"Nothing."

"Jackass! Every bloke dat comes inter dis here joint has ter take somethink!"

"Then give me a glass of beer," I replied hardly above a whisper. In my embarrassment, I imbibed the beverage almost at a swallow. That gave all the witnesses hysterics. They assured me: "We only sip it!" They addressed me as "Siss!" "Pet!" "Fairie!" I did not immediately perceive the significance of the last appellation. I was encircled. Particularly two sailors ingratiated themselves. They requested me to purchase "schnapps" for them because impecunious. I provided glass after glass, for they were bewitchingly gallant. All the other individuals were kidding me: "The doll-baby likes the blue-jackets, sure Mike!" "Sailor-boy, take off your suit and make it a present to her!" "How I wish I was one of Uncle Sam's boys and I'd git steeped in schnapps too!" I was mortified by such observations, and as soon as the sailor-boys invited me, departed under their escort.

I hired a chamber at a third-class hotel nearby. I gave them funds to secure another. For we did not desire that the clerk perceive that we were all to occupy the identic room. We pretended the sailors and I were unacquainted.

They finished by inserting a handkerchief into my buccal cavity, tying a strip of the bed linen over it, binding my hands behind my back, and fastening my lower extremities to the bed springs so that I could not even kick. They then departed with my wallet and outer clothing.

After an hour of helplessness, I discovered that the partition to the adjacent chamber was scarcely more than card-board. Because I perceived sounds of the entrance of an individual. I could even hear his breathing. I discerned the words: "How I wish I had three hundred dollars!"

I commenced a continuous jouncing up and down. The uninterrupted tintinnabulation of the springs attracted the individual's attention and he addressed me. I could respond only with a low gurgling. The clerk soon liberated me. I had to confess everything. But he manifested sympathy and donated a nickel for carfare.

One blue-jacket was of about my own measurements. Evidently he intended to desert. For he had abandoned his uniform. I was compelled to attire myself therein and boarded a car for my domicile.

My house-key had remained in my appropriated habiliments. How to enter was my problem. If I rang, my arrival at midnight costumed as a sailor would disclose everything. I hoped the butler had neglected to secure the covering of the coal-hole in front of the basement windows.

Every one had retired. Able to raise the covering, I dropped to the coal-pile. I discovered that the door at the head of the cellar stairs was also fortunately unsecured. With trepidation and in absolute silence, I ascended, in stocking feet, to my chamber and devoutly thanked Providence for restoration to my family without a hair injured.

I had only recently purchased the appropriated habiliments. The subsequent day I visited the same establishment and succeeded in securing an exact duplicate so that my family would not observe the disappearance of the original.

II

THE PUG HEAVEN

I henceforth visited the Pugilists' Haven one evening each week. After the appropriation of one good suit, I always attired myself rather shabbily. After seven o'clock dinner, I would change to the cast-off apparel and noiselessly glide down the two flights of stairs from my chamber. Fortunately father always had prayers after dinner. While the family were in the prayer-room and all the servants in their dining-room, I succeeded in engineering my exit for an evening's revel with little risk, in my poverty-stricken disguise, of encountering any individual in the halls. No one ever suspected the reason for my absences. It was several times remarked that I had been out late. But I threw the observer off the scent by the pretext of a perambulation to obviate insomnia.

As I proceeded rapidly from my domicile, I would, if I detected a familiar figure advancing, cross to the other side of the street and make a feint of ringing a doorbell. In order, in my dilapidated apparel, to avert the danger of encountering on the public conveyance some one acquainted with my identity, I would perambulate more than a mile in order to attain the Bowery by an east-side car. On the way I would conceal my house-key and an emergency greenback in a crevice in the Central Park stonewall—always the identic cavity in order to be regained with ease.

At Pug Heaven—as my dive was nicknamed—I was universally given a hearty welcome and secured the society of adolescent ruffians fairly clean and sprucely attired. Of course they always ransacked my pockets the first chance that offered. Before it could happen, I had treated liberally half-a-dozen of the handsomest, and thus insinuated myself into their good graces. I always kept a reserve five-dollar bill sewed in the waistband of my trousers—a pair worn on these sprees alone because too shabby to be a temptation for appropriation.

On my second appearance at Pug Heaven, the heroic gunmen entertained me with episodes about other female-impersonators they had encountered. I particularly remember stories about the "Duchess of Austria," from whom, they recounted, "some lucky guys had pumped" hundreds of dollars. One narrated anecdotes of a physician located south of Fourteenth Street. Young fellows would visit his office to be medicated and he would reveal his own bisexuality. My pals did not marvel at all over my strange appetencies. They entreated me to bring around other female-impersonators. They were merely anxious for the money it would bring them. When I apologized for my queer penchant, they said: "It is nothing. It is Nature." Ralph, those adolescent Pug Heaven sluggers knew more about the psychology of instinctive female-impersonators than all the M. D.'s in America combined! From that single hour's conversation, I ascertained more about my own personality than in my prior fourteen years pilgrimage on this planet. For the first time, the riddle of my existence was solved; I perceived that I had been born a biological sport—a female with male genitals.

I soon acquired half-a-dozen permanent favorites. These adolescent sluggers and gunmen lost no time in assuring me: "You're only a doll-baby, Eunice, and so need us big, strong fellows to fight your battles. But you must stay with our gang! If we should catch you running around with any other, we'd murder you!"

I coveted to be their slave, Ralph, and did all I could for them without disclosing that I belonged to a wealthy family, because a female-impersonator of a higher social stratum associating incognito with gangsters must conceal his status. At Pug Heaven, I became an expert detective and actor—an accomplishment requisite for every upper-class impersonator destined to sprees in the Underworld.

A thousand times I desiderated female corporeality so that I could have married one of these magic gunmen. How I have envied many a young mother before my eyes with babe in arms! How could a God of love have created me physically a male when I have always so coveted personal female corporeality, and, in adulthood, the mothering of offspring!

These weekly female-impersonation explosions continued more than two years, when my father relegated me to a university several hours from New York. I leave it nameless—to spare it the disgrace of having once numbered "Frank White" among its students. These evenings in Pug Heaven were the most beatific feature of life. During college vacations, and for several years following graduation, I occasionally visited the joint. But finally, on my return from an extended residence in Europe, I discovered a haberdashery occupying the site. I was informed that an application for renewal of license had been denied. Its habitués became thus scattered.

III

A University Friendship

Would it interest you, Ralph-Jennie, to hear how I was blackmailed in college? The episode commenced only in my junior year. Throughout the first two years, because of the safety-valve I possessed in the Pug Heaven gunmen, I had succeeded in restraining my appetencies and presenting no occasion for *chantage*. But early in my junior year, the janitor of my dormitory happened to be an exquisite chocolate cream-drop. Only twenty, and with such a "divine" countenance! I could have gazed into it throughout eternity without a second's intermission—until I detected the rascality underneath! Such dreamy brown eyes! Perfect, arched eyebrows! Sun-flower cheeks! And soft chestnut hair! Ralph, you never saw anything so fascinating! For weeks I experienced anguish at being denied a declaration of my admiration! I then commenced making the "divine" creature presents. And it was then not long before I began inviting him around to my room after all the other students had retired and there was little risk of any individual discovering the unequal friendship. For I would have been ostracized for entertaining a janitor. And again it was not long before Jack manifested a roguish streak in his character, which any one but an intimate would have opined equally beautiful with his countenance and figure. After I discovered his true character, my fascination died down. But there was absolutely nothing to do but tolerate him up to graduation.

In the course of my two decades of adulthood, I have repeatedly fallen victim to the physical charms of some adolescent stalwart menial in my every-day environment. I have lived much abroad. In the United States and Great Britain, three out of four, if of generally good reputation, demonstrate themselves diamonds in the rough. They refuse to take advantage of a step-child of Nature whose secret they happen to unearth. But on the continent of Europe, the proportion is as high as nineteen out of twenty. There a correct knowledge of sexual intermediates is widely disseminated and the courts deal out justice to the woman-man. Even the Paris apache realizes that these bisexuals are worthy of commiseration and not responsible for their idiosyncrasies. But English-speaking countries give *carte blanche* to every prude actuated to pillage and even murder us women-men. We are outlaws; enjoy no police protection; and are denied recourse to the laws and courts. In English-speaking lands, as already in other civilized countries, even the scum of society should be educated, first by newspaper propaganda whenever the murder of an intermediate is described, and then from mouth to mouth, that the woman-man and the man-woman are irresponsible for their exceptional sexuality and should not be tortured on account of it.

Notwithstanding that I immediately entered into an arrangement by which Jack benefited fifty dollars a month, I soon perceived evidences of whisperings that "Frank White is abnormal!" An exasperated classmate once even exclaimed sarcastically: "You are not a proper person to associate with!"

In my senior year, I failed of a much coveted election to a senior society—an election which many indeed had prophesied on the basis of my wealth and scholarship. The failure was explicable only in the rumors apparently being circulated. But fortunately they were only *rumors*. In my college days, I would never have been so reckless as to have permitted any individual ever to discover me, even for a second, in conversation with such as Jack. Thus Incredulity followed closely on the steps of Rumor. Because of my general goody-goodiness, the fellows probably thought it impossible for me to be so utterly depraved! But the actuality was far beyond rumor. The only mistake was the rumormongers *a priori* assumption of deepdyed depravity. I was not a whit more corrupt than those Pharisees themselves! The worst of the matter was that I am a girl incarnated in a fellow's body, and nevertheless doomed to be segregated exclusively with males. If the world could only realize that nearly all their anxieties and horrors are as groundless as this abhorrence of myself in the university!

Because no busybody engaged a detective to ferret out my secrets, I was privileged to graduate. But commencement day was like that of my own funeral. For I realized I was bidding *alma mater* a farewell forever. First, on account of Jack's treacherous character, who had remained with the university because of his advantages with me; and secondly, on account of my questionable reputation. Tears even trickled down my cheeks during the commencement exercises, Ralph. For I felt that I was in my death throes so far as the university is concerned. I was compelled henceforth to keep out of touch, including all alumni gatherings. In all class letters and address lists published the first five years, I engineered things so that there appeared after my name: "Whereabouts unknown."

Otherwise Jack might have ferreted me out. The Pharisees doubtless concluded my "depravity" had wrecked my life. But the fact was that I rose rapidly in my business career.

Primarily in order to give Jack the slip, I spent the year after graduation in Europe—for the most part in Paris. I despatched Jack several cards in order to put him on a false scent.

On resuming residence in New York, I had to make the best of its Overworld. I ascertained that they are incredibly bigoted as compared with the liberalism of continental Europe. Only a person who has resided there has acquired the acuteness of vision to discern the legend on the hatbands of upper-class New Yorkers: "I am holier than thou!"

I had heard that the Rialto is New York's stamping-ground for amateur female-impersonators. Accordingly I commenced devoting one or two evenings a week to its resorts. As soon as I learned that "the Hall" is the home of cultured female-impersonation, I made it my own headquarters.

IV

The Masked Ball

You inquire, Ralph-Jennie, if I have been blackmailed during my business career. I confess I have been more negligent than most cultured women-men, and as a punishment, have suffered more blackmail. I have insanely betrayed my secret to several dishonest young bloods who knew who I am and therefore forced large sums out of me. I shall describe the most remarkable case.

But first, why have I been the victim of blackmail? Because my strongest passion is to get into feminine finery now and then and play the coquette. I also occasionally yield to instinct in the way Nature ordained for me. But in all this I transgress not in the least against God or man. Of course I have offended against laws that are a legacy from the Dark Ages.

No man should cast a stone at me who indulges in marital joys more than once a week. For since my Pug Heaven apprenticeship, I have not myself averaged once a week. True I have changed partners about thirty times. But if circumstances had rendered it possible, I would have been satisfied with a solitary permanent one. But in the case of women-men, there do not exist the reasons for monandry and the permanency of the bond.

But while I have been guilty of nothing to be ashamed of in the eyes of the All-Wise, I have—owing to irrational laws, fear of imprisonment, and particularly of bringing bitter disgrace and sorrow on my family—suffered myself to be bled unmercifully.

Ever since resuming residence in New York, I have taken advantage of all the public masked balls to gratify my instinct to pose as a belle. Even those under the humble auspices of the Draymen's Union, the "Tonsorial Artists," and the "Société Universelle des Cuisiniers."

A particularly great event has been the annual Masked Ball of the Philhedonic Society. Every pair of trousers may attend which can scrape together $10 for self and "lady." The patrons range from scions of the aristocracy out for a lark, to crooks bent on thievery. For conditions at the Philhedonic Ball are ideal for the light-fingered fraternity, particularly because every patron is in disguise, with a mask covering at least the upper third of the face, and the millionaire and the thief dance and flirt together.

Our families have, of course, no suspicion that we hermaphroditoi are only pseudo-men. While marvelling because we have never courted a girl, they have not been so far enlightened as to discern what that signifies. That they may always remain in their ignorance, we hermaphroditoi—as you are aware—set out from our respective domiciles for a public Masked Ball in masculine attire. Later, with hired masculine escort, we depart from (Paresis) Hall bewigged, bepadded, bepowdered, bejewelled, and begowned to shine as belles on the bewaxed floor of X——Garden. After arrival there, we associate, without waiting for an introduction, with whatever pair of trousers— that is, presumably—appears fair to look upon. We hermaphroditoi do our best to converse like real belles. An accidental gruff note does sometimes betray us. But usually the gallant comprehends, sympathizes, and merely laughs at a good joke on himself.

The Philhedonic Ball is the spectacle of a lifetime. I do not approve all that transpires. The two large orchestras, playing alternately, pour forth continuously into the inebriated ears of the three thousand revellers the thrilling music of the most voluptuous dances, rightly tabooed by all decent society. The revellers are as impious a crowd as ever gathers in America. I would approve the police's radically restricting the present license. I am sure we hermaphroditoi are not among those who give the ball a bad name.

Some of the costumes have been ordered from Paris and London. Many have already graced the Mardi Gras of New Orleans or Nice. Practically every romantic or grotesque character ever heard of is on the floor: monkeys, parrots, geese, yellow kids, foxy grandpa, Happy Hooligan, Cupid, Mephistopheles, and a thousand others.

At a Philhedonic Ball of about ten years ago—at which the most remarkable blackmail episode of my life had its origin—I impersonated Euterpe. Down to my debacle, money fortunately came easy with me. I therefore endeavored to adorn every Masked Ball with the most elaborate feminine costume on display there. My Euterpe gown, terminating at the knees, was of turquoise satin. It was ornamented with several flounces of miniature sleigh bells washed in gold. Whenever I moved, they emitted a melodious jingle. My silk, open-work stockings were of an azure hue, and the pumps of purple kid, with mother-of-pearl buckles. My chevelure was surmounted with a gold-plated lyre, studded with hundreds of Paris diamonds, which, under the myriad gas flames, scintillated dazzlingly. I had had my beardal hair eradicated so that I could glory in a countenance of an infantile softness and an exquisite glabrity.

Until about three, everything transpired after a beauteous fashion. My unrivalled costume had attracted a score of flirts, begging a dance with me. I finally fell to chattering with an individual in a bearskin. He soon declared his conviction that I was merely a female-impersonator. But by exception he manifested irritation at being hoodwinked, and nausea at the very idea of cross-dressing. A panic supervened upon his strident tones. I was overwhelmed with mortification and trepidation on discovering myself in the clutches of what I supposed one of those charlatans who attend the function in order to unearth a moneyed female-impersonator of some prominence with *chantage* as objective. I lost all heart for mimicking a belle. Most terrible of all, the fellow next denuded my face of the mask. Horrified lest my identity be disclosed, I pressed the lacerated fabric to my countenance and proceeded toward the dressing-room.

In the corridor, the fellow blurted out: "I think I know you. Those eyes of yourn—how far apart they are! They give you a queer look that no guy kin for-git who has seen you several times. Any bloke'd recognize you anywhere, even with a girl's wig on. I have often passed you down on Wall Street."

Though actually employed a stone's throw from that street and promenading it almost every lunch hour, I responded almost inaudibly, I was in a state of such trepidation: "You are in error. I am employed on 42d Street."

"Don't think I'm a fool! I'm so sure of meself that I'm goin' to hang 'round Wall Street till I run into you agin. And I'm sure comin' up to say 'Hoddo!' Sure I remember your sissie stride and, most of all, the way you stare at young fellers as if you were goin' to eat them up! I work on that street meself; elevator man in the Z—Buildin'. Me name is Tony Neddo. I'm not ashamed to let any one know who I am! But you! Do you know you've done an awful dirty, disgustin' thin' in comin' to the ball in a girl's rig? For this you'll have to pay dear! But if you know on which side your bread is buttered, no guy 'll ever be the wiser on account of what I've just found out.

"But get rid of your tremblin'! You needn't be 'fraid of me. I ain't the mean guy you think. When you meet me in my every-day clothes, you kin see for yourself. You'll see I'm a young feller of strong, pure manhood. You'll see I've the build of a pugilist. Whoever you are, Mr. Skirt, I know, from the diamonds in your harp, you're rich! On the other hand, I know I kin do for you far more than you kin for me. Any how, let's you and me be best friends? We'll part now, but you'll sure see me comin' up to you on Wall Street soon. Bye-bye, sweetheart!"

O Ralph-Jennie, the fellow was really cute as he took his departure. He captivated me by his good-humored farewell. It dissipated all my depression. While I realized he would descend to *chantage*, I already perceived he possessed innumerable compensating characteristics. Every individual is derelict in some respect. Tony had never been enlightened on the immorality of *chantage*. So I hardly devoted a second thought to his cupidity. At the time I possessed no "best friend"—no "adopted son", as we older hermaphroditoi designate our sweethearts. I immediately commenced to gloat over Tony as *my conquest—my boy!* How proud I already was of him, although not yet having visioned his countenance! But he had strutted away in such a manly fashion and possessed such a deep bass, ultra-masculine voice! I could perceive he was athletic and a little larger than the average man. And I was particularly obsessed with his blatant, nonchalant description of himself: "Strong, pure manhood"!

Henceforth my stream of thought was surfeited with visions of conversing with him again. But the opportunity did not supervene until two awfully long hours—in the closing half-hour of the ball. The floor was ankle-deep with confetti, rendering further dancing impracticable. A goodly proportion of the revellers were anyway too tipsy or too fatigued to be on their feet. The hundreds promenading the arena, besides the couple of thousand in the boxes and balconies, were sprinkled with red, white, and blue confetti and wound round and round with paper streamers of all colors. A steadily flowing river of humanity was discharging into the street. I would myself have already taken my departure, but had devoted the last half-hour to dragging myself wearily to every nook and corner in search of my bear.

Finally, in the main corridor, a handsome adolescent stepped smilingly out of the stream of humanity slowly moving streetward: "Are you looking for me, sweetheart? I am Tony Neddo."

He dared excuse himself, for a moment or two, from his "lady"—considering to what class she belonged! We withdrew out of her hearing. I was tickled to death on now beholding what I had drawn in the lottery. I had known the fellow was ultra-masculine. But not until that moment did I discover that he was handsome into the bargain. Indeed he was indisputably the best looker of the hundreds of young fellows who, with their "ladies," streamed by as we whispered together.

"How old are you?" I began.

"Nineteen is all."

"Eleven years younger than myself. Just my ideal age for a young man to be adopted as my son. Tell me frankly: Did anybody ever tell you that you are unusually good-looking?"

"That's not for me to say. But you yourself see me now when I have my own clothes on. I don't look as if I belonged to the weak, crippled sex—as you do yourself—do I? I look to be a he-man, don't I? While you are one of those awful she-men! Mr. Skirt, just think of your own shameful, disgustin' nature! Your secret and character have come into me power. And it wouldn't do you any good to hit back. I have nothin' at all to lose.

"But I'm only talkin' business now. Every bloke puts his foot into it now and again. And I did at our first meetin'. Because I was then just crazy for money. That's all. But it only *looks* as if I'm after your money. What I really and truly want is the chance to make your life happy. I want to be your best friend. Just let me see what you would do for a young feller who would give himself to you, body and soul. No one is poorer than me these days. All I got is the suit on me back. I only rented that bear rig for the evenin'."

"Well, Tony, how much would you expect?"

"Two hundred bucks a month."

I argued for one hundred—all that at the time I cared to part with, although my infatuation soon after augmented so that I voluntarily presented him three times my first offer. But on this first night I repeatedly assured him coaxingly, though sincerely, that he was just the type of young fellow that appealed to me. Over and over again he replied: "I wouldn't sell me goodwill so cheap! All your fine talk, Mr. Skirt, doesn't get us anywhere. It doesn't have the least effect on me. Only money talks. If you'll part with two hundred bucks, I'll know you think that much of me. Besides, if we don't fix up matters now, don't ever show your face again on Wall Street!"

But when he had bluffed to his limit, he accepted my first offer. And I didn't mind the promise of that stipend to *him*—so winsome and handsome and assuring me he would be my soul-mate.

Because his "lady" was dancing attendance, our conversation had to be broken off before the end of five minutes. In parting, I said: "The more I have heard you converse, the better I like you, Tony. You are a pretty smart boy. I would be glad to give you an education, so that you can rise to my own social level instead of continuing in the servant class. We shall not regard our agreement as blackmail. Instead I now adopt you as my sole well-beloved son. I will even be your slave. We shall enjoy together all the good things of life. But, remember, you must never do anything to betray my character and our relations to anybody. And, Tony, always call me 'Frank.' I would prefer that in private you called me 'Eunice,' but if you acquired the habit, you would sometimes make a break before people."

V

Frank-Eunice's Indiscretion

Would you like, Ralph-Jennie, to be enlightened as to how I came to reside, five years of my prime, within prison walls? You have censured me for black-guarding the Church and religious people. But do you marvel thereat after I disclose that it was *they* who were instrumental in robbing me of five years of man's all too brief sojourn on earth? In my youth, I was naturally religious. While no longer a church member, not a Sunday passes but I attend morning service. I continue to be a disciple of Christ in my own way, and estimate church attendance as one of the greatest privileges of existence. But religious people, the Church, and the Bible have occasioned me such terrible persecution that I can no longer do aught than revile them for their hypocrisy. And the average preacher, while meaning well, is so bigoted! Only recently I heard one declaim about the deluge: "God then drowned humanity as rats with the exception of Noah's family because Monsters were being born in considerable numbers." He claimed that "monsters" is the correct translation for "giants" of King James' version. And he made evident that he understood by "monsters" us bisexuals. Must we poor sexual cripples bear the blame not alone for the decline and fall of nations, but also for the Noachian deluge?

You ask, Ralph-Jennie, my philosophy of life. First: To brighten the lives of unfortunates. Secondly: To get out of existence all the good times one can without transgressing against any one else. We are certain of nothing in this life except the passing moment. I even do not *know* that you exist, Ralph, otherwise than as a percept in my stream of thought.

My incarceration supervened, but not immediately, upon my reception of Tony Neddo as adopted son. Nature created me impotent. I could never possess wife and children. And for the reason that I accepted the only alternative of an adopted son, society incarcerated me! Ralph, do you call that Christianity and enlightenment? You, Ralph, recognizing that I am a congenital goody-goody, are in condition to accept my declaration that I have never in all my earthly pilgrimage transgressed against a solitary individual. In addition, Mother Nature endowed me with such cerebral capacity that at the university I was one of the leaders in scholarship. Nevertheless policemen and jailers—who of course are not responsible for their meager education in the rural districts of Ireland, where they were instructed merely to spell out the primer and scrawl their own names—have tyrannized over me, handcuffed me, and compelled me, when absolutely guiltless of any offence against the Deity or society, though having transgressed against mediæval jurisprudence, to accompany them whither I strenuously did not desire, and to perform hard labor for years without remuneration, and to abide in a cell, amid vermin, and subsist on disgusting nourishment! Do you marvel that such impositions, continued for years, have rendered me a misanthrope? For while I sympathize with and alleviate the sufferings of humanity up to my capacity, I experience only detestation for hypocritical humanity surfeited with exuberant health and in influential positions.

After the Masked Ball of ten years ago, Tony Neddo continued, for a longer period than any other young fellow, to be my adopted son and soul-mate. With the exception of his initial roguery, he rang true. Of course the consideration that I loaded him with benefits exercised an enormous influence. He realized that solely by cultivating my affection, he could play a good thing for all it was worth. My ambition to educate him for a profession was doomed to disappointment. While sufficiently intelligent in practical affairs, he lacked the gray matter for acquiring book knowledge.

The immediate reason for my incarceration was merely an indiscretion. I had resided two years on the continent of Europe, where every individual comprehends bisexuality and nobody oppresses those so unfortunate as to be afflicted therewith. That tolerance unfitted me for residence in the United States, where the words "sex" and "sin" are synonyms. I erroneously opined I could be as overt in New York as in Paris.

Therefore, while continuing to reside with my aged parents, I, soon after adopting Tony (not legally of course) leased for him a furnished apartment at a high-class residential hotel. Two successive hostelries finally refused to rent further to Tony and me. In the third year, we were in our third caravansary. But its personnel proved of unexampled bigotry—because the manager was a narrowminded Methodist. He opined that simply expelling Tony and myself ignominiously was not sufficient. He was busybody to the extent of praying for my incarceration. Therefore he engaged an unusually handsome youthful detective to enmesh me.

Attired as a Beau Brummel, the sneak first scraped acquaintance and then insinuated himself into my confidence. Soon he succeeded in seducing me where it was possible for a confederate to employ a camera without my suspecting anything. It was on the basis of that photograph that I was sentenced. My accomplice, who had been the sole occasion of the so-called felony, and who alone had proceeded deliberately and wilfully, received merely the thanks of the court and of society.

You inquire about the element of suffering during my incarceration. The first week in the Tombs jail, I lay awake half of every night in mental anguish, for I realized I was a martyr. Every one was accusing me of deepdyed depravity when my life was actually on a high ethical plane. All the journals announced in big headlines that I had been surprised in a double life—intimating wilful immorality. "Immorality"! "Immorality"! That was the keynote of all newspaper accounts of myself, as if hitherto "immorality" had been an unknown quantity with Knickerbockers. People could not get through singing the refrain: "At last a New Yorker has been discovered who is infected with *immorality!!!*" The journals stated that I had been incarcerated in the Tombs to await trial, the evidence against me being so incontrovertible and the felony charged so revolting that bail had been refused. At the time I was unenlightened as to what that evidence was and a thousand possibilities coursed through my stream of thought, none of which, however, emerged in my subsequent trial.

I was terribly browbeaten by the plebeian police. They resorted to subterfuge and endeavored by every means to betray me into confession of the secrets of my heart that they suspected. They adopted insulting language. They inquired point-blank over and over again in the common indecent expressions whether I had not with such and such persons (particularly Tony) been guilty of what jurists denominate ridiculously, though solemnly and with bated breath, "the crime against Nature," when in fact nothing is more *natural* than the conduct in question. It is exclusively Nature's feat. But I scrupulously guarded myself from making a single incriminating statement. I refused in any way to admit being a bisexual—because all my inquisitors presented evidence that they considered that condition the most horrible of crimes.

This was before I ascertained the existence of the photograph and I fully expected to elude incarceration. And the result proved that they were impotent to lay their hands on any other legal evidence beyond the detective's statements.

That first week in the Tombs I would have committed suicide if I had been vouchsafed an instrument. For I was continuously immersed in the deepest melancholia. But the jailers were careful to deprive me of my pocket-knife and everything else by which it was possible to do myself harm. Even while at meals, I was continuously observed lest I utilize the table knife on my body.

> *"Who ne'er his bread in sorrow ate,*
> *He knows you not, ye heavenly powers!"*

Before I experienced it, I did not believe an individual could survive years of such depression. But, as you see, Ralph, it turned my hair white. Fortunately it has not rendered me bald or wrinkled.

And the judge's charge was so absurd: "The crime of which you, Frank White, have been convicted, is of such a disgusting character that it can not even be defined!"

To think of relegating an individual to state's prison on a charge that no one comprehended; that no one had ever been permitted even to investigate—because the subject is beyond investigation, no intellectual even being willing to define it!

The judge said: "It is as heinous as murder, because it strikes at the very existence of the race! No one but a criminal of the deepest dye could descend to it! Frank White, you have been convicted of the awful felony of race suicide!"——Unreason and prejudice! There was hardly an individual within the hearing of the judge who had not been guilty of race suicide, though in a different way from my own! And they for the most part deliberately, whereas I was compelled by Mother Nature. They imprisoned me for what they conceded to themselves: Following Nature's behests other than solely for the perpetuation of the race!

And then the day following my sentence, in the yard of the Tombs jail, being thrust into an iron-barred bus along with a score of hardened male criminals—just as if I were myself a male!—to be driven to the Grand Central to board a train for Sing Sing. I, the goody-goody girlboy, having evolved into a felon!

But my prosecution by self-righteous Christians for what were really offences against no one—simply to satiate these Christians' thirst for tormenting people whose views differed from their own—had more serious results than my five years in prison. My life has been a wreck ever since. My having been incarcerated on a conviction so utterly loathsome to the ordinary mind—because it has never been permitted access to the truth of the matter and is governed solely by mediæval bias—completely alienated every member of my family, who now regarded me as dead, and disinherited me on the ground of deepdyed hypocrisy and degeneracy. If we encountered one another on the street, they would not speak.

When liberated from Sing Sing, I was compelled to adopt a new appellation and strike out into a new field of labor, where it has been possible only with difficulty to make ends meet.

As for Tony, he escaped to parts unknown immediately following my arrest. My deprivation of his friendship was the severest blow of all, for he had shown himself so devoted—but only, as results demonstrated, because of the fortune he derived from me. He merely left a memo declaring he would write me some day, but never effectuated his promise.

If only the Javerts who prosecute Nature's stepchildren realized the world of woe they thereby occasion these most unfortunate of mankind, they would reflect twice before inaugurating the prosecution. But society prohibits the reasons for the conduct of bisexuals becoming known. Which knowledge would prove a death blow to such prosecution.

PART V
ANGELO—PHYLLIS

I

ANGELO ANGEVINE'S DEBUT AS PUBLIC
FEMALE-IMPERSONATOR

That fancy masculine name was only an alias, androgynes having a penchant for such as are musical and of exalted connotation. Further, its first element was after Michelangelo, an arch-bisexualist.

In 1895, Angelo-Phyllis divulged what I have here recorded as nearly as I can remember. As I said in the first chapter of this book, I remember only the general outlines of the originals of the monologues I give. But I have listened to numerous confessions of the sort of which I now present a sample. Where definite memory fails me, I have had recourse to my sea of general memories of the way the hermaphroditoi talked, how they looked upon life, what they did, and what befell them. I aim at a fairly full, but essentially true, portrayal of the inner history and life experience of cultured female-impersonators who were my bosom-friends during my own heyday in that avocation in the Rialto. In order to economize the reader's attention, I present all of Angelo-Phyllis's life story as if confessed to me at one sitting.

In referring to Frank White it seems more natural to use the masculine alias and pronoun, but the feminine with Phyllis. For the latter was conspicuously womanish: beardal growth sparse and always clean-shaven, if not eradicated; breasts as large as in some women; hips very broad; spine disproportionately long and legs correspondingly short. "His-her" body approached the feminine to a higher degree than that of any other androgyne I ever set eyes on with the possible exception of myself. Phyllis surpassed me in meagreness of beardal growth, sissie voice, feminine strut and gestures, and craze and taste for feminine finery. As a cross-dresser and female-impersonator, the bisexual now to be portrayed was one of the two or three extreme hermaphroditoi, while ranking low in erotic *furor*.

(In a physical male, cross-dressing is the instinctive wearing of feminine apparel, or, in default, of the loudest and fanciest male styles. In a physical female, it is similar adoption of masculine habiliments, or in default, of feminine attire and aspect approaching the masculine as nearly as possible: hair bobbed, stiff linen collar, a man's neck scarf, and always severely plain tailor-made waist and skirt. The reader will recall such photographs of brilliantly intellectual women, particularly authoresses. Cross-dressing is generally an earmark of sexual intermediacy. It is not at all due—as bigots claim—to moral depravity, but entirely to irreproachable instinct. It is not at all due to childhood's training, such as the stories of parents' bringing up their boy or girl as a girl or a boy when they particularly wished a female or a male heir. Such child, as soon as he or she became old enough, would wholeheartedly rebel against such a travesty. In nearly every case, cross-dressing is due to the fact that Nature injected a psyche of the one sex into a corpus of the other. The cross-dresser is not usually conscious of the oddity of taste for apparel. His or her manner of dressing indicates what he or she considers artistic. All ultra-androgynes—such as made up the membership of the Cercle Hermaphroditos—would always, if society permitted, clothe themselves as women.)

In 1895, Angelo-Phyllis was a plump little body looking to be a decade younger than "his-her" thirty-three, and of decidedly brunette, Mediterranean type.

Ralphie, *mon cheri*, the sexual cripple now speaking was born in 1862 and brought up in a town of 50,000 within 300 miles of New York City. I did not move here until twenty. As soon as I became financially independent of father, I chose New York as the stage for my career because only in a great city can an instinctive female-impersonator give his overwhelming yearnings free rein *incognito* and thus keep the respect of his every-day circle.

Father was one of the leading lawyers in my home town and wanted me in his office, for he seemed blind to my being a sissie. But just because of this fate, I could not stand living in my home town. Furthermore, I had no taste for law, and pined only one year in father's law office after leaving high-school. I was all for Art, with a capital A! Art! Art! Which taste turned me into millinery channels as soon as I began life in New York in 1882.

Excepting the years that George Greenwood was with me as "adopted son," I have in New York lived all by myself in a 5-room apartment. Thus I have been able to transform myself into a young woman and set out for a female-impersonation spree without any one getting wise.

If I had had my say at birth, Ralphie, my lot would have been that of a full-fledged woman, or, less to be wished, a virile man. Not half-and-half. But at twenty I cut out the foolishness of all the time shedding tears over my fate. Those tears were chiefly due to the world's forbidding a bisexual's living according to his-her nature. I could not assume the responsibilities of a man and pay court to women—an ordeal so horrible, but expected of me if I stayed in my home town. I balked at having my life forced into a masculine groove. In New York one can live as Nature demands without setting every one's tongue wagging.

I was unconscious of sex until my fourteenth year. Up to that age, I went to pay school. My dozen schoolmates—including four sisters—were all of the goody-goody type. No one ever tried to seduce me.

From fourteen to eighteen I went to public high-school. Several boys hugged and kissed me now and then. While I liked this, I shrunk away for shame. Now for the first time I felt sorry I was a boy. I stole a sister's discarded garb, from corset to hat, which I kept under lock and key in my room and put on now and again in order to strut before a full-length mirror and feast my eyes on myself as female-impersonator. Because of shame, I never told a soul.

So counter to the fate of most hermaphroditoi, I was a virgin until the beginning of my female-impersonation sprees. Because in high-school, morbid bashfulness kept me from becoming well acquainted with a single boy. Down to twenty I lived as sheltered a life as any girl. I had really never been under any kind of temptation.

Ralphie, *mon cheri*, I can never forget the entire day spent in getting together my woman's wardrobe on arrival in New York. I went to a ladies' store in the Ghetto. I lacked the cheek to buy feminine finery uptown. I gave the Russian Jewess the usual hoax of amateur theatricals. And women are so dense as to believe it! She helped hugely to the end of my being able to turn myself into a stunning soubrette.

An evening or two later, in my flat, I dressed for my first spree. I touched up eyebrows with a stick of charcoal and cheeks with rouge; applied padding where needed, laced on a corset, and adjusted a soubrette's wig. Lastly I put on my art gown, pinned on a picture hat, threw an opera cloak about me, and was ready to set out.

On my sprees I have always been careful to avoid a clue to my identity. No one would have ever learned who I really am even if I had been sent to Sing Sing. Since the world thinks female-impersonation utterly disgraceful, I had to spare my family all risk. Furthermore, they themselves would disown me if they ever learned of my mania for cross-dressing and female-impersonation.

It is bitter to be so misjudged! And people balk at being set right! While I get much joy out of life, I often feel crushed to earth when seeing how I am scorned, and now and again weep a full hour. When, in the pride of their manly vigor, the virile throw at me a glance full of hatred or of ridicule, I feel like killing myself!

I always closed my hall-door noiselessly and used the stairs. The elevator boy might have recognized me in my disguise. If, on the several flights, I heard an approaching footstep, I would slink for a moment to a dark corner of the spacious hall. Reaching the street, I had my regular hiding place for my key and a yellow back. It was most necessary to be able to let myself in on my late return, when the street door was locked, instead of ringing up the janitor.

On my first spree, Ralphie—as on all for several years—I boarded an elevated train and alighted at a Bowery station. Several times in later years, I spied acquaintances of my every-day world either on the train or on the Bowery. I always gave them a wide berth, although having a great advantage in means of recognition.

And why, on my very first spree, did I seek the Bowery, Ralphie?

Because only a few weeks before, in my home town, I had seen a comic opera staged on that avenue, its keynote the oft repeated refrain:

> *"The Bowery! The Bowery!*
> *There they say such things!*
> *And they do such things!*
> *The Bowery! The Bowery!*
> *I'll never go there any more!"*

So I was dead crazy to bring to pass there the female-impersonation sprees of which I, for several years, had had merely waking dreams in my home town. Such realization was why I moved to New York. It was, *mon cheri*, all because I wanted to live within half-an-hour's journey of the enchanting old Bowery!

On my first spree, I made my way up and down the crowded sidewalks for an hour, staring with all my eyes at the brilliantly lighted fronts of beer-gardens, the many gaudily dressed girls strutting up and down all alone, but, most of all, the sporty-looking youthful laboring men seeking their evening's fun. How longingly and beseechingly I gazed into the latter's eyes! A hundred times I had accosting words on the end of my tongue. I but barely lacked the brass for utterance, notwithstanding that in my every-day life I had always been morbidly bashful. How I wished I were acquainted with at least one of these powerfully built—and, to me at least, bewitchingly handsome—foreign-looking young fellows!

Who, *mon cheri*, that knew me as a goody-goody boy in my home town, always going to Bible school twice on Lord's day, and not merely once as nearly all children of pious parents, would have foretold that some day I would be tapping the sidewalks of America's greatest red-light district as a common strumpet?[1]

Doctors claim to understand such as me *a priori* and are too squeamish to investigate. They would say I am insane. I have never shown any sign of a diseased brain, nor has there been any taint of insanity in my family. Ours, *mon cheri*, is simply the case of half-and-half as to sex. The only taint in my family is that father is somewhat

---

1. In the year of writing (1921) sight-seeing busses feature the Bowery at night. Years ago that formerly quaintest of New York's streets lost most of its character as red-light and amusement center for New York's manual-laborer foreign stock. For a brief history of New York's bright-light districts since 1800, see the author's RIDDLE OF THE UNDERWORLD, in its Table of Contents.

womanish: falsetto voice, sissie mannerisms, and never any mind for things thoroughly masculine. He ought never to have married to perpetuate, and probably strengthen, his own mild sexual intermediacy.

As I walked the Bowery on that first spree, I was puzzling my mind as to which of the brightly lighted dance-halls or the dark and fearsome dives—through whose doors I saw pass only sailors, guttersnipes, and slovenly gangsters—would be the best stage for my virgin effort at female-impersonation. At last I slipped into the least prosperous-looking and, to the stranger, most uninviting, dance-hall, the notorious "Rabbit." And why the "Rabbit"? Because it looked to be the most crime-inviting of all the dance-halls. I had stood and watched as there passed in and out the most criminal-faced of the Bowery boys: coal-heavers, dock-rats, and fierce-and-cruel-stalking gunmen—not to speak of the poor, deluded "fallen angels."

I dropped into a chair. Almost in less time than I can tell it, four youthful coal-heavers came up grinning: "Hello Bright Eyes!"

Those three words were the most soulful, the most infatuating, that had ever fallen on my ears. I was also delighted because so lucky as to take in, right off, some of the many bewitching Bowery boys I had stared at that night, and cement them to myself. I smiled back: "Hello!"

For the next few hours, I was in hitherto un-dreamed-of bliss because of being wooed by all four in their delightfully wild and rough way. Ever since my later teens, I have always yearned to be treated by young fellows as a girl, and on my female-impersonation sprees now and again, I have had such yearnings fully met. On that debut at the "Rabbit," I was for the first time in my life with sexual counterparts before whom I could be myself because they did not know who I was. And they treated me as *their* sexual opposite. They danced with me in turn. Only after four hours, I had to own up that I was not an out-and-out female. But that knowledge seemed to count for nothing with these lovesick coal-heavers.

Already two hours before, I had felt that I had had more than enough flirtation for one night. All my efforts to get away, however, were useless. At two A.M., the "Rabbit's" doors were locked. I had to allow one of my beaux to escort me somewhere: to the Grand Central waiting-room, for there I would be safe. I now warned my beau that if he did not leave me, I would sit there for a week. But it took him two more hours to give up all hope of my yielding to his goodhearted pleas.[2]

2. A warning to any unsophisticated androgyne who may be moved to an impersonation spree in a red-light district. It is necessary to go slow and be ultra-cautious. Numerous

Five minutes after he left, I sought the street. I turned half-a-dozen corners, lurking a minute around each to see if the coast was clear. I then boarded a car. I slowly dragged myself up the three flights of stairs and noiselessly let myself into my flat. Tired out, I threw myself on the bed only half undressed and slept until noon.

But, *mon cheri,* I had now found myself. For seven years afterward, I sought the "Rabbit" or the "Squirrel" once every other week, giving the rest of my time to business or self-culture. One evening out of fourteen was all I could spare for the female side of my being. But the balance of my waking hours were filled with blissful thoughts of my flirtations— memories which will last as long as I. These sprees have been to me the first thing in life. I would have given up anything else for them. When now and again something has blocked my fortnightly spree, I would be the most melancholy person in New York.

On the Bowery, I always went with the same gang of about a dozen savages. If any one took a look at me, Ralphie—so soft-spoken, so chicken-hearted, so wishy-washy—they wouldn't set me down as leader of a Bowery gang, would they? But that's just what I once was. All the members of my gang were of foreign parentage, sturdy, possessed of well chiselled features, and tolerably clean. I found nothing disgusting about them. None had had more than three years' schooling, or the least training in morality or religion. Nevertheless they were not a bad lot; far from being as evil-minded as the upper class would judge from the outside. None was more than twenty-five while a member of my gang, and none bright enough to earn his bread at an occupation of higher grade than coal-heaver.

The average age remained low because one after another settled down in marriage, having brought to an end his sowing of wild oats, and some budding gangster took his place with me.

On my fortnightly hegiras, I was well supplied with money so that I could give all a first-rate treat in exchange for their wonderful kindness. They kept good friends because I loaded them with gifts. Only after seven years, a born criminal, who had happened to worm his way into my gang, now and again sought to dog me home. Twice I had to sit for

androgynes have been murdered by gangsters. Frank-Eunice, Angelo-Phyllis, and myself were exceptionally fortunate. Every time an androgyne puts himself in the power of a stranger gangster, it is at the risk of murder. Several times I myself have been half-murdered. A poverty-stricken aspect and concealment of one's culture constitute the best protection. By no means show fight if assaulted.

an hour in the Grand Central waiting-room to get him off my trail. Up to that time no one had broken my firm command that I should not be tracked the moment I chose to fade away for a fortnight. For I was like a good fairy—in the twinkling of an eye bobbing up in the midst of my gang, gathered by appointment in the "Rabbit," and a few hours later as wierdly dropping out of sight. Of course I could not let any of the gangsters find out in what part of the city I lived. At last, to put a stop to high-handed and high-figured blackmail by this one rascal, and, most of all, to escape murder, I was forced to say good-by forever to the whole Bowery. Of course I did not dare let even the most trustworthy gangster know that I was never to see him again. It pained me fearfully to leave them in the lurch, but I could do nothing else.

I henceforth made the Rialto my stamping-ground when yielding my bisexual body to the woman in me. And fortunately, for I thus met Roland and the other hermaphroditoi who had likewise turned to the Rialto to blow off now and again their ordinarily pent up, but at last overwhelming, craze for female-impersonation.

II

Jailed for Wearing Petticoats

A scrape that I like to tell about, *mon cheri*, although very bitter in the happening, is my only arrest for flaunting myself in feminine finery. Don't you think a jail a queer home for a wishy-washy gentleman and art connoisseur? A softy whose swatting a fly was the worst act he was ever guilty of, and he almost had to weep when he did that.

Ever since driven from the Bowery six years ago, I have, one evening out of fourteen, clad in my beloved feminine finery, tried to get on the string strange young fellows in the Rialto ladies' parlors. My nerves need such a lark now and again. Otherwise years ago I would have gone crazy or killed myself.[1] In my later teens, while living in my home town, where I had to crucify my cross-dressing and female-impersonating instincts, I was its most melancholy being. Because I, a female soul, was imprisoned in a male body. How dark life looked from inside my male prison! How I pined to be free! To have my soul wholly clothed in woman's bone and flesh instead of man's for the most part—the latter so hated in my own body, but slavishly worshipped when breathing out yells of joy in sport or the cry to battle and the clash of arms!

One evening five years ago in the Rialto I ran across two youthful artillerymen from Fort Q and spent the evening with them. Regimentals have always overpowered me. Even when I was as young as ten, when an acquaintance enlisted in the national guard, his mere donning the regimentals brought about, in my eyes, a magic transformation. If already handsome, the young fellow became supremely, unearthly enchanting. If plain and unattractive in civilian dress, he grew handsome. Blue clothing and brass buttons surely bring out whatever charm was born in a young fellow. Furthermore, his taste for warfare, shown by his

---

1. Just the day I retyped the above (Jan. 24, 1921) I read how a girl-boy of eighteen committed suicide in New York City by jumping from a thirty-five foot bridge upon railroad tracks. Adolescent androgynes are continually putting an end to their lives because bitterly persecuted merely on account of their bisexuality and most unfeelingly told by their closest associates that they are deeply depraved, and because prohibited by the leaders of thought from acquiring scientific knowledge of their idiosyncrasy.

volunteering, proves him a demigod. For I think warfare the highest function of the real man.

Whenever I catch sight of a youthful soldier, I rivet my gaze every second possible, even halting at the curb to look back at the wonderful vision. I yearn to fling myself at the soldier's feet and cry out my worship of all his magic traits. As the vision fades away, a pang goes through my heart that he must pass out of my life forever and I never be able to make known to him that for the rest of my days I shall be continuously burning incense in my heart to his memory.

O Ralphie, I am overwhelmed when I call to mind the hundreds of the cream of physical youngmanhood with whom I have flirted, and whom I wholeheartedly loved! I have to weep at thinking that the way the world is made, I must be forever barred from them. In spirit, I am eternally joined, knit, dovetailed to every man of them, but in the flesh, must never lay eyes on the demigods again. How I wish I could have continued to heap blessings upon them and make their sojourn on earth happy! But I am not God! In the next world, how I wish, as a reward for my always having tried in this to make my associates happy, I might be placed by Providence in the position of a sort of sub-deity to the hundreds of rough, uncultured young bachelors whom I have made protegés in this life, in order that I might be the means of affording each the eternity of bliss I so covet for them! . . .

I do not lose an opportunity to see a parade of the national guard, and particularly of regular soldiers, marines, and blue-jackets. I do not give a straw to see any other type of men marching. But while witnessing warriors stalk by, I am seized with a craze to prostrate myself in the roadway and have those fierce, pugnacious young tigers—as they tramp, tramp, tramp!—trample upon me until dead.

The two artillerymen I met in the Rialto begged me to make an hegira out to the barracks to give a female-impersonation before their buddies. One afternoon I made the hour's journey, clad as an extreme dresser of the gentle, and at the same time harebrained, sex.

Around five P.M., I knocked at my friends' barracks. Being in woman's garb, I would not step inside, but jollied with them on the large porch. The news spread that I was only a female-impersonator and half-a-hundred crowded around, flirting for all they were worth. That was, *mon cheri*, my apotheosis—far above all other adventures. I was overjoyed at hearing at one time from half-a-hundred demigods cries of admiration and affection. For I would sacrifice myself more for,

EARL LIND

and give more richly to, youthful common soldiers than any other class of men.

When, after half-an-hour, the bugle sounded retreat, how overwhelming, how unearthly, how infinite and divine, its notes! The bugle-call, because closely associated with the clash of arms and with that type of human who shine as demigods, always lifts me up into an unutterably blissful female-impersonate and cross-dress intoxication. I seem to be raised to the very zenith of the universe as The Supreme Woman, The Fairie Queen, and to have all the fighting men that ever lived bowing low in worship of my feminine attributes. During the minute that the bugle-call resounds and reverberates, I live infinitely! I live out a whole eternity!

But to come down to earth again, Ralphie: When I went away at the supper call, my two friends said they would meet me in a beer-garden in a neighboring village. It was the favorite evening resort of the common soldiers. My two friends arrived with four buddies. Of the half-a-hundred patrons, none else, excepting several additional soldiers of my friends' company who happened to drop in, knew, up to the very last, that I was only impersonating a female.

But toward eleven, some of my party had drunk a drop too much. Their behavior became boisterous and improper. When the waiters tried to curb them, a terrible fight started. The waiters were themselves ex-soldiers and born fighters. Heavy glass schooners were thrown back and forth. I had to get under a table.

After several minutes, two constables burst in and put all my party under arrest. I had now to 'fess up that I was not really a girl. My faltering words filled the constables with disgust and hatred. This is not to be wondered at, because village constables do not know psychology like Bowery and Rialto policemen.

The seven of us were locked up for the night. The next morning the Justice-of-the-peace discharged my companions with a mere reprimand because members of the army. But he was wild to punish me for putting on woman's garb. He sent a constable with me to the White Plains jail, where I was to spend thirty days, or until I could pay a hundred dollars fine. The Justice thought I was a low-down poverty-stricken fairie from New York's worst slums. I did not have the brass to tell him I was really a person of good character, a regular church attendant, well educated, and able to pay the fine.

The jailer, however, was sorry for me. I felt safe in telling him the worst of my secrets. I let him feel my woman's breasts. That made him my best friend and he helped me get into communication with my New York lawyer. After only a second miserable night in a cell, the lawyer paid my fine and escorted me back to the city—even in my feminine "regimentals," as he had forgotten to bring along one of my male outfits.

After that scrape, I made an hegira to the barracks now and again, but always in male garb. The whole fort marvelled at the "woman-man," as they called me. They always gave me a great time. Nothing would I have liked better than to live with them in the barracks as their most devoted slave. Because they were my farthest opposites.

III

George Greenwood[1]

Ralphie, I am now going to tell you about the foremost specimen of young manhood I ever met. If a man show had been held five years ago, on the model of the horse show, the young fellow I am going to tell you about would have won first prize.

You know that most of us hermaphroditoi have a single soul-mate. Of course they are uncultured. Mere diamonds in the rough. For the past four years, George Greenwood, whom you have seen with me, has been my own soul-mate. For while I have flirted with many others, he alone has been like an adopted son—as we older hermaphroditoi look upon our soul-mates. At present, George is twenty-nine, and in outer attractiveness, only a wreck of what he was when I "adopted" him.[2]

I must explain, *mon cheri*, that George is not well bred. About twelve years ago a portrait painter of my acquaintance ran across him selling papers on Broadway. George was then only seventeen. At first sight, the artist felt George's unique beauty and asked him to pose. Later other artists did George in oils and with the chisel.

He has never known who his parents were. For he was a foundling. When discharged from the orphan asylum at fourteen, he was apprenticed to an upholsterer. But on account of George's quick temper and nasty tongue, he could hold no position more than a month. When

---

1. The reader might omit this chapter because thinking it not **a propos**. It is given because describing an actual episode in the life of the sexual cripple being depicted. It also paints the type of fast young bachelor after whom the cultured ultra-androgynes of New York commonly "run." To avoid any chance of a suit for slander, I merely substitute the real name of one of my own half-dozen New York favorites—the half-dozen who will live forever in the **sanctum sanctorum** of my memory—that one favorite who physically much resembled Phyllis's "adopted son," but whose character was ideal. The real George Greenwood—of immaculate beauty and charm, and unsurpassed friendliness to a sexual cripple like myself. In the words of Phyllis, I am "continuously burning incense in my heart to his memory." I would wish to confer on him immortality.

2. At the time I knew him slightly, he was very bald and possessed a rather "passe" countenance. He was nearly six feet tall, perfectly proportioned, and had a negroid complexion, charcoal eyes, and the blackest of curly hair—that is, what was left of it. He was apparently of Spanish extraction. Only when he had his hat on was he still of entrancing appearance.

my friend ran across him, George's thoroughly bad record had left him only one means of earning his bread: selling papers. But ever since his ideal physique was discovered by my friend, George's path through life has been strewn with roses.

Four years ago I happened to lay eyes on George as he posed in my friend's studio. Right away his lines of face, head, limbs, and body—hitherto even undreamed of—held me spell-bound and I took him into my home. For I thought George was Michelangelo's Adam stepped down into flesh and blood out of the painting on the ceiling of the Sistine chapel. Angelo's nude figures of youthful men have alone approached George's ideal lines.

But he has been such a drunkard and high-liver in general that his beauty—particularly his head and face—is now far below par. For two years he has not been hired as a model. And he does not want to earn in any other way. He has leaned wholly on me to keep up his life in the Rialto as all-around sport.

I breathe to you, Ralphie, under pledge to keep it forever locked in the chambers of your heart, that George's face and figure, once driving me beside myself, have become hideous and loathsome. How I hate his billiard-ball head! In order to stand his presence, I have to ask him to keep his hat on. And a man's wig disgusts me even more than a bald pate. Three months ago we stopped living together. I could no longer put up with his all the time scolding and cursing me, and spitting tobacco juice and vomit on the rugs. While we see each other now and again—because he wants a few yellow backs—we have come to hate the very sight of one another.

Ralphie, I heartily wish I were forever rid of the brute beast! It now comes hard, when I see nothing of the hero in him, to fork over a roll of bills every few days. Our relations the past year have been hardly more than a case of blackmail. I do not wholly drop him for fear of his telling abroad how I pass now as a man and now as a woman.

Most of all I want to get out of George's clutches because five months ago I met a wonderful young fellow whom I plan legally to adopt. When I took George Greenwood, I planned the same thing. But his character proved so terrible! I am now getting on in life, *mon cheri,* and my health is delicate. I need a close intimate in my home to wait on me during my many sick days. It is difficult for any of us hermaphroditoi to take a wife. One hates so to explain to a woman that after marriage, the life must be that of brother and sister. And no woman—excepting only the most old-maidish—would marry under these conditions. But I know one of us hermaphroditoi—before your time, Ralphie—who did marry, after thirty, under that arrangement, and only because he had political ambitions, and his being known as a married man would give pause to enemies who were backbiting him because of the indiscretions of his youth. This hermaphroditos was one of the brightest of men and rose, as a result, to one of the foremost posts in the nation. But if he had not been married, the politicians and the voters would have turned him down. A legal marriage surely covers a multitude of sins. But I myself have such a horror of women that I could not live with one even as a sister.

I have a maiden sister, whom I could get as housekeeper, and who would take the best of care of me. But I can not receive her into my home for fear she might discover my bisexuality. I could not allow a servant to live in my flat any more than my sister. For even at the age of thirty-three, I, although half the time almost too feeble to drag myself about, do not feel like saying goodby forever to my female-impersonation sprees. They are still such fun; about all I have to live for! And God has made young fellows so wonderful, so charming! I still admire their beauty as much as I did ten years ago. And it is still so easy to get them on the string, almost as easy as it was ten years ago. But if I am able legally to adopt Calvin—about whom I will tell you in a minute—I feel that I then can, having him with me always in my home, always in my office, always travelling with me wherever I go: I then can say goodby forever to female-impersonation sprees. For he would be to me a husband as well as a son. He would be everything to me! I would live only in and for him! Only to make him, his female wife, and his offspring happy! For I would not put anything in the way of his taking a full-female wife in addition whenever he felt like it, because a full-fledged young fellow is restless without one.

Of course I could have another hermaphrodites live with me, as Ruby, Berenice, and the Duchess live together. But it has always been my fondest dream to adopt as son a young fellow who comes up to my ideal.

For several months I have had my ideal under my eyes every day as stenographer in my millinery house. As "women's men" are prone to take for private secretary the prettiest face or "divinest" form among the gentle sex, likewise *I* picked out the applicant standing highest as an Adonis. He is only twenty and possesses golden curly hair; deep-set, marine-blue eyes; and radiant red cheeks. From his having been baptized "Calvin Luther" you can tell what kind of parents and breeding he was blessed with. He is thoroughly pure-minded and unspoiled, having, until fifteen months ago, lived on a farm.

I slavishly worship the youth. The biased world would tremble at the thought of the harm I would surely (as they fancy) do this pearl of great price. For he is truly an angel; God's child; very religious—a trait so rare among the strongly virile. I have already made something of a confidant of him in order to learn his feelings toward a woman-man. Most young fellows with a puritan bringing up would turn the cold shoulder. But I found Calvin Luther open to reason. He told me he has always, as a good church member, struggled against his wanting the gentle sex. While at business school in a small city, he earned his board by delivering for a baker in the early morning. A natural thing followed upon his being rarely good-looking. I barely wormed it out of him when I was administering the third degree. He 'fessed up that a number of servant girls where he delivered played on him the trick of Potiphar's wife on Joseph. Twice—he 'fessed up with face as red as a beet—he did not show Joseph's strength of character. And I did not think the less of him.

And you, Ralphie, of course know that I would never be guilty of anything that could bring the least harm to this adored innocent. His health of body and mind will not be damaged a particle. I shall give him the best educational and cultural advantages. As I have said, he will some day marry the girl of his choice, and I shall live with the pair as a parent. He and his children will be my heirs.

Is such an outlook for a poverty-stricken young fellow just cause for Pharisees holding up their hands in holy horror?[3] The sexually

---

3. In the July, 1921, number of a prominent American medical journal, I saw a tirade against androgynes, whom its author declared merited no mercy, but ought to be crushed as a social menace. The invective proved merely that its physician-author clings to the sexual ethics of the Dark Ages, and at the same time belongs to the mildly virile type. That type lacks a superfluity of sexual vigor. It is inconceivable that a young man of that type should be intimate with an androgyne except for a rich reward—which has occurred when the individual androgyne was cut off from all access to the ultra-sexed, toward whom alone he gravitates. The mildly virile young man shudders violently at the very thought and is confident—**a priori**, as it is only a traditional phantasy—that his **vita sexualis**, health, and morals would be seriously undermined. I concede, however, that such might be the case with the mildly virile because possessing only a modicum of sexual vigor (perhaps, for example, merely enough for relations with his lawful wife once a fortnight

full-fledged cannot get into their heads that we women-men are just as high-minded and conscientious as themselves. They are continually hurling insults—calling us "degenerates." But my only thought is to heap blessings on those whom I worship. I have always lived up to the maxim: Act in such a way as would be good if universally followed. Those who through self-righteousness condemn and crush me are a hundred times worse sinners. Perhaps some day, *mon cheri*, the world will come to believe that the actual presence of women-men in all communities—which Nature brings about—is a distinct blessing to society in several ways.

---

or so) and because tending to be overconscientious. I concede that the mildly virile's morals would be damaged, simply because he fancies such relations the unpardonable sin. If once in his youth overcome by the offer of a "bonanza," he would ever afterwards regret the experience and feel deep guilt. As I myself in my youthful verdancy, he would cry out a thousand times: "'O wretched man that I am, who shall deliver me from the body of this death!'" And because of his meagre sexual energy, he might possibly feel ill effects physically. But that by no means proves that the ultra-sexed would also feel them. And morally, the latter look upon the experience as entirely natural and sinless—the same as the eating of a piece of mince pie. Instead of ever regretting it, they look back with satisfaction that they had the experience.

Mildly virile writers on sex forget that there exist tens of thousands of men of far superior sexual energy. While they themselves, for example, may care for the services of their legal wife as seldom as twice a month, the tremendously virile "fellow" is not satisfied with less than an opportunity every night, and is at the same time "the husband of all women." In my opinion, Philippics against the androgyne have their basis only in prudery and bigotry.

Aᴜᴛʜᴏʀ's Nᴏᴛᴇ.—Within a year of the above confessions, Angelo-Phyllis was found dead in "his-her" apartment. The skull had been fractured with a hammer.

PART VI

NEWSPAPER ACCOUNTS OF MURDERS
OF ANDROGYNES

AUTHOR's NOTE.—These excerpts from New York dailies are presented in order to impress upon the public that such murders of inoffensive androgynes are a fairly common occurrence because that public has tabooed, on the basis of prudery alone, enlightenment of the general reader on the facts of androgynism. I withhold names of journals and dates of issue, and cover identities, out of respect for the victims and their families. But I assure those families that one of my present objects is to avenge, by enlightening the public, the unmerited assassination of their dear ones and thus prevent in the future such martyrdom of innocents. The families have my most sincere sympathy, particularly because I myself have several times been brought near death's door in the manner in which their unfortunate—but not in the least immoral—relatives were put out of the way.

Each of the first three murders was apparently the work of some prude not at all criminally minded, but feeling himself the mandatory of society in ridding the world of "a monster of deepdyed depravity," according as he was taught by church and synagogue. The harebrained prude had been prohibited by public opinion from learning the truth that *androgynism is solely a matter of abnormal psychology and anatomy, and not at all immorality*. The term which best calls up the sensations of revulsion of such a murderer is "sodomite." To its highly malodorous and fundamentally false connotation and application can be traced every year, in every corner of Christendom (particularly puritan), murders of inoffensive androgynes.

The author's comments are in brackets.

I

Two Murder Mysteries Which, Strangely Alike in Many Ways, Baffled All Efforts to Solve

(Much condensed, and slightly edited for diction, by author of The Female-Impersonators, from article in a New York daily.)

Victims Were Two Elderly Bachelors of Means, Living in the Same Section of City—X and Y Were Both Fond of Personal Adornment and Display and Both Habitually Chose Young Men as Associates—Each Was Slain in His Own Apartment—Only Twenty-Nine Days Separated the Two Murders—Many Circumstances of the Two Crimes Bore Curious Resemblance

Consideration of recent terrible crimes in New York which have halted agents of justice at dead walls of mystery must bring to mind the X-Y murders of a little more than a year ago. They were committed within five weeks, the scenes within a few blocks on fashionable Murray Hill.

In both, extraordinary interest was stirred by the maniacal savagery unleashed. The settings of the crimes were alike bizarre. The characters of both victims were most peculiar, yet alike. And the men had been friends. (Androgynes, in all large cities, form little cliques like the Cercle Hermaphroditos.)

X was a bachelor of fifty-six, an electrical expert, an art connoisseur, and collector of jewels and weapons. Though in more than comfortable financial circumstances, he resided entirely alone, doing his own housework (common manner of life of androgynes) in a 6-room flat on the ground-floor of the Q Apartments. (I know one androgyne who purposely chose a ground-floor apartment in a house without hall-boy so he could go and come in his disguise with less chance of encountering other tenants.) He had made it his home for ten years. (This proves his outward decency, as well as liberality to blackmailers.) The artistic luxury of its furnishings was striking. The walls were galleries of fine old prints, original oils, and copies of masters, and displayed a strange collection of swords, sabres, and barbarian spears. (Well-to-do androgynes possess the most highly ornamented homes of any class of society. While congenitally too "yellow" themselves to handle the weapons of warfare, such are generally sexual fetishes with them, being symbols of the highest function of the true man.)

In this handsome, lonely abode, the detectives made a discovery of significance: X had lived in extraordinary fear of the lawless invasion of his rooms. (Cultured androgynes, realizing how bitterly they are hated by prudes, live constantly under the sword of Damocles. Every night they fall asleep in the fear of being murdered. They are uncommonly careful in locking themselves in. The author tries his locks twice before retiring. While a child, he, every night before getting into bed, looked to see whether there was not a murderer under it. Androgynes are extreme cowards.) For he had used his expertness with delicate electrical devices to set his rooms with a maze of traps for any person who might try to enter it by force or stealth. Doors, windows, etc., were invisibly strung with delicate wires. With the controlling alarm device set, scarcely an article might be touched without the ringing of sharp bells of warning.

But that thieves were those of whom he lived in dread was contradicted by other facts. X, far from being a recluse, frequented hotels and cafes and was prone to make chance acquaintances, especially of young men, while going about extravagantly bejewelled and habitually carrying a large roll of bills which it was a pet vanity to display.

His social hours were spent almost entirely with young men. He had been known to comment: "I keep young because I associate with the young." The Q servants said these young-men callers never behaved boisterously. All were decorous and well dressed. (A small proportion of cultured androgynes who live alone in their own homes entertain there adolescents who bear the earmarks of trustworthy gentlemen. X's murderer could have been of no other type, but was in addition an extreme prude so far as concerns homosexuality. The cultured enjoin extreme noiselessness so as not to arouse suspicions of co-tenants of the same apartment house. The uncultured commonly receive any adolescent at all in their homes because having no fear of disgrace and blackmail. By "young men" the author of the excerpt evidently means those from eighteen to twenty-five, the age-group preferred, and almost exclusively cultivated, by androgynes.)

The Q servants further said that X frequently started alone on strolls, many times, however, returning with a youthful companion, who would spend an hour or two with the elderly host. (The favorite New York localities for evening "strolls" of cultured androgynes for scraping acquaintance with a strange Hercules or Adonis are, in cold weather, the Broadway and the Fourteenth Street Rialtos and cafes; and in summer, Madison Square, Union Square, the southerly quarter of Central Park (the three park spaces most frequented at night by idle adolescents who would be glad to pick up a few dollars), the Battery (because frequented by common soldiers), and other localities frequented by uncommissioned warriors, the ideal occupation, as I have already said, for a real man in the eyes of androgynes. In the case of X, the Q men-servants probably saw through everything. The servant class often respect a cultured moneyed androgyne who treats them well, and they act only in a protecting capacity.)

Of woman visitors, there could be recalled but one—whitehaired, a few years older than X, said to be an aunt.

Investigators were astonished by the nicety, the fond care, with which X had done his own housekeeping. Floors, rugs, and every article were flawless of dust. In spick and span appearance, thoughtful and orderly arrangement of utensils, neatness of china closets, refrigerator and provision store-room, a feature of which latter were shelves lined with jars of homemade preserves labelled in handwriting, the bachelor's kitchen was fit to excite a housewife's envy. (Androgynes take naturally to woman's tasks.)

Discovery of the Murder

IT WAS NOT DISCOVERED UNTIL many hours after commission. At noon of (date omitted by author of THE FEMALE-IMPERSONATORS) the Q janitor saw a light shining out of a transom of X's. He was immediately convinced such a methodical man would not have gone away leaving the light turned on. He tried X's entrance and found it unlocked. He went to the room where the light was burning. Stretched on the floor beside a divan, with a couch pillow resting on the face, was X. A few feet away was the sabre with which he had been murdered.

The divan covers were half ripped off where the falling man had clutched them as he was repeatedly felled—repeatedly, for it was evident X had fought hard for his life against the sabre-armed assassin. The sabre had been ripped off the wall of the hall-way of the apartment.

The retaining wires were strong and the hand must have been strong that snapped them. (Androgynes cultivate only the best physically developed.)

The deduction was made that the assassin had not entered X's home with the intent to murder. He was pictured as having, in all probability, left his host in the "den" and started down the hall to make his exit from the flat when the resolution to attack and kill—a resolution which the weapons on the wall may have suggested—came suddenly upon him. Ripping the weapon from the wall, he is pictured as having dashed back to the "den" and surprised X with a fury of murderous attack. (X probably entertained at his home for the first time that night his well dressed and apparently trustworthy assassin. Only when the two adjourned to the "den" did X probably disclose his desire, so nauseating to the unsophisticated and those ignorant of abnormal psychology. Doubtless a minute after the disclosure, the prude left X's side in insane disgust, and on passing through the hall entertained his first thought to do his "duty by society and put this monster where he could corrupt no more young men"—an absolutely unfounded way of looking at the matter. I have myself scraped acquaintance with a youthful Hercules, who would lead me on hypocritically, and when he got me where there could be no witnesses, has half-murdered me because of disgust at androgynism. My adventure with Harvey Green is an example.)

Physical examination disclosed that despite his fifty-six years, X possessed the preservation of a man of thirty-five. (Perennial youth is an earmark of ultra-androgynism.)

The autopsy showed that every character of blow had been inflicted—deep stab wounds, slashes, and fracturing strokes on the skull either with the broad side or dull back of the sabre. The coat of X, who was fully clothed when killed, had been slashed to tatters. (The assassin wished not merely to kill, but to hack X to pieces because of his loathing of androgynism. I myself have not alone been half-murdered, but mutilation has been practiced for its own sake. See page 132 of my AUTOBIOGRAPHY OF AN ANDROGYNE.)

A Midnight Caller

X's CONDITION OF BEING FULLY clothed proves of course that he had not yet retired. (It also indicates that his assassin had repulsed his amorous advances immediately after the pair entered the "den." On such occasions, androgynes usually undress.) Further evidence was that his web system of alarms had not been set. It was his invariable custom, on retiring or when he went out, to do this. There was no sign of forcible entrance of the ground-floor apartment. Therefore X is believed to have freely admitted the man who was to murder him—probably such a chance acquaintance as he appears frequently to have made in his saunterings through the city's streets and visits to its resorts.

The examination of medical experts resulted in the hour of the crime being placed between nine and eleven of the evening previous.

Made No Outcry

IT BEING EVIDENT THAT X had survived the first attack at least for a few minutes before he finally succumbed under the raining blows of the sabre, the police were puzzled to understand why, with his life at stake, the man did not make an outcry. There was only a single wall separating the scene of combat from the public lobby where were stationed throughout the night a telephone operator and an elevator attendant. Tests made showed that a shout of medium volume from the "den" could be distinctly heard in the lobby. The attendants were positive they had heard no calls for help.

One of the puzzles, therefore, was to determine the character of X's murderous guest and the circumstances of his visit. Had X reason so grave for concealment of the presence of his slayer as to prevent him from calling for aid even with death immediately upon him? (X's consciousness of being a sexual eccentric would likely be an inhibition to his alarming those who lived in the same house. He probably did not suspect that the servants saw through everything. Between death and the disclosure to his co-tenants that he was a sexual eccentric, he probably chose the former.) None of the wounds was in his throat. The blow that fractured his skull must have been among the last as indicated by the evidence that X had fought his slayer long and hard.

Motive Not Clear

A DIAMOND RING, WHOSE VALUE must have been close to $1,000, habitually worn, together with X's gold watch and chain, were taken. Very little money was found in his clothing, whereas it was known he usually carried large sums. But there were at hand heavy solid silver articles, and gold ornaments, and valuable jewelry in a frail desk—none of which had been taken. Only X's body had been stripped. The police were convinced that the robbery was committed to conceal another deeper motive, as suggested by the savage maltreatment of X's body.

Whatever the motive, the murderer entered the apartment unseen that night and departed unseen. The police made haste to interview all persons whom they could trace as having been associated with X. There was a young sailor whom X had lately befriended and who had been his guest for several days. This youth was traced to his ship and his presence aboard the night of the murder established.

One clue was a bit of cardboard on which was scribbled, in X's handwriting, the latter's address. It looked as if made hastily for the guidance of the stranger guest to X's apartment. (And in the apartment thrown away as being no longer of use.)

No slightest clue to the identity of the slayer was uncovered.

The Murder of Y

ON THE NIGHT OF (DATE omitted by author of THE FEMALE-IMPERSONATORS) just twenty-nine days after the murder of X, Y was slain in his home nearby. The two murders instantly linked. For the two crimes presented an almost perfect parallel. The scene was the same—an elaborately furnished "den." As with X, Y's murderer had been his guest. A secret guest—in that nobody saw him enter Y's residence, no sound betrayed him in the act of killing, and he managed to leave the "den" and Y's house unobserved.

Of astonishingly the same stamp were X and Y. Both were elderly bachelors and art connoisseurs. (The latter an earmark of cultured androgynism.) Both had specialized in the collection of ancient and curious weapons. Both were addicted to an extravagant display of jewelry on their persons. (Androgynes are loud dressers.) Both lived in dread of attack in their homes and had made elaborate preparations against the possibility. Inspection of the lives of both found them oddly empty of attachment to or association with women. Both had a disposition for the society of much younger men, and had many such acquaintances.

Living in the same neighborhood, frequenting the same hotels and restaurants, visiting the same art galleries and antique shops as they were tireless in doing, it was rather to be expected that they were found to have been close friends.

The indicated motive for both murders was robbery but in both cases only the valuables used in personal adornment were stolen, while other jewels, and silver and gold objects of art and service, plainly in sight, were ignored. (Robbery being only a blind, loathing of sexual eccentricity being the true motive.)

In only two particulars did the crimes differ: X was hacked to death; Y was strangled by the bare hands of his assailant. The marks of relentless fingers were deeply imbedded in the victim's neck. The other difference was that in Y's case, there had been no struggle. He had had no chance to put up a fight for his life. He had been taken by surprise and the strangler's grip been clamped on his throat before he could make outcry.

Y was fifty-nine years old, and a native of rural Illinois. He had prospered as owner of a fashionable ladies' dress-making concern in New York. But he had retired and at the time he was murdered was renting an ex-mansion of a millionaire, where he conducted a boarding-house of the highest class. There were twenty lodgers, but scores of additional persons living in the aristocratic neighborhood took their meals at Y's. He frequently organized card parties and dances for his guests, and to these were always invited freely young men in war service on leave in New York. (Warriors are androgynes' special heroes. A common soldiers' and sailors' club was situated next door, where Y apparently made many acquaintances.)

Y's body was found at seven A.M. (date here omitted) by George, one of Y's eleven negro servants. (Y conducted his establishment on the plan of a multimillionaire's residence.) It was George's daily duty to go to his employer's room on the first floor, directly over the kitchen, awaken him at seven, and serve him breakfast in bed. On that morning, George, receiving no reply to his knock, pushed the door open and entered the elaborately furnished "den" and bedroom.

Strangled to Death

THE BED WAS IN ORDER, and the body of Y on the floor nearby was clad only in pajamas. (Apparently the assassin had pretended he was going to retire with Y. Therefore Y got into his night clothes, as also probably the assassin. But just before the bed covers would have been turned down the latter fulfilled his mandate from society by "ridding New York of the monster!") An autopsy showed that indubitably Y had been strangled to death. The deep, purple marks on his throat were valueless as furnishing finger-print evidence, but they did stamp the murderer's hands as large and very strong. (Androgynes cultivate only the best physically developed.) Y had been suddenly attacked by the strangler and immediately choked into helplessness, for nothing in the room had been disturbed. He had been borne down to death on the very spot where seized.

Y's "den" was the scene of many late-hour parties, in which young men figured exclusively as guests. Frequently also he returned very late with a single companion. His late-hour guests were never boisterous and never gave cause for complaint by Y's refined lodgers.

As in the case of X's apartment, Y's house gave no evidence of a forcible entry. Physicians determined that Y's death had occurred at eleven the night before the body was discovered. At that hour the outer doors of the house were always locked. Many of the lodgers and some of the negro servants had not yet retired, and must have heard, it would seem, a ringing of the doorbell. None did.

Probably an Expected Guest

THE CONJECTURE WAS CONSEQUENTLY MADE that Y had appointed a late meeting with his murderous guest and given him a key to his house that he might enter quietly. Of fully twenty-five persons in the house at the time, not one heard the slightest sound of distress or noise of any kind from the "den" at the hour of the murder.

Even more futile than in the case of X were the efforts of the investigators to round up the many young men (evidently bachelors from eighteen to twenty-five) whose acquaintance Y was constantly making.

Three diamond rings of a value of $2,000 had been stripped from the dead man's fingers, and his gold watch and chain were taken. But as at X's assassination, many articles of jewelry and of gold and silver easily accessible were not touched.

Alike in mystery, the cases of both X and Y manifest the strong likelihood that the same man effected both murders, with a suggestion of a deeper motive than robbery, of a desire to do violence aroused to frenzy, judging by the stark ferocity with which both crimes were committed.

(The motive of course was to rid New York of androgynes; at least, extensively promiscuous ones. It is quite likely the same prude was guilty of both murders. Perhaps at first the assassin had known merely through hearsay that both X and Y were sexual eccentrics. But he was reasonable and merciful enough not to put them out of the way until he possessed ocular evidence. (I have myself associated with torturers who would act only on such.) For X's and Y's murderer was solemnly and conscientiously acting as the mandatory of society.

(From the murder of X he had learned that an androgyne might put up resistance. Therefore in the case of his second quarry, Y, he must adopt a safer, more sudden, and an absolutely noiseless means of execution. In sabre-slaughtering, there was too much risk of the victim calling for help. Moreover, X lived all by himself, whereas Y's residence was alive with people. Androgynes like to be treated by their virile associates as if women, and the ultra-virile always humor that liking. The assassin probably started in with a pretended "love" embrace, and, before Y could realize, turned it into a strangling death-grip.

(I will admit that X and Y were extensively promiscuous. But they could not have been particularly intemperate because my own experience proved that excessive venery soon wrecks the health of an androgyne.

As both were close to sixty, their lives had doubtless been temperate. They had probably indulged (the more humiliating role in fellatio) not more than once a week throughout their adulthood. But although they apparently sought intimacy with almost every adolescent Adonis or Hercules (only one out of every twenty adolescents could qualify under either of these types) whose acquaintance they made, they harmed these youthful rakes not in the least; nor did they, throughout their lives, bring detriment to any one else since all androgynes possess the inoffensive psyche of women. For proof of the harmlessness to an adolescent of an androgyne intimate, I refer to my AUTOBIOGRAPHY OF AN ANDROGYNE, pages 88, 89, and 194.

(Far from the adolescent suffering harm, he is loaded with material benefits by the well-to-do androgyne who worships him. He is preeminently a "lucky dog."

(X and Y were entirely irresponsible for being androgynes and sexual eccentrics. Absolutely no harm came to any individual or to society collectively through their condition or instinctive functioning. They did not deserve that any one interfere with their life, liberty, and pursuit of happiness.)

Z Mystery Baffles Inquiry
at Every Angle

(Much condensed, and slightly edited for diction,
by author of The Female-Impersonators,
from article in a New York daily.)

No Proof of Suicide and No Motive for Murder Found in Case
of Youth Strangled Aboard His Own Power Yacht—Friends
Insist Death Was an Assassin's Work—Dressing of the Body
in Woman's Clothing Furnishes No Clues to Family or
Police—Full Details for Students of Crime to Study

After two weeks of many-sided investigation, the death of Z remains
as great a mystery as on the evening of (date omitted by author of The
Female-Impersonators) when his mother discovered him strangled
aboard his power yacht in New York Harbor dressed in woman's apparel.

"No reason for suicide and no motive for murder—no proof of suicide,
no positive evidence of murder." Such is the conclusion reached by the
police, private investigators employed by Z's family, and by newspaper
reporters who have worked on the baffling case unique for its mass of
contradictory theories and circumstances.

(And to the present writer, himself an androgyne and instinctive
cross-dresser, the strongest of reasons for suicide and the strongest of
motives for murder! Androgynes, because so terribly misjudged by their
associates, are the most melancholy and prone to suicide of any class of
mankind. Moreover, they are often murdered on the strong motive of
intense loathing felt by prudes ignorant of abnormal psychology, in whose
eyes the androgyne is a "sodomite," with all the terrible, though false,
connotation of that term. Such prudes believe themselves mandatories
of society to rid the world of the "monster." The present writer did some
detective work in this case "on his own hook." He ascertained that in
the circle of those who knew Z by sight but were not personal friends,
he had the reputation of being a fellator. I interviewed several of this
circle, but did not dare thrust myself into that of Z's close friends.)

The view of the police generally is that the death was clearly suicide. But as to how the suicide was accomplished, police officers hold theories no two of which agree.

Family Sure Z Was Murdered

Z's FAMILY, HIS CLOSEST CHUM, and his friends generally, maintained from the first, and still believe, that Z was murdered aboard the yacht by an assassin who secreted himself in one of the cabins and afterwards escaped in a fashion equally mysterious.

The fact that young Z wore woman's clothing is to the police the strongest evidence of suicide and supplies to them evidence of a psychopathic individuality. (That fact is to myself the strongest evidence of murder since I have repeatedly witnessed the intense revulsion of prudish bigots at any cross-sex phenomenon, and have been myself half-murdered solely on this incentive.)

Opposed to this is the most positive assertion from Z's family and friends: (1) That he was a normal boy in every respect. (In nearly every case of a cultured androgyne in the past, his family have never suspected anything because of the veil of silence that the deluded public has insisted be thrown over the phenomenon of androgynism and the consequent absolute ignorance of the *truth* about this phenomenon on the part of the entire Overworld excepting a handful of sexologists. Just to throw their associates off the scent, some cultured androgynes purposely do some courting of females, and have even contracted a marriage (of course, Platonic) as mentioned by Phyllis in the last chapter of PART FIVE. Moreover, some androgynes are psychic hermaphrodites and capable of sincerity in courting a girl, while at the same time Nature insists on occasional female-impersonation sprees. Z might have been a psychic hermaphrodite.)

(2) That he had never shown any suicidal tendencies. (Readers of my AUTOBIOGRAPHY OF AN ANDROGYNE know that I probably showed more suicidal tendencies than almost any one else who has failed to carry them out; yet I always hid them absolutely from my family and every-day associates. Androgynes, because they do not want their friends to become aware of the cause of their melancholia (fearing it would alienate them, as at present no one can forgive cross-sexism in an intimate) habitually suffer in silence and seclusion the most intense mental torture.)

(3) That no kind of woman's wear was ever known to be in his possession. (For years together I have myself kept woman's wear under lock and key and occasionly put it on, but none of my every-day associates ever discovered these facts. Cultured androgynes always conceal such practices because their every-day bigoted circles would make them pariahs.)

And as yet nobody has been able to find where Z got the feminine apparel. (It was later discovered he had bought it of a ladies' outfitter.) Nearly every article found on him was soiled and showed unmistakable signs of wear. (He had probably worn the articles on scores of female-impersonation sprees. Cultured androgynes never let their families get an inkling of these psychic explosions.)

Z was twenty-one. The boy received a common-school education, but left high-school in the second year to work in the large manufacturing establishment of his father. He had a strong bent for mechanics. He took care of the family's three automobiles, as well as a motor-cycle. Three years ago his father gave him a motor-yacht, which he himself took care of.

During the World War, Z enlisted as mechanician in the navy, but was assigned to shore duty near New York throughout the war.[1] (There

---

1. This comment so developed that I was compelled to make it a footnote. The assignment to shore duty might indicate that Z's immediate superiors might have noticed that he was of soft disposition, an earmark of androgynism. An androgyne acquaintance, though perfectly sound physically, was rejected in the World War draft merely on account of his softspokenness and generally "soft" mannerisms. Another young androgyne acquaintance enlisted in the Hospital Corps during the war so as to be able to pass all his time among idols. Moreover, androgynes long to serve as nurses to wounded virile young men, as did Walt Whitman during the American War of the Rebellion. Androgynes make the best nurses of youthful warriors because they slavishly adore them. From an eyewitness I heard of a third androgyne who was drafted in the World War and "bobtailed" out of the army because discovered to be addicted to fellatio. From another eyewitness I heard of a fourth androgyne who was similarly "bobtailed", and as a result of the indignities heaped upon him at the time, immediately committed suicide. Of course those who heaped up the indignities thought the sexual cripple wilfully depraved. From still another eyewitness I heard of another drafted androgyne who, on the eve of his first battle in France, ate the heads off matches so as to assure getting back into the hospital while his virile "buddies" were valiantly "going over the top." Virility confers bravery.

At the date of writing, I still "pal" only with regular soldiers, but am instinctively such an industrious worker that I go into any kind of fellowship only about once a fortnight. I still look upon youthful regular soldiers as magic demigods to whom I wish to enslave myself. Two days before the present writing, I happened to take a walk to Fort Y, which played a large part in my AUTOBIOGRAPHY OF AN ANDROGYNE, and which, from 1902 to

exist all degrees of psychic effemination in androgynes. I estimate my own proportions as woman, 80 per cent; man, 20. Evidently Z was around 60, woman and 40, man, judging by his willingness to take a fire-arm into his hands, a thing which I would never do, even as a child shrinking from a cap-pistol. X and Y likewise were less extreme

---

1905, I visited, in the role of female-impersonator, one evening out of fourteen, and where I was acquainted with practically every one of the four hundred men not above the grade of sergeant. That of two days ago was only my second trip there in the past sixteen years. Because it is inconveniently located for a visit. After sixteen years, I happened to be recognized by one soldier who had stuck to that post and risen to the rank of sergeant. He told me there were still only about four at the fort who served there when I had the honor to be "the daughter of the regiment." He expressed his amazement at my being so well preserved, saying I look twenty years younger than I am. He told me that only four or five fairies had run after the men of that fort in the past sixteen years. That small number is due to the remoteness of Fort Y from the city. At two other forts formerly frequented by me as a female-impersonator which are right in the city, androgyne cultivators of the common soldiers are numerous. A man serving at one of these forts told me that common soldiers often speak with one another about their "fairies." Whenever any one of the former appears with a new watch, ring, etc., a common query of his "buddies" is: "Did your fairie give it to you?" Seven out of ten common soldiers appear exceedingly glad to have a prosperous young androgyne in their midst, particularly because he showers them with gifts and entertainment. Only one out of ten is such a prude as to walk away from the circle of which I have hundreds of times had the privilege of being the star. Some of these prudes would murder an androgyne but for fear of being punished.

Because of this remoteness of Fort Y, however, I had found there, during the hey-day of my career as female-impersonator, a specially hearty welcome and specially rich pickings.

(See **"Emotion"** in Part VIII.)

The sergeant I met two days ago—as common soldiers in general—was very much interested to hear the experiences of an androgyne as I narrated my life-story for the sixteen years since I talked with him. I habitually tell soldier associates the complete story of my life, and all who stay in the circle to listen appear very glad for the chat. Of course I never use any indecent language, although dealing frankly with sex questions. I am a lecturer on sexology to them. Moreover, within three minutes after becoming acquainted with a common soldier, I sometimes ask him, if he is beyond twenty-five, if he is married. For I do not care to chat with married men. I also commonly ask why he never married. I ask him to enlighten me as to his feelings toward the gentle sex, and as to what transpires when he and a girl are out for an evening's stroll on a rural road. They are very frank in telling me their outlook on life. If there is no opportunity for assault and robbery (A large proportion of the uncultured thinking the first thing of robbing a stranger androgyne, if not of "beating him up") I have, to strange young soldiers, confessed myself an androgyne within three minutes after we exchanged our first words, because their learning that fact proves, in general, the strongest kind of a drawing card.

The sergeant of two days ago wanted to make a date with me. I absolutely turned my back on such a proposition, chiefly on account of the dread of the physical and mental debility always supervening the following day. He urged me to resume my visits to Fort

effeminants than myself. They would put up a resistance if attacked, whereas I depended for escape merely on entreaty or flight (Nature gave me the legs of a gazelle); or if they failed me, I pretended loss of consciousness after the first terrific blow. Through this complete

---

Y, to flaunt myself before all the soldiers as female-impersonator, as sixteen years before. I replied that I was now too old and too feeble. While sixteen years before I never left the vicinity of the post without dalliance with intimates, two days ago I did not entertain the least idea of, and hardly any wish for, such relations. Age has sobered me. "Intimates" I just wrote—some of whom, however, I had never laid eyes on until three minutes before. Providence gave me this wealth of one kind to counterbalance the almost unparalleled anguish I have been called upon to suffer because of my fate of being a sorely persecuted androgyne.

Lest I should be misjudged (the reader will any way judge me the warmest body that ever breathed, as intimates have told me) I further confess that during the year ending March, 1921, I visited at another fort about once a fortnight a 20-year-old private whom I planned to adopt (not legally) as son to live with me the rest of my life. I previously looked over, at ball games at the post, the entire common-soldier personnel of several hundred in order to pick out one of the three or four handsomest. Even at my first visit, one or two of the privates with whom I exchanged words evidently took me for an androgyne looking for a sweetheart, and did their best to be "the lucky dog." But I passed the poor fellows by until I could get intimately acquainted with one of the three or four pre-eminent Adonises. I later ascertained that the one selected—greatly to his joy and to the envy of numerous "buddies"—excelled in disposition and character as much as in good looks. I also learned he had been brought up in the back woods and had never attended school a single day, although he had learned to read and write a little after entering the army. After I had known him intimately for nine months, his enlistment expired. Only now I disclosed my true name and station and took him to live in my own home, where I had been all by myself, doing my own housework like a woman. Although I had loaded him with gifts, this my "third adopted son" took French leave after only three days' residence with me. His "buddies" told me he had gone away to marry the girl with whom I had known he had been corresponding.

Having lost him, I immediately started in to cultivate at the same barracks its pre-eminent Adonis, and almost its preeminent Hercules, with a view to his non-legal adoption to live with me as son the rest of my life after a nine-months apprenticeship during which he would not know my real name, station in life, or place of residence. It is easy to conceal these things from common soldiers. They are not inquisitive. They believe my misrepresentations of myself—necessary because androgynes are the favorite victims of blackmailers. But after a month, this latest favorite committed theft and I never saw him again. His "buddies" told me that he had stolen two blankets, **"government property,"** and was therefore sentenced to two years in military prison. If I am correctly informed, court martials often impose on an enlisted man caught in a misdemeanor a prison sentence several times as lengthy as would a civil court. I take this opportunity to enter a plea for better treatment of common soldiers, who have been my "pals" for a quarter of a century—particularly for punishments by court martial no more severe than by civil courts. Sometimes I have thought that when an uneducated young man enlists to defend his country as a common soldier, he thereby forfeits all rights of citizenship and all

passivity, I came out far better than if I had shown fight, and probably saved myself, on several occasions, from being one hundred per cent murdered.)

Z often practiced with a revolver at a target in the basement of his home. (He was pay-master in his father's factory and often had in his possession large sums, and had to know how to defend himself from robbers.) His rifle was found on his boat, together with cartridges, on the day of his death. Why, if he intended suicide, did he not use his revolver, or else the rifle that was handy at the time on the boat? (This, to me, is conclusive evidence of murder or manslaughter.)

Z possessed the only key to the cabin of the boat. The family say there were originally two keys, but the duplicate was "lost" about a year ago. (Possibly Z staged all his female-impersonation sprees on his yacht and so gave the duplicate to an idol before whom he regularly posed, just as I have given a trusted idol a key to enter my own apartment whenever he felt like it.)

In High Spirits

ON THE AFTERNOON PRECEDING THE day of his death, Z took his motor-cycle apart in order to renew some mechanism. On his last evening alive, he was in high spirits, setting every one of his

---

privileges guaranteed by the American constitution. The cow-boys of the Rockies have mingled with common soldiers because of the numerous forts scattered throughout the "Indian country." I asked one with whom I was well acquainted why he did not serve a few years in the army. His words were: "Do you think I want to be a slave?" But the lot of the common soldier has steadily improved during my association with him, excepting during our war with Germany. In 1921, he is better treated by his officers than ever before.

The context of this footnote moves me to reflect: Do I prefer an Adonis or a Hercules? I incline to the latter slightly. My first "adopted son" (for nine years, as described in my AUTOBIOGRAPHY OF AN ANDROGYNE) was an almost unmatched Hercules and at the same time an almost unmatched Adonis. He was one young man out of ten thousand. My second "adopted son" (for only a half-year, as described in same work) was neither a Hercules nor an Adonis. Not more than one out of twenty adolescents can qualify under either of these physically superior types, and I must confess that these types are very much lacking in mental acumen. Bright intellects nearly always go hand in hand with poor physical development. My second "adopted son" (while only tolerably good-looking) commanded my adoration because of his beautiful disposition and extreme passion for myself. My third prospective "adopted son" was a pre-eminent Adonis, and a fair Hercules.

There exist other attractive qualities in males that knit females to them. The chief is intellectual brilliance. That to me has always been, sexually considered, decidedly detractive—because I am myself of the intellectual type. As a rule, only opposites attract.

circle laughing. So far from being depressed, he seemed flushed with happiness at the prospect of future success in business, having only just received a promotion. (His unusual happiness on the very eve of the murder might indicate that he had just succeeded in coming to terms with a *new* idol, who, however, the next afternoon, on discovering how "deeply depraved" Z was, strangled him with the rope. I myself have several times been half-murdered under similar circumstances. I have also been elevated into the third heaven of bliss on receiving a favorable message from an idol.)

On the morning of the day of Z's death, he called on a friend who was to give a party in a few days, and assured the latter he would be present. He then ate noon lunch with his family. It was his father's birthday, and Z promised to take the family out for an automobile ride in the late afternoon. Right after lunch, Z remarked: "I'll first make a trip to the boat to pump the water out. It hasn't been touched for a week, and you know how the water accumulates under the engine. I won't be gone long." (It was two miles from Z's residence to the boat; twenty minutes, by motor-cycle, to get on board. The reason given impresses me as a mere pretext to hide his appointment on the launch and prospective female-impersonation—because the pretext sounds just like *me*. I am one who has been compelled to falsify much because if my associates had been granted the truth, they would have impiously crushed me. In my university course in ethics, I was taught that it is proper to tell a lie if the persons deceived have no right to the truth. Always those whom I deceived had no right, because the truth would have rendered them insanely cruel.)

In a jovial mood (because about to meet his idol, I suspect) Z departed on his motor-cycle at 1:30. On the way he stopped at a dealer's—full of laughter here also—and filled his cycle tank with a gallon of gasoline. (Two indications against suicide.) At the wharf, he was seen to take oars out of his locker and row to his power-boat anchored fifty yards out. He was next seen, by two men on a yacht anchored fifty feet from his own, to disappear down into his cabin. (The last declaration by any one of having seen Z before discovered dead in his cabin.) These two men remained on the deck of their anchored launch all the afternoon until 5:30, and both are positive that Z did not reappear on his deck. They are equally positive that no one came from or went to Z's launch.

The owner of the power-boat continuously anchored on the other side of Z's was aboard from 2:30 until 4:30, and is positive no one approached Z's boat from that side. The owner of a third power-boat continuously anchored thirty-five feet from Z's in another direction also spent the afternoon on board, and tells the same story. Two men (custodians and renters of boats) busy all the afternoon around the wharf fifty yards away saw no one go to or come from Z's launch.

(To me the most probable solution of Z's death is that it was neither murder nor suicide, but accidental man-slaughter. Perhaps Z had the habit, to satisfy his mania for female-impersonation, of taking on his yacht as an audience young bachelors who owned launches usually anchored near his own. Perhaps a launch, on that Sunday afternoon ideal for yachting, was kept at anchor near Z's because its owner had plotted to teach Z a lesson, with the "good" intention of curing him of his habit of female-impersonation, believing—as nearly every one does at present because prohibited by public opinion from learning the truth—that it is a *wilful* bad habit. When Z had rigged himself in feminine garb (because the female side of his duality demanded it), one or more of the young men from one of the anchored yachts—according to my theory—had tied ropes around him, even around his neck, the latter merely in order to frighten him and prevent his calling for help. The newspapers stated that only a "seaman" could display such skill in tying ropes, and these yachtsmen were amateur seamen. They then, late in the afternoon, after they had had their "fun" with the pitiable androgyne, went ashore, having no thought that the rope around the throat would tighten sufficiently to strangle Z. They designed merely to punish him for his androgynism (1) through his being compelled to lie helpless on the cabin floor for several hours, with a rope tight around his neck to prevent him calling for help, and, (2) more than that, through humilating him before his family, who finally, anxious over his not returning home, would visit the yacht and discover him in his most ignominious garb and predicament.

(But Z, in his writhings to free himself from his bonds, unfortunately tightened the rope about his neck and was fatally strangled, the young men having departed and no one being at hand to succor him in his death agony. Z was only one more of the many martyrs to the public's prohibition of the showing up of the myth that bisexuals are monsters of depravity, deserving the cruelest forms of torture and even murder. Those guilty of Z's death—under the theory now being propounded— were fundamentally irresponsible. The guilt lies with the Church and public opinion, both of which teach that no punishment is too bad for an androgyne.

(A few days after Z's death, I wrote letters to Z's father giving all my theories. I desired to do all I could to avenge my brother in calamity by bringing his assailants to justice. It would not be surprising if Z's father was disinclined to press matters because of shame over the son's being an androgyne combined with the public's so terribly misjudging androgynism. Z's near neighbor, a young college graduate whom I "pumped," told me first that the fact at the bottom of Z's death "was of such nature that it could not be discussed"! I could get at the truth only by putting repeated frank questions, since he labored under the terrible delusion that sex is a subject beyond discussion. This college man expressed the opinion that Z was wilfully depraved and "got all that was coming to him." I interviewed several others who knew the Z family merely by sight and reputation. They all showed intense antipathy, being of the opinion that a family's having an androgyne relative was sufficient cause for its ostracism.

(A personal parallel: To only one member of my own family—a brother—have I ever confessed my addiction to female-impersonation sprees. I did it twenty years ago, at the age of twenty-seven, because I then had enemies at Ft. X (at the time my regular stamping-ground) who hated androgynism so fiercely as to be capable of murdering an individual in whom the phenomenon cropped up. I therefore explained matters to a brother: that if ever I was found murdered, to look for my assassin among the common soldiers of Ft. X. He replied: "Ralph, if you are ever murdered on one of your female-impersonation sprees, the family would be too much ashamed ever to take the first step to bring your murderer to justice!")

At the supper hour, Z's mother telephoned to the wharf and was informed her son had not returned from his yacht. Fearing he had met with an accident, she and her daughter went by automobile to the wharf, arriving at 6:30. It was then almost dark. A boatman rowed the mother, shivering nervously, to the launch. As Mrs. Z descended the forward hatch, her foot struck a human body lying at the foot of the steps, face downward. She felt the hands, which stuck out above the body, and found them cold.

"Linnie has fainted!" Mrs. Z exclaimed. She hastily lighted a lantern, while the boatman remained at the top of the short flight of stairs, apparently paralyzed with fear. But having a light, Mrs. Z discovered the inert body to be clothed in a long blue dress, while the head was covered with a black oilcloth bag. (Such covering of the head indicates non-suicide. The man-killer covered Z's head because, before abandoning him with the rope around his neck, he (or they) tormented and tortured Z. I have myself had a handkerchief thrust into my mouth to prevent an outcry and been thereupon tortured merely because of insane loathing of androgynism.)

Mrs. Z now exclaimed: "Why, it's a woman! She's been strangled, and Linnie's not here!"

Overcome with terror, she left the boat without further examination. Mr. Z, when his wife greeted him with the frantic cry: "A woman has been strangled on our yacht!" immediately visited it. He removed the hood from the form on the cabin floor, and in amazement recognized the face of his son. Around the neck was a tightened noose of Manila rope tied with a *hangman's* knot. Mr. Z is positive the knot was at the *back* of the neck. (This position is an indication of non-suicide. A suicide would naturally have placed the knot in front.) Unable to loosen the knot, Mr. Z cut the rope. He noticed that both his son's hands were behind the back, apparently tied with a sash cord, although he did not think to make sure *both* were tied. For, finding the body cold, he was convulsed with grief and immediately left without making further examination.

The next arrivals were policemen.

The Homicide bureau contends that although there was a slip-knot around the left hand, the right was free and Z used one or both hands to draw the hangman's noose about his neck. This theory presupposes that the knot was at the throat, and discards the father's assertion that it was at the *back* of the neck.

Z's ankles were tied together with rope, as were his knees and arms. (A queer way to commit suicide for the victim to take the greatest pains to make people think he had been murdered! And when there were a rifle and cartridges on board the launch! And only an hour or two before in a jovial mood, and laying in a supply of gasoline!) A medical examiner calculated that death had occurred between four and five P.M. The two men on the deck of the power-boat on one side of Z's launch had gone ashore at 5.30, and the single man on the power-boat on the other side, at 4.30. None had heard any cry or other sound from the Z launch (35 to 50 feet distant and on an ultra-still Sunday afternoon when sounds carry unusually well.) When these witnesses went ashore, Z's rowboat was fastened to his launch—in the same position as when his mother arrived.

EARL LIND

The woman's apparel in which Z was found clad consisted of a chemise; corset; corset-cover with rose-colored baby ribbon running through the lace; a pair of pink bloomers with ruffles at the knees; high black stockings fastened by garters to the corset; a pair of high laced woman's shoes, with French high heels; and finally, the blue-checked gingham dress. All the apparel fitted Z well.

The clothing in which Z had left home was found on a bunk in the cabin—excepting an overshirt, which was pinned over the porthole nearest the launch fifty feet distant on whose deck two men spent the afternoon. Aside from this circumstance, the police discovered no sign of disorder in any part of the launch. They discovered no other articles or circumstances having a bearing on the case. (Androgynes are in general non-resistant. Z probably did not struggle against his tormentor, as I myself have always been absolutely passive on such occasions. Any way he probably did not even imagine that he was under any risk of death. He probably expected to return home within an hour—as he had previously done after dozens of female-impersonation explosions.)

But reporters, who later examined the boat, found a thick hickory club in a drawer. (My theory is that Z was accustomed to entertain on the boat, in the absence of any of his family, adolescents before whom he had a craze to impersonate a mademoiselle—the common practice of the more extreme type of androgyne. He probably entertained only one at a time. Fearing he might be attacked by one of these perhaps doubtful characters, he kept the club for self-defence, as well as the rifle already mentioned. The fact that he did not attempt to avail himself of these weapons on this occasion indicates that his assailants were young men whose high morality was known to Z.) In a chest in an out-of-the-way place, the reporters found a bundle of wrapping paper stained and torn. Inside was a metal shoe-horn. (My theory is that Z stored his feminine wardrobe in this paper and chest. The paper was probably that in which the feminine outfit had originally been brought to the launch and was preserved for possible use in carrying it away.)

The Z family kept a supply of beer on the yacht, but affirmed: "Linnie hated beer and never learned to drink it." (Very androgynesque. Girl-boys are inclined to be puritans in every respect except female-impersonation and coquetry.)

The only feminine article that Z wore which the family recognized was a multi-colored silk ribbon fastened around his waist and belonging to a sister.

The autopsy showed that death had resulted solely from strangulation. All the ropes used in binding Z belonged to his yacht. (The reason Z was done to death with ropes is that there naturally were many on board a yacht and it was a *noiseless* death. There was a loaded rifle on the yacht. That a noiseless method was chosen indicates murder rather than suicide. The use of ropes also indicates a yachtsman as author of the crime—because accustomed to handling ropes. He lives and breathes ropes.)

Z was five feet four in height and weighed 145 pounds. (Short and plump build characteristic of androgynes.) The city medical examiner noted that the lower ribs were "retracted, possibly due to the use of corsets." He also noted that "the beard and moustache are scanty." (Meaning if not shaven close. Such scantiness is common in androgynes.)

If the murder theory is true, the assassin must have planned to murder with great care. (It was all done on the spur of the moment, and the death probably an accident.) He must have had an accomplice who brought him to the boat before the murder, and took him away afterward, and he must have known in some mysterious way that Z was going to visit the boat that Sunday afternoon. (If Z was murdered, he had had an appointment on the yacht with his assassin. The latter must have arrived before the yachtsmen who spent the afternoon on the closely encircling decks, and watched that they go ashore before himself. At dusk he could have swum away without being seen. At that hour on a Sunday, there were many desolate points on the nearby shore at which he could have unobservedly emerged. But the most daring criminal would hardly have committed a murder with several men only a few feet away on the decks of the encircling yachts. A single shriek from the victim would have immediately brought several men on board.)

The care with which the clothing was put on certainly seems to indicate that Z himself put it on, every article being properly adjusted.

(The authorities, because ignorant of androgyne psychology and habits and despising a bisexual (myself) too much to listen to his-her theories, were on a false scent. At the date this volume goes to press (December, 1921), the Z mystery—as well as the X, Y, and Q—has not been cleared up by the authorities, although none of the four is much of a problem to myself, knowing how the world treats androgynes.

(It is a strange coincidence that about a score of years before Z was strangled, within two miles of his yacht's point of anchorage, in a large patch of woods at night, I was, as an aftermath of a female-impersonation, being roughly teased by six "young fellows." To cap the climax, they led me toward a tree and said they were "going to get a rope and hang" me. Horrified, I feigned an epileptic fit to save myself. See my AUTOBIOGRAPHY OF AN ANDROGYNE, page 208.

(While I have never believed Z a suicide, it is a possibility. A new idol with whom he had had an appointment on the yacht that afternoon might have shown utter disgust at Z's revelations—as I have myself witnessed in a confidant—and pitilessly abandoned him. This misguided attitude might have brought on Z a sympathetic disgust with himself as female-impersonator and cross-dresser. According to this theory, Z wished to punish and heap indignities on his own body—just as I have myself, in my verdant middle teens, taken a whip and chastised my own body because lustful, homosexual thoughts had invaded my mind, while crying out: "'O wretched man that I am, who shall deliver me from the body of this death!'" Perhaps Z wished to punish his own body by depriving it of breath while in female garb and so publish to the world the despicableness of his own physical personality. In no other way could Z's spiritually minded psyche better revenge itself on his carnal body than to have the latter's grossness proclaimed on the housetops.

(In case Z was a suicide, the idol who had only a few minutes before pitilessly scorned his advances was very likely an adolescent spending that afternoon on one of the three nearest yachts. As I have said, the case came to a curious abrupt ending in the papers, as if the entire solution had become known to those immediately interested, but the public was not let into the secret in order to shield unblameworthy parties.

(If Z was a suicide, I have myself passed through a very similar experience. (See my AUTOBIOGRAPHY OF AN ANDROGYNE, page 235.) Because heartlessly jilted by a new idol and afraid I would as "a monster of depravity," be cast out of the caravan with which I was travelling in an uninhabited region of the Rockies, I walked away in the forest alone at dusk a mile from camp having in mind suicide by being torn to pieces by bears, with which the forest abounded, and several of which I saw that night roaming within a hundred feet. Like Z, I had not left behind a single oral or written word as to suicide. I was acting on the spur of the moment. For several hours I experienced such depths of sorrow as not one human out of ten thousand ever tastes. Continuously for an hour, out of hearing of the camp, I wailed at the top of my voice over my terrible lot in life—that of a despised, hated, and outlawed "degenerate" (as the hypocritical nine-tenths of civilized humanity delight to call me)—and over the possibly impending unfathomable disgrace among a party of rough men with whom I must travel until we got back to a railroad. I experienced a violent desire to be devoured by bears. But the All-Seeing overruled that they did not attack me.)[2]

---

2. I had fully described this adventure in my AUTOBIOGRAPHY OF AN ANDROGYNE, but the details were cut out by its editor. I append them here because tending to show that the sparser the population of a district, the greater the repugnance of civilized young roues to androgynism and the rarer is the latter phenomenon per thousand males. In other words: My conclusion from extensive travel and intimate mingling, as an ultra-androgyne, with native adolescent roues in every corner of the United States and Europe is that among civilized nations, the frequency of male bisexuals per thousand inhabitants and their tolerance by the full-fledged are in general in direct proportion to the density of population.

I, a woman-soul, but reputedly a young man, was delegated to write up an unusual affair transpiring in a Rocky Mountain wilderness. I was in a caravan with fifty men of the roughest type, cowboys, miners, etc. All were bachelors or grass-widowers. Day in and day out, they hardly talked of anything but prostitutes, some of whom enlivened every mining or lumbering camp of any permanence, although their rates were seven times city prices and they laid away fortunes. Some of the decidedly lucky prospectors, as well as occasional city-ites on hunting trips, were always accompanied by their mistresses—the city-ites doubtless glad to get away from "friend wife" for a few weeks.

I found the adolescent cowboys and miners of the Rockies the most prejudiced against effeminate males of any of the hundreds of circles of adolescent roues with which I have mingled as a girlboy. The first hour, when I had not compromised myself in any way, they began to heap up insults, particularly taking pains to refer to me within my hearing by the obscene term most often used by roughs for a girl-boy. (My own age was then thirty-three, but my friends told me I looked to be only twenty-five. I still possessed the "small-boy" aspect common among ultra-androgynes.) I feared my forced sojourn with those who so despised effeminacy would be intolerable.

But my plan to win their respect succeeded. I exhibited my credentials as representative of a journal of national reputation. They never again insulted me and I even became popular. The more sensual began to resort to terms of endearment and embraces. But, while fascinated by these attentions, I distrusted them to the extent of not disclosing my secret desires. I knew that prudes occasionally murder bisexuals in cities. In the wilds of the Rockies these same prudes (only so far as concerns homosexuality) could so easily push me over a precipice after tempting me to a stroll, and no one ever learn my fate. The tradition is wide spread that bisexuals must be murdered. Perhaps the practice of murdering is akin to that prevalent among some savage tribes of children killing their parents as soon as the latter become too feeble to hunt and work. It was racial economy to put out of the way those who could not contribute their share to the food supply, as well as those impotent to procreate children. But as civilized man no longer finds it necessary to the continued life of the nation to knock in the head all citizens as they reach the age of sixty, equally there is now no call for murdering (or even chastising) individuals incapable of generation.

But sleeping in the same tent and continuously having to listen to confessions of their amorous adventures, I became wrought up as rarely in my life. Therefore after a week of continuous Platonic association with the cowboy who seemed naturally the most high-minded and trustworthy, I invited him for an evening's stroll in the forest primæval. He had been brought up on a Wyoming ranch, never been inside of a church, never heard a word read out of the Bible, and could not read nor write. He asserted he had once been a rough rider in Buffalo Bill's show, and my test of his descriptions of the surroundings of Madison Square Garden in New York evidenced his truthfulness. I worshipped the very soil on which this "Nature's nobleman" trod. For he was, in addition, the handsomest adolescent in the caravan. On our stroll I confessed myself an "hermaphrodite," using that inaccurate term because it is known to every rough (though by them always pronounced incorrectly). He would not have understood "androgyne." Since he was only a servant in the caravan, I offered a large bill. But much to my surprise and almost to my death, he abruptly jilted me with an unparalleled display of horror. But he promised to keep the incident locked in a chamber of his brain, and events proved him true blue. My desolate stroll in the bear-infested wilderness followed immediately.

If these cowboys and miners, as well as all other men, instead of having been, from boyhood, fed on the most crime-provoking of falsehoods, namely, that homosexuals (so called, though psychicly and often in part physically belonging to the opposite sex) are monsters of depravity for whom no punishment is too severe, had been taught that these sexual cripples merit only compassion, I would myself have been spared those hours of excruciating anguish in the forest, and hundreds of youthful androgynes would not have committed suicide.

III

College Student's Death is Unexplained

(The following are excerpts from a New York paper. Every few months the press brings to light a similar death of an androgyne. All because the world misunderstands and grossly misjudges them, as well as because public opinion has always deprived them of the means of coming to an understanding of themselves. Bracketed words and italics are those of the author of The Female-Impersonators.)

Student's Death Mystery Baffling—No Known Basis in Q's Life to Suggest Murder or Suicide Theory

Overdone detective fiction seldom presents so many significant but mostly inexplicable circumstances surrounding the victim of death by violence as those developed concerning (Jimmie Q), twenty, *quiet, studious, religious* (earmarks of androgynism), a (North Atlantic) college junior, popular, not morbid, a clean-cut American youth, whose body was taken from the river last Thursday night. . .

Q loved to roam the slums of large cities. (An earmark of cultured androgynism. They thus roam because realizing that in their Overworld, they are prohibited outlet for the feminine side of their duality. They roam with day dreams of how they would like to impersonate a female in the Underworld, where alone female-impersonators are welcome; and finally, in many cases, they are carried away by their mania for an actual female-impersonation spree.) . . . His college room-mate commented on the large number of neckties, all Q had, which the latter was taking along. (As he *said,* for a few days' visit to his father, which visit did not take place. My theory is that he went to the great city, in whose harbor his dead body was found, to spend an evening with chance-met gangsters in the slums, as I have myself done, and he took the many neckties as presents for them, just as I myself have carried *neckties* with which to shower them and thus win their goodwill. The androgyne, of course, wishes the gangsters as an audience for his loved impersonations. Androgynes always wish an audience of tremendously virile "young fellows.")

Q did not drink and *never took special interest in any woman*. But he did like to rove about in the districts of big cities in which the poorest classes live and work. . . Whenever he was in New York, he spent most of his time in such districts. . .

At the Morgue, Mr. Q identified the effects of his son. When the body was exposed for his inspection—it appeared to have been in the water about ten days—the father bowed his head and tearfully exclaimed: "Poor Jimmie! How you must have suffered!" . . .

The fisherman who had pulled the body ashore had used a grappling hook. . . To it they attributed the incision which the (City's) Medical Examiner had reported to have been made by some weapon. The Medical Examiner denounced this report and suggested that the police were forwarding a suicide theory to escape responsibility for solution of a crime. He declared there was evidence of hemorrhage in this wound not producible by such an injury inflicted long after death. He further recalled that the left arm of Q was dislocated at the elbow, with the arm muscles twisted—positive indications of external violence. (I myself have been tortured by a ruffian's seizing me by the wrist and twisting around my arm so that I had to shriek in agony.)

The Medical Examiner declared the absence of water in the lungs developed by the autopsy showed beyond question that Q was dead when his body entered the water. . . He had seventy-seven cents in his pockets when his body was found. (Evidence of robbery, considering that he was a well-to-do youth on a visit to a great city distant from his college. My theory is, on the basis of intimate knowledge of the practices of androgynes, that he scraped acquaintance with one or more gangsters, while adopting a girl's role. Many gangsters cordially hate bisexuals. Because of this hatred, as well as to escape prosecution after robbing Q, the gangsters murdered him and threw his dead body into the river—probably in the vicinity. Again the fundamental cause of the death of another androgyne is the terribly false teaching of the Church and public opinion as to the nature of bisexuality.)

PART VII
MEDICAL WRITERS ON ANDROGYNISM

I

What a New York Official Physician Has to Say about Fairies

In MEDICAL LIFE of December, 1920, I had an article: *The Biological Sport of Fairieism.* Readers completely out of touch with Underworld life evidently thought I was telling a fairy tale. Apparently the editor of the MEDICAL REVIEW OF REVIEWS appealed for corroboration to a physician likely to be one of the best authorities in the United States on my subject, Perry M. Lichtenstein, M.D., Ll.B., Physician to City Prison, "Tombs" (New York's principal jail), House of Detention, etc., all of New York City. Apparently there resulted the valuable and interesting article, *The "Fairy" and the Lady Lover,* in MEDICAL REVIEW OF REVIEWS of August, 1921. Its writer has enjoyed almost unparalleled opportunities for examination of the very fairies whose existence had been called in question. I quote a small fraction, but the whole paper should be read by every devotee of Aesculapius. Knowledge of its contents is very necessary for every practitioner. I use my spelling of "fairie." My own comments are in brackets. The REVIEW for November, 1921, contained quite a lengthy reply of mine. Dr. Lichtenstein begins his paper:

"Does the 'fairie' or 'fag' really exist? This question has been asked time and again. There is no doubt but that this type of degenerate is a reality. (Unprejudiced science has not yet decided the matter of the degeneracy of the androgyne in general, as I have already shown in detail. There exists as much evidence that the bisexual is a superman or genius as that he or she is a degenerate. The truth of the matter probably is that degenerates are no commoner per thousand among bisexuals than among the sexually full-fledged, but that geniuses occur far oftener.) He is a freak of nature who in every way attempts to imitate a woman. In my official capacity I have come in contact with several hundred of such individuals, and have in every instance felt sorry for the unfortunate being. (Such sympathy indicates that fairies are not wilfully of that *genre,* and should not suffer term after term in prison, as now, for acts that do nobody harm beyond offending the æsthetic sense of the unsophisticated. Of course, in the matter of accosting on the street, etc., they should be treated the same as full-fledged females. But their punishment should not be augmented because they are "homosexuals"—a word that is a misnomer.)

"In practically every case I have found the man to be a young person of age ranging between sixteen and thirty. ("man"!—Only a *pseudo*-man. Really a woman whom Nature has disguised as a man; a woman with male genitals.) . . . They are by no means mental defectives. Most of them have had a good education and come from respectable families. . . Since early childhood they have been seclusive and kept close to their mother. They are emotional and affective. . . They. . . imitate the female as closely as possible. They take feminine names, use perfume and dainty stationery which frequently is scented, and in many instances they wear women's apparel.

"Recently one of these individuals was arrested, charged with soliciting. When he ("he-she" would be the accurate pronoun) arrived in the city prison, he was searched, and on him were found. . . artificial busts, a wig, and a box containing powder and rouge. This young man ("androgyne" would be the proper term) was twenty years of age. He was beardless (evidently natural), had an effeminate voice, and a distinctly feminine walk. He lisped and in speech closely approached a bashful female He. . . had graduated. . . from high-school. . . He ran away from home and met some boys ("girlboys" would be the proper term) whom he considered good company. These young men ("androgynes" would be the proper term) were of the same type as he. . . In this way (after a fashion, taking the place of the female of the species), (he) made enough money to live.

"These individuals. . . often occupy handsomely furnished apartments which are paid for by men who patronize them. As a rule several 'fags' occupy an apartment. On one occasion ten such individuals were arrested in a raid by the police. . . I had an opportunity to observe them closely. In every respect they resembled the female. The names they used in calling one another were feminine. . . They had a typical feminine walk. . . (Because androgyne legs are sometimes those of a woman.)

"I can distinctly recall two cases which occurred quite recently. . . The first. . . was arrested for soliciting and was sent to the female prison. This person had wonderful hair which reached to the waist, and it was not false. His face was as smooth as a woman's (naturally beardless evidently), his voice was distinctly feminine, and his hands and feet were small. He wore high-heeled shoes. In examining this person the matron insisted that he strip. The prisoner refused, and thereupon I was notified to make an examination. . . When questioned, he stated that he preferred to dress as a female because he found that he was effeminately inclined. . . He was sent to the workhouse, and after serving his time was released. Several months later I learned that he had again been arrested for a similar offence. This time he wore a wig in addition to the feminine garb. (Because during his prior imprisonment, he had, under pressure, consented to have his hair cut short, like a man, and promised to live henceforth as a man—a promise hard to keep since "he" was psychicly, and in part physically, a female.)

"The next case. . . was arrested. . . When taken to the female prison, he refused to allow the matron to search him. . . I was called in. I found that the prisoner wore a wig and artificial breasts. Every bit of his attire was feminine. . . The voice and mannerisms were distinctly effeminate. . .

"Many of the so-called 'social elite' are to be included among these people. . ." ("Many" only in the aggregate. Proportionately, only about one out of one-hundred-and fifty men. But the ratio is probably higher among the cultured than among manual laborers. They are not at all blameworthy, because they were born with the strongest kind of instincts in that direction, and do not thereby harm in the least any individual or society as a whole. They carefully keep their idiosyncracy under cover.)

II

What One of America's Foremost Medical Writers Has to Say about Fairies

D r. Robert W. Shufeldt, author of STUDIES IN THE HUMAN FORM, has included at least one fairie among the many human beings the results of his physical examination of whom he has published. The following are excerpts from his valuable and interesting article, *Biography of a Passive Pederast*, in the October, 1917, issue of the AMERICAN JOURNAL OF UROLOGY AND SEXOLOGY. I use my own spelling of "fairie." My comments are in brackets. Those interested should read the entire original article. Particularly two photographs of the subject are given, one nude and the other in full feminine garb.

"J. W. . . . is a fairie from the slums of Brooklyn, N. Y. . . . twenty-three years of age. When fourteen. . . the lobes of his ears had been pierced. . . for earrings, and these ornaments he commonly wears when dressed in female attire. . . He invited my attention to the fine development of his breasts, whereas there was not the slightest evidence of gynecomasty. . . The impression was left upon my mind that he was morphologically male in all particulars. . . I became thoroughly convinced that the man was laboring under. . . a most extraordinary delusion. . . He claimed to have his menses regularly every month. . . (Evidently bleeding piles.)

"In July he admitted that he had never been pregnant; while in November, when he brought with him one of his numerous 'husbands' or lovers, he claimed that he had been pregnant a few years previously and been operated on in a hospital and the conception removed 'through his side.' . . . I am convinced that this mendacity is due to his delusions.

". . . While he could sing soprano well, he could not whistle. . . and he threw a stone like a girl. (Common earmarks of androgynism.) . . . He did not, as he moved about. . . give one the impression that there was anything in his demeanor simulating femininity, nor did his behavior in any way betray the remarkable manner in which his sexual life was being lived. . . Apart from his extremely meagre education, he is no fool or dullard in other particulars. . . It would seem that his trade (professional female-impersonator and fairie) is plied chiefly for the money there is in it. . . He claims he has never been arrested or otherwise interfered with by the police. . .

". . . He has always been possessed of the contrary sexual instinct. He always shunned women and girls more or less, while yearning at the same time to assume female attire and enter into their domestic vocations. . . Believing himself designed by Nature to play the very part he is playing in life, it was truly remarkable to hear this nervous, loquacious, foul-mouthed, and foul-minded fairie of the most degraded slums of the multi-millioned city chatter about his experiences. . .

"Few writers in the field of psychiatry have enjoyed what I had next the opportunity to observe. . . The putting on of female attire by a contrary sexed male. (The paper details the putting on of the various articles.) . . . He became very talkative. . . telling of some of his recent escapades. . . gesticulating as we often see agitated girls do. . . remarking that he was very tired, owing to the fact that he had been 'ironing all the forenoon.' (Androgynes gravitate toward peculiarly feminine tasks.) . . . 'What do you think of that hat? Is n't it a dandy? I trimmed it myself.' . . . He was, without the slightest doubt, thoroughly in earnest in all he said and did, and by no means was he playing a part. . . 'Dear me,' he said, 'I've forgotten my ear-rings; but you won't mind that?' Upon my assuring him that I liked young girls better without them, he seemed relieved and proceeded to fit to his head a. . . blonde wig. . . As he had recently shaved, his face was quite smooth, and in a twinkling he made it up with. . . pink powder, with red pomade for the lips. . . 'Ha!' he said (after fully transformed outwardly into a soubrette, in the style of costume prevalent among courtesans at the date of J. W's appearance before the doctor for wear in their resorts only, but in 1921 affected for street wear by all butterflies of fashion) 'I feel more like myself now, and I am ready for the picture!' . . ."

PART VIII
ANDROGYNE VERSE

The first of the following attempts to penetrate into Plato's "world of ideas" and get at the real essence of things, and then to express them in an ideal manner, was inspired by a chance visit to the Whitestone station in October, 1921. Subsequently I was seized with the desire to try out my muse in incorporating some of my other emotions and experiences in verse. I had essayed no metrical composition since 1905, the year of writing the last of my Fairie Songs, the best of which were published in the **Autobiography of an Androgyne.**

I understand by "poetry" the version of things seen incorporeally; things spiritualized or with a halo around them; things as they exist in substance, in reality, back of their superficial or phenomenal presentation—the version of things that an individual's subconscious or subliminal self utters.

At present when I evolve verse, I try to lose myself to the phenomenal world—the domain of sensation—and to let down my bucket into the well of the subconscious, the subliminal; to peer into the eternal, the infinite world (the domain of fundamental substance). The sensuous, material skin or crust of this world of ideas is all that most children of Adam can grasp. Only to poets and metaphysicians has Nature given a rope of sufficient length that their buckets can reach as far as the water level in the well of ideas. Nearly all poets even of the first rank manage to flop into their buckets a few exquisite thoughts as to eternal realities, and clothed in appropriate language, only about once out of a score of attempts. Nineteen-twentieths of their verse would better have been forever withheld from the public's eyes, since it is merely artificial, nonsense doggerel. In that proportion of their work, these poets of the first rank show themselves up merely as bad rhymesters.

The editor of The Female-Impersonators declared "the book would be better off without" my verse, but has kindly humored my wish to include it. The reader's verdict may be that I, too, am merely a bad rhymester, and thus put my work on a level with the vast bulk of the outpourings and outdronings of our best poets.

But I, as a would-be poet, labor under the disadvantage of expressing sentiments of an androgyne. Even if there should really be any poetry in my own outdronings, no one but another androgyne could recognize the fact, since it is next to impossible for anybody to appreciate any literature unless they can make its sentiments their own and identify themselves with one of the characters. And the sexually full-fledged, who constitute more than ninety-nine per cent of the reading public, are obsessed by an irrational horror of androgynes.

I therefore beg the reader, in judging the following verse, to bear in mind that it is not written by a *man* about *men*, as the reader first thinks; but about men by a *pseudo*-man; by a physical "man" who is psychicly a woman, and even physically a woman at least thirty-three per cent.

I have read some of Mary Baker Eddy's verse, which her disciples place on a level with the Psalms of David. But I think the former weak and the latter perfect. Here again we see that to judge verse to be good, one has to imagine it one's own outpouring. I therefore do not expect any sexually full-fledged person to declare of my verse (even if it were the best ever written) anything else than that it is "far beneath the worst doggerel. The mere thought of it is painful!"

For—I repeat—it is impossible for any one to judge poetry objectively—only subjectively: that is, not according to the merits of the verse, but according to whether the reader can make the sentiments his own.

A sexually full-fledged literary confidant, who has read the first two books of my trilogy, declared of my verse: "If you publish it, it will cast ridicule and contempt on your whole book. In the book, you have claimed culture, but when your readers come to this verse, they will say that no one with the culture of a longshoreman would try to pass off such stuff as verse even in fun, and that if you had the slightest tincture of literary taste, you would realize this. You will go down to posterity in ridicule, and destroy all the good your books might otherwise do."

But I persist in including the verse. If the quoted verdict is correct, than I have "a screw loose" intellectually, as well as being sexually and anatomically "a freak of Nature." The published pieces show the psychologist what ultra-androgyne verse is like. Besides, possible androgyne readers may be able to appreciate this verse.

As three out of the four following "attempts" were first conceived only in January, 1922—after **The Female-Impersonators** had gone to press—it has been impossible that they benefit by the author's judgment after they have grown cold.

I

Emotion[1]

(Inspired by sight of Whitestone station in 1921.)

Still stands the selfsame Whitestone station,
    So sombre as night's shades fall;
At its north front do still halt trains,
    While brakemen "Whitestone! Whitestone!" call.

My trysting-place in nineteen three
    With warriors of the nation,
When I was frivolous and wild,
    Was this old Whitestone station.

Yea, holy ground its platform is;
    It makes me sigh and ponder;
In my mind's eye those blue-clad forms
    Still wait for me just yonder!

They met me at the train when I
    From New York came, directed
To see and stroll about with "braves"
    Of manhood unsuspected!

On balmy eves we stalked dark lanes,
    No other person near us;
No other's eye upon us gazed,
    No other's ear could hear us.

What gallant, passionate lovers they!
    Considerate of my pleasure!
Uplifting to the highest bliss
    That Eve on earth can measure!

---

1. Attempt at poetical expression of experiences described in prose on page 255 following.

Returning to the porte cochere
    Of that selfsame old station,
We lingered, till the whistle blew,
    In blissful conversation.

What eyesore thou, old Porte Cochere,
    To every traveller seemest!
To me, howe'er, thou shelter gave;
    With memories dear thou teemest!

The station's waiting-room with seats
    Extending all around it,
'Whelms me with recollections fond,
    Because unchanged I found it!

For 'twas on these rude benches there,
    When winter's winds were hurtling,
And travellers few and far between,
    All evening sat we flirting.

In words our conversation lagged;
    In substance it was silly!
For all I said the evening through
    Was: "How I love thee, Willie!"

We every confidence but breathed,
    Lest some strange ear o'erhear us;
They guessed not—travellers—what we said;
    There were none very near us.

Whene'er the train I took for town,
    And we "Goodnight!" repeated,
"Farewell!" o'erwhelmed me as I left
    And in the coach was seated.

Once rode with me a gallant three
    To College Point, first station;
To have with me five minutes more
    Before farewell ovation.

How charmed was I that period brief!
    Its memory ever lingers;
As we sat holding hidden hands,
    I felt their horny fingers.

"Three cheers for Jennie June!" they cried,
    When finally they must leave me;
"The soldiers' friend, and sweetheart too!
    Let not our parting grieve thee!"

      *   *   *   *   *   *

Gone are ye from my life for years,
    You heroes! Wonder boys!
In memory though I hold you fast—
    Forever perfect joys!
        Farewell!

II

Recollection[1]

O thou FAIR as the sunrise on deep sea's green surge,
    While the whitecaps seem dancing all around!
FAIR as sunset from mountain's sheer precipice's verge,
    Seen o'er maze of high ridges snowbound!
Even FAIRER than the rose, of all flowers the fairest;
    Beyond Vatican's Apollo Belvedere;
BUD McDONALD, youth's soulmate, of beauty the rarest,
    ADOLESCENT wert thou without peer!

First, BEAU BRUMMEL wert thou, so fussy about clothes,
    O immaculate BUDDIE McDEE!
Dirt and slovenness cat, never more than thou, loaths;
    Must be brushed every hour from dust free;
Every lock of thine hair with worried care laid in place;
    As a girl didst thou prink—I can vow!
But of all the young bloods of Rialto's fast race,
    Not one sweller was costumed than thou!

Beheld one the shining patent leather of thy shoe,
    And both hands decorated with rings;
Marked thy wiles through which dude *hoi polloi's* favor doth woo,
    One would say: "All from effeminacy springs!"
"Not a bit!" I must answer. For MACK, SPORT as well,
    Was a crack shot with pistol and ball;
How he hunted, coldblooded, dumb beasts he did tell;
    Furry creatures clubbed dead; cursed them all!

Best of all:—an ADONIS wert thou, BUD McDEE,
    With incomparable red peachlike cheeks;
Threads of eyebrows so cleancut!—in memory I see—

---

1. For prose description of the personality that I have here attempted to depict poetically, see page 114 following.

As o'er her eyes a soubrette alone seeks;
With thy pearls of teeth, cherry lips—beloved sir—
    And as well chiselled nose as can be,
How I've wondered that thou and I intimates were!—
    Explanation:—God gave thee to me!

I again in fond memory behold before me,
    Pinkish mountain of loveliness tower;
Buddie's *forma divina, au naturel,* see;
    How his charms, yea unmatched, did o'erpower!
An "eyeful" his two breasts, with fine gold scraggy hair;
    Graceful curves; rotund body and limb;
With his robust ribs bursting through skin O so fair,
    And his deep-channeled back breathing vim!

Once Unequaled "Young Fellow"! Six-and-twenty long years
    Now have rolled by since thou wert All That!
Art today gibbering sot, maybe suffering jeers,
    With foul trousers and torn greasy hat?
For the cup cherished thou that glad makes the sad heart.—
    How I wonder! Where sleptest last night?
Is vitality wasted? In grave resting art?—
    Us together soon lead, Kindly Light!

III

Memories[1]

I dream tonight of the gay bright lights
    Where I sought recreation;
While meek I sat at feet of profs
    To gain an education:
I studied hard six dreary eves,
    But when the seventh came,
Bade "au revoir" to books and grind,
    And skipped to RIALTO's game.

There where lurked pleasure's devotees
    Giant Kill-joy never came;
I met there New York's wildest swains,
    And buxoms of ill fame:
We revelled all the evening through—
    Fine fellowship, I say!
I ne'er happed on politer folk
    Than in RIALTO gay.

And which was I, kind sir, dost ask?
    Was I a bad roué?
Or shameless demi-virgin wild,
    In paint and powder gay?—
"But I was neither this nor that!"
    Such answer here I set;
While youth in form, I chose to take
    Diversion as soubrette.

The young bloods pardoned me—they said—
    For wearing hated breeches!
"For thou art not a real male;
    Thou'rt like yon winking witches

---

1. See page 103 following.

Who throng these noisy promenades
    Their favors fair to sell;
And kissing thee we deem as sweet
    As kissing ma'moiZelle!

"Lik'st thou that we thee sweetheart call?—
    We'll humor thy desire;
Sit on our laps while we sip wine;
    Let's flirt until we tire;
To break thy shapely corset stays,
    We'll try our best, dear Jenn;
But thou must mimic maid thy best;
    For us:—the part of men!" . . .

To have love made by youthful swains,
    To me was highest bliss;
In the bright dives where scores beheld,
    No,—shrinked we not to kiss:—
Of yore in gay RIALTO's halls
    Knew folk no self-restraint;
Insane e'en sometimes acted fools!
    Those dens no place for saint! . . .

I'm prone tonight to philosophize:—
    Why did I gravitate
Toward RIALTO's racy denizens
    When moved to dissipate?
'Twas just because I sought and found,
    In RIALTO's "swell" gallants,
The opposites and complements
    For whom my spirit pants. . . .

O comrade of RIALTO's halls
    Of nineties of century past—
Should'st read these lines, some former pal,
    "Jennie June" remembered hast;
Now after twenty-six years,
    I hail thee with heartfelt greeting;
Beseech Benediction on thine head,
    In lieu of present meeting.

IV

French Doll Baby[1]

Young bloods prom'nade Fourteenth Street's pave—
    Each eve out for a lark;
Their eyes "peeled" for French doll babies;
    With whom they sigh to spark;
    Why admire the fraidcat babies,
        Who weep easily?
The helpless crippled sex e'en *seek!*—
    Harebrained gentility! . . .

Cheeks a beauteous red through rouge puff;
Pink powder (pretty, pretty! ! !) 'pon nose;
    One inhales as she nigh minceth,
        Such soothing scent of rose!
Locks—so silklike—reach to shoulders;
    Gown of "art" design;
Coquette extreme must she be sure;
    All signs she doth combine.

When a young blood spieth dolly,
Cutely mincing Fourteenth Street;
Then the young blood smileth sweetly,
    And, stranger e'en, doth greet:
Replies she smilingly "Good evening!"
    Surely she is fly!
Too, overjoyed because of having
    Bewitched a stalwart "guy."

"Little tootsy-wootsy!" cries guy,
    "Art ravishingly cute!
Thou art, yea, a pretty Pussie! Pussie, Pussie ! ! !

---

1. See THE FEMALE-IMPERSONATORS, page 153. Second stanza is a free translation from Beranger. For original, see AUTOBIOGRAPHY OF AN ANDROGYNE, page viii.

Ne'er saw I such a beaut!"
Answereth she in mellifluous voice:
   "And I 'Strong Hans' thee call!
Thy frame so large and powerful!
   Not spindling thou, yet tall!"

They acquainted barely minute,
   Such confidences express!
As only hubby—hidden, secret—
   Doth glad to spouse confess:
Bold gallant the French doll calls "Wifie!"
   While she e'en feels that he
To her already united is—
   The twain, twin souls, to be!

Reader, never heardst thou such words!
Much mush! (as "Kiddo! Kiddo!"—"Kitty! Kitty!"[2])
Passing strange the way of young blood
   With French doll baby pretty!
That sexual difference existeth
   Renders twain insane;
Except for Nature's procreative plan,
   These instincts—how inane! . . .

Holdeth French doll from "guy" a secret;
   Yes, surely she can *act!*
Only after hour's deception,
   Revealeth she the fact;
When she's found that she can trust him;
   Can reveal her whim:
In burst of laughter doth disclose:
   "My real, true name is 'Jim'!"

---

2. Seemingly natural language of "pup love", the girl repeating the former a hundred times in five minutes, and the adolescent the latter. Both also cry these words simultaneously while gazing into each other's eyes.

Announcement of Third of Trilogy

The Riddle of the Underworld

Sequel to *Autobiography of an Androgyne* and
The Female-Impersonators

By Ralph Werther—Jennie June

Edited by
Alfred W. Herzog, Ph. B., A. M., M. D.
(Editor Medico-Legal Journal)

To be published, in the fall of 1922, by the Medico-Legal
Journal. At least 65,000 words and a dozen illustrations.
Cloth. Price three dollars, including postage within
United States. The three volumes of the Trilogy,
(an aggregate of over 200,000 words) ordered on
the same date, eight dollars, including postage.
The Autobiography of an Androgyne,
ordered on the same date with one
other of the Trilogy, six dollars.
Price of Autobiography alone,
four dollars including
postage.

The author of the Trilogy, one of the half-dozen most remarkable bisexuals known to medical science, while living in New York City as college student and subsequently professional "man," had, incidentally, a six years' variegated experience (age nineteen to twenty-five) in the Underworld of the metropolis. In the Autobiography, besides an exhaustive analysis of his own intuitions, beliefs, courses of reasoning, emotions, penchants, and instincts, the author merely *outlined* his manner of life and adventures, particularly while impersonating a female. In The Female-Impersonators, he undertook little more, in description of Underworld life, than to detail the experiences of cultured ultra-androgynes.

In the Riddle of the Underworld, the author of the Trilogy—

GIVES the history of New York's white-light and red-light districts since the beginning of the nineteenth century; analyzes the causes of vice and crime on the basis of his intimate mingling with the Underworlders; shows why a "vicious tenth" exists in all cities, and how the Overworld (which constitutes nine-tenths of the population of Christian lands) should regulate the former.

DEPICTS life in New York's poorest immigrant quarters and tenements—*in its reality* because he saw it as an *insider,* the denizens of the slums and the Underworld shamefacedly veiling the fundamental facts of their existence from charity and sociological investigators, but admitting the author to everything because he mingled with them as a non-intellectual and fairie.

DEPICTS life in the lowest type of slum lodging-house, once the author's home, and the night life in general of the Bowery at the height of the latter's vogue as New York's principal red-light street, the author at the time being one of its *"filles-de-joie."*

DEPICTS, lastly, in great detail, his career as female-impersonator in New York's slums and red-light and white-light districts and the life of "bosom friends" of the Underworld: Young bloods sowing their wild oats; middle-aged extreme alcoholic wrecks; extreme drug addicts; intellectual mild androgynes during the hours when Nature drives them to a double life in the Underworld; low-class "fairies"; *filles-de-joie* in their hey-day; wrecks of such in their thirties; "confidence men"; gangsters, gunmen, and burglars (whom Providence gave the author as soul-mates).

THE CLOSING VOLUME OF THE TRILOGY DEPICTING THE
LIFE-EXPERIENCE OF A BISEXUAL UNIVERSITY "MAN"

A Note About the Author

Earl Lind (1874–unknown) was a pioneering transgender autobiographer. Born into a Puritan family in Connecticut, Lind—who also used the pseudonyms "Jennie June" and "Ralph Werther"—asked others to call him Jennie as a child, and soon began identifying as an androgyne. As a young adult, Lind moved to New York City and began participating in the homosexual nightlife centered at Paresis Hall. In 1895, Lind cofounded the Cercle Hermaphroditos, perhaps the first advocacy group for transgender rights in American history. At 28, Lind underwent an operation to be castrated, hoping to suppress his masculine features. Although he identified as feminine, the term "transgender" had yet to be coined in Lind's lifetime, leading Lind to self-identify as an "effeminate man," "androgyne," and "invert." His autobiographical works—*Autobiography of an Androgyne* (1918), *The Riddle of the Underworld* (1921) and *The Female-Impersonators* (1922)—are considered pioneering works of LGBTQ literature by scholars around the world.

A Note from the Publisher

Spanning many genres, from non-fiction essays to literature classics to children's books and lyric poetry, Mint Edition books showcase the master works of our time in a modern new package. The text is freshly typeset, is clean and easy to read, and features a new note about the author in each volume. Many books also include exclusive new introductory material. Every book boasts a striking new cover, which makes it as appropriate for collecting as it is for gift giving. Mint Edition books are only printed when a reader orders them, so natural resources are not wasted. We're proud that our books are never manufactured in excess and exist only in the exact quantity they need to be read and enjoyed.

bookfinity™

Discover more of your favorite classics with Bookfinity™.

- Track your reading with custom book lists.
- Get great book recommendations for your personalized Reader Type.
- Add reviews for your favorite books.
- AND MUCH MORE!

Visit **bookfinity.com** and take the fun Reader Type quiz to get started.

Enjoy our classic and modern companion pairings!

Classic & Modern